Love and Marriage in Africa
in the Novels of Elechi Amadi, Buchi Emecheta and Chinua Achebe

Dr. Richa Jha

PARTRIDGE

Copyright © 2022 by Dr. Richa Jha.

ISBN: Softcover   978-1-5437-0821-9
            eBook   978-1-5437-0820-2

All rights reserved. No part of this book may be used or reproduced by any means, graphic, electronic, or mechanical, including photocopying, recording, taping or by any information storage retrieval system without the written permission of the author except in the case of brief quotations embodied in critical articles and reviews.

Because of the dynamic nature of the Internet, any web addresses or links contained in this book may have changed since publication and may no longer be valid. The views expressed in this work are solely those of the author and do not necessarily reflect the views of the publisher, and the publisher hereby disclaims any responsibility for them.

Print information available on the last page.

To order additional copies of this book, contact
Partridge India
000 800 919 0634 (Call Free)
+91 000 80091 90634 (Outside India)
orders.india@partridgepublishing.com

www.partridgepublishing.com/india

CONTENTS

Preface vii

Acknowledgement xiii

Chapter I: Introduction 1

Chapter II: The Concubine 47

Chapter III: The Bride Price 93

Chapter IV: Things Fall Apart 141

Chapter V: Conclusion 187

Bibliography 225

Webliography 235

Preface

An attempt has been made in the following pages to study and analyze the theme of love and marriage in the novels of Elechi Amadi, Buchi Emecheta and Chinua Achebe. The recent years in the past have witnessed the world critics exhibiting a newfound interest in the literature of Africa, which had been suffering in ignominious darkness for long, yet the perspective of their study is generally focused on postcolonial themes and human/interpersonal relationships have largely been ignored in their studies. The white man's perception and portrayal of Africa as a land of savages, devoid of finer emotions, could be a major influence in this regard. This study strives to prove that the Africans have a rich history and culture of interpersonal relationships and the twin themes of love and marriage run across their literature. The novels under study in this book present the importance of love in various aspects – man-woman relationship, parent-child relationship and an individual's love for his native land. Various types of matrimonial alliances, with the different aspects of an African marriage – settling of marriage, settlement and payment of the bride price, gender equations, polygamy, widow remarriage etc., have all been studied in the backdrop of the three novels taken under consideration. For purposes of a systematic exposition of the research question and clarity of presentation, this work has been spread out and organized in five chapters.

The first chapter is the introductory chapter that has been divided into two parts. The first part holds a comprehensive study of the oral and written literature of Africa. In it, the orature of Africa and the development of African literature in English after the advent of colonisers in the continent has been discussed in brief. The development of the written form, inspired by the oral folklores and local tales of the region, in the colonizer's language forms the content of the initial part of the first chapter. The shift in focus from the novels written by men to the development of women's literature, making way for a broader expression of the reality, with the discussion of feminism that better focuses on the situation of marriage in Africa forms the crux of this chapter. The effect of the colonial invasions on the African literary tradition and the novels depicting the cultural significance as well as role of love and marriage in African societies has also been mentioned. The second part of this chapter deals primarily with the depiction of love and marriage in literature and their different types practiced in the African society, as seen through the novels. Literature across the world views love and marriage as the ultimate aim of the female kind, the woman's success defined by the economic and social worth of her husband or lover. African society is no different, and here too, the woman is seen through the patriarchal lens. Different types of matrimonial alliances make no difference to the basic treatment of the woman as a possession, as a commodity, that can bought, sold, or her ownership transferred. The latter half of the chapter studies the various types of matrimonial alliances acceptable in the African society and the theme of love and marriage in the novels selected for this research work has also been discussed in brief.

The second chapter, titled after the name of the novel it focuses upon, i.e., *The Concubine*, analyzes the treatment of love and marriage in this work by Elechi Amadi. The power of love has been studied in detail, which runs across the novel, enabling a simple man to stand against the supernatural powers, and not backing down even in the face of imminent defeat. Love has been studied in both its aspects – positive and negative. The positive love of Ihuoma and Ekwueme cures the latter of his mental illness and serves as an anchor for both of them to plan for a better future together. Though Ihuoma was a widow, and Ekwueme had been married to another, yet their families and the society support them in their love and accept their relationship seeing their virtuous and pure love for each other. On the other hand the negative aspect of love can be seen in the jealousy harboured by Ahurole (Ekwueme's first wife) and the Sea-King (Ihuoma was his concubine in the previous life). Ahurole, jealous of her husband's affection for Ihuoma, was desirous of his love only for herself and in her mad rage she administers a love potion to Ekwueme that has a reaction and he loses his mental balance. Instead of standing up and facing the consequences of her action, she chooses to abandon him and runs away. The Sea-King, on the other hand, had chosen to humour Ihuoma's curiosity for human life by sending her on earth as an ordinary mortal, yet his possessiveness for her did not allow him to see anyone come near her. All her lovers or husbands meet untimely death due to the envy and wrath of the Sea-King. This second chapter also studies the different rituals and traditions associated with marriage. For example, the role of the elders in the family and the society is highlighted in the match between Ahurole and Ekwueme, which was settled upon much before they could speak properly. As the society would not have taken kindly to the annulment of this child marriage, Ekwueme and his family go ahead with the marriage negotiations knowing well that his happiness lay with Ihuoma and not Ahurole. Another aspect brought to light is the settlement of the bride price, or the money paid by the groom's family to the bride's family before marriage, which forms an integral part of an African marriage as seen in all the three novels taken for this research work. The issue of widow remarriage also forms a centrepoint in the novel. Though a widow becoming the first wife of an eligible bachelor was deemed unthinkable, yet it was quite acceptable for young widows to consider remarriage in the African society. The fact that a woman becomes the property of the husband's family also comes to fore. After Ihuoma's first husband, Emenike's death, it is upto Emenike's brother to give her away in marriage to another man, as seen when Ekwueme seeks Nnadi's permission to marry Ihuoma. The African myth and its hold on the people is also studied in the novel, with reference to the lives of the characters in it.

Buchi Emecheta's novel, *The Bride Price* has been studied in the third chapter by the same name. This chapter critically analyzes the theme of love and marriage that runs across this novel, from the social, mythical and feministic perspectives. The third chapter studies the tradition of bride price which plays a major role in the African marriage and the myth attached to it. The effect of the myth of the bride price, that is, the imminent death of the bride in case of its non-payment during her first childbirth, is the running motif in the novel. The hold of this myth on the psyche of the main protagonist of the novel, Aku-nna, alongwith her rebellion against the constraints of society in her love for Chike, a slave descendant, and consequent marriage to him. The bride price myth, negotiation, marriage by capture, importance of virginity for a girl, the treatment of women as a child-bearing machine, inheritance of a dead man's property by his brother, including the wife, through the system of levirate marriage, etc. have all been studied in this chapter in detail. There are enough evidences and instances in this novel to stress on the importance of love and marriage in literature as major themes. Emecheta's novel, out and out, deals with these twin themes, based on the life of Aku-nna in Ibuza. The young girl, coming from the modern town of Lagos is confronted by the age-old customs of her native village Ibuza that over and over again prove the hold of traditional rituals and myth on the minds of the people of the village and also establish the secondary status of the womankind in society. Each custom fills her with a longing to turn away from this society and she is finally able to break away from it through her love for Chike that empowers her to rebel against the stagnated laws; yet her rebellion stays incomplete at the psychological level. Even after shunning the native norms and leaving the village Ibuza for the new, modern and progressive town of Ughelli, her mind keeps swinging back to the age-old customs and adheres to them due to the life-long conditioning the litte girl had received. It seems almost impossible to totally deny the hold of the traditional culture and her young mind, unable to deal with so much stress, bows down to the vicious myth of the bride price. Aku-nna dies. But even in her failed attempt, she is successful in proving that love can conquer all. Had her health not failed her, perhaps she'd have lived. Even though she did not live long, the short life she had with her love and the freedom she enjoyed with him, gave her the happiness of a lifetime which she might never have got had she not dared to rise against the constraints of her society.

The fourth chapter, titled after the novel by Chinua Achebe, is *Things Fall Apart*. The focus of study for this chapter is multi-dimensional. The secondary status of women in marriage, along with the practice of polygamy, the dynamics of the co-wives and their children is studied in depth in this chapter. The bride price, integral to any African marriage also finds description in this chapter through the episode of Obierika's daughter's marriage. Love, in different forms, is a constant motif in this novel and has been duly analysed. The different female characters, exhibiting different kinds of love and submission, like the mute obedience of Okonkwo's first wife, or the fierce love of the outspoken Ekwefi, his second wife – both present totally different types of love in marriage. Gender roles in a marriage, where the women mostly receive a secondary status is evident through the course of the novel, and is studied in this chapter. The male ego, the fear of the feminine, and the tradition-bound roles of the male and the female in the society have been analyzed and discussed. The chapter also deals with women-women relationships portrayed through the co-wives and the priestess' friendship with Ekwefi. Parental love, shown through Okonkwo's and Ekwefi's love for Ezinma and the girl's concern and love for her father is studied in this chapter. Okonkwo's love for his land and its tradition is also discussed in depth. This chapter mainly focuses on these different aspects of human relationships, all showing different types of love that exist in the society. The portrayal of these characters in the novel highlights the importance of love and marriage in the African life with distinctive features of attitude, desires, norms and cultural ways of the society.

Finally, the findings flowing from chapters two, three and four have been penned down in the fifth chapter, which is the concluding chapter, titled '*Conclusion*'. Major arguments of the research have been mentioned in brief in the conclusion stressing upon the importance of love and marriage as the consistently playing themes in the novels taken under study. This research work seeks to establish that love and marriage are closely intertwined with the social and cultural norms of the Africans and hence a complete understanding of the African way of life calls for an earnest study of the novels in the light of these two themes.

In respect of the mechanics of writing, documentation, citation and works-cited list, MLA Handbook (Eighth Edition) and MLA Handbook for writers of Research Paper (Seventh Edition) have been constantly followed. It is also to be put on record that established conventions of research, both written and unwritten, have been faithfully followed throughout the book.

Acknowledgement

I, first and foremost, thank my Gods – Shiva, Shakti and Surya. Without them, this book would never have seen the light of the day. I am equally indebted to my family and friends, whose constant help and support made this research work possible.

It was my good fortune that my guide Dr. Vinay Bharat was not merely my supervisor but also the one, who moulded my thoughts and perceptions towards such a complex literary phenomenon with patience and fortitude. It was he who inspired me to study black literature and respect it as a unique and valid literary pursuit.

Access to primary texts as well as secondary texts, especially those published in the recent past was a problem that I encountered many a time during the whole process. However, the librarians of JNU, New Delhi, Sahitya Akademi, New Delhi, International Library, Ranchi and The Maharaja Sayajirao University of Baroda helped me in a big way by responding generously to my requests and giving me access to the requisite texts for this thesis.

I am also indebted to the Faculty of Humanities, Ranchi University, Ranchi, and specifically the Department of English for their support. I extend my heartiest thanks to St. Xavier's College, Ranchi and Ranchi University, Ranchi for enabling me to stand on this platform of literary scholarship through its eminent professors and vast resource base.

I bear the deepest sense of gratitude to my family and friends for their words and kind gestures of inspiration. My father Mr. Prem Kumar Jha, and my mother Dr. Rani Jha, extended constant support throughout this journey and instilled confidence in me to complete this research. To them I owe my growth and development, my consciousness, and my sensitivity to literature.

I wish to thank my sister Shaily, brother-in-law Kaushik, my brother Kshitij, sister-in-law Shalini and my friends Chandan and Mishtu for lighting up my mind with their buoyant energy and vitality. This paper and the research behind it would not have been possible without their exceptional support. Their enthusiasm, knowledge and exacting attention to detail have been an inspiration and kept my work on track from my first encounter with the African literature to the final draft of this paper. Their unwearied energy, constant concern for my work, and precious suggestions have helped me throughout. They have proved to be my most valued people and truest friends, in every sense. I am highly indebted to them for their constant support in all respects.

I would also like to specially mention my little nephew Shlok who made it possible for my sister to help me with the typing and formatting. Without his patience, this would not have been possible. I extend my heartiest thanks to him.

My husband, Avinash never for once let my spirits flag by constantly stimulating me with his valued words and inspiring advice, I am also indebted to my mother-in-law, Mrs. Nita Jha, for her sensitive approach to my work.

I also express my heartfelt gratitude towards my grandmothers, Mrs. Sharmishtha Devi and Mrs. Anjali Jha, whose prayers and blessings have helped me a lot in course of my research.

And lastly, but most importantly, I would like to express my gratitude towards my son, Shaurya, who came half way through this journey but supported me in his own little ways to ensure that I completed it.

– **Richa Jha**

Chapter - I

Introduction

The introduction of this research work is primarily a crisp view of the development of African literature in English, and the influence of the missionary education that shaped the written literature of Africa. The Africans, who had a very rich oral tradition adopted the foreigner's tongue and spun their indigenous tales in the new language, making it their own. The oral tradition is clearly evident in the written works of most African writers. There has been a constant interaction between the deeply rooted oral tradition and the developing literary tradition of the twentieth century. This interaction is revealed perfectly in the works of the writers taken under this study. This introductory chapter traces the development of African literature in English. It takes a quick look at this development from the historical perspective, identifying the western influence through the stages of *adopt*, *adapt* and *adept* in African literature and the growing stress on interpersonal relationships between man and woman that has been largely ignored uptil now. The more popular angles of study, like the post-colonial or mythological etc have mostly overshadowed the theme of human relationships in literature of Africa. This research work has sought to mend this trend by focusing on the themes of love and marriage in literature of the region to establish that Africans have a very deep-rooted culture and tradition. They are in no way the brute savages that some western writers portrayed them as, and are, in fact, as capable of harbouring and exhibiting finer emotions as any other individual from any other civilization. This chapter, in two parts, has attempted to portray the history and development of the African novel, and the different types of love and marital alliances shown in the African novels. Love and marriage may be portrayed very differently in diferent societies, but the more we compare it to other cultures, the more similarities we find. Though the way these interpersonal relationships work may be different for different people, but the underlying reasons and purposes of marriage remain the same.

Love, whether platonic or romantic, fleeting or lifelong, has the power to nurture meaningful relationships, shatter our hearts, teach important lessons, and change lives forever. So it is no wonder that love is one of the most frequently delved-into themes in literature. It defies boundaries by appearing across all genres, age groups, and periods in history. And just like in real life, the presence of love in a novel can make its story acutely heartfelt and memorable, regardless of the outcome. Novelists like Chinua Achebe, Elechi Amadi and Buchi Emecheta have beautifully presented the different hues of love in their works. Romantic love is not the only kind of love that is explored in their novels. They also touch on kindness, compassion, friendship, forgiveness, patriotism and parental love, all of which are platonic forms of love.

Marriage in Africa works as a bond for not just two individuals but for the community as a whole. Writers like Amadi, Emecheta and Achebe, the three novelists whose works have been studied in this research work, have depicted the different customs related to marriage in all its fine aspects. The involvement of the whole community in a wedding, various rituals associated with a marriage can be witnessed in their novels.

This research work studies the theme of love and marriage through analyzing the involvement of the community in setting up a marital match, the love affair of a couple being the concern of the society at large, the influence of caste and class structure of the society on love and marital relationships, various rituals and customs related to a marriage in Africa etc. have all been analysed in this chapter, in the context of the works of Amadi, Emecheta and Achebe. This introductory chapter gives a brief account of the theme of love and marriage in their novels, namely, *The Concubine, The Bride Price* and *Things Fall Apart.*

The African Novel: A Historical Perspective

The African continent, which had for long been associated with darkness and savagery, is now being seen in the well-deserved new light of post-colonial generosity. It is now viewed as a storehouse of a long and rich cultural legacy endowed with a varied corpus of literary traditions, handed over from one generation to the next through the medium of orality. The orature of Africa that was preserved by its native people in the form of folktales, poems and songs, helped in retaining their culture and tradition against the colonial interference. Oral literature is, and was, by far the most integral part of African literary tradition but gradually the fear of the colonizers and the need to compete with them in order to establish an individual indigenous identity, led the natives to gain on the educational front – to learn the language of their masters. The western education system not just gave them knowledge about a world other than their own, but also the scope to spread out and tell the world about their own world. This acquired knowledge and language helped them to convert their oral literature into the written form.

This transformation was the result of the education that the native African was compelled to receive by the colonizers and the missionaries from the initial stage of their advent into the continent till the end of colonial regime. But soon they realized its advantages and started taking help of this very forced education to narrate their own stories–their myth, their culture, their people and society. Their stories shattered the world view that had been created by the likes of Joseph Conrad and Joyce Cary. They were never the land of the savages, the image that so unceremoniously had been bestowed upon them. They just had their own ways and system of living different from the white man's idea of civilization. The foreigner's language was imbibed into their own, narrating their stigmatic journey from pre-colonial to the post-colonial era. Though the structure was foreign, they used the English language filled with their own native terms, proverbs and riddles to make it their own.

African writing in English emerged primarily as a result of the Euro-African colonial encounter and its aftermath. African literature in English, although its origin goes demonstrably far back into the country's past, is of comparatively a recent time. In 1952, Amos Tutuola's *The Palm Wine Drinkard* was published. It was the first novel in English by an African, to be published and widely read. Since then there has been an outpouring of plays, poetry and prose, a kind of Renaissance, the flourishing of a new literature that has drawn sustenance from both, the traditional oral literature and the present society that is rapidly changing.

Most literary productions and their criticism revolve around the socio-historical process of colonial domination and the subsequent movement for decolonization. European colonial expansion on the African continent in the nineteenth century, as in other parts of the world, was initiated primarily for economic exploitation. It was impossible for European imperial powers to physically control such a vast continent and the great imperial project had to be sustained through ideological mechanisms, the operation of which has been much discussed by the postcolonial theorists. The famous stages of *adopt*, *adapt* and *adept* pretty much summarize the colonial agenda.

Ideological imposition in the African context was of a much harsher nature than in the Asian colonies because of the predominance of traditions of oral communication in most indigenous African cultures. The absence of a written tradition allowed for the imposition of the colonizer's language through the mechanisms of education in English, and this consequently led to the control of one form of communication over the other, that of writing over orality. Taking overt advantage of the absence of a documented past, people south of the Sahara were denied an existence in the writing of the Western master narrative of colonial history. With the established control of the Church over education, the power to block out indigenous narratives passed into the hands of the various colonial authorities. One of the most effective tools of colonial hegemonic control became the negation of identity through the denial of a collective history. Ngugi wa Thiong'o summarizes the complicity of religion, language and education over the dissemination of knowledge in the following words:

> *'... the missionary carried the Bible, the soldier carried the gun, the administrator and the settler carried the coin. Christ, commerce, civilization, the Bible, the coin, the gun.'*[1]

The history of the African novel, as D. Ivezbaye explains in *Issues in the Reassessment of African Novel*, has been "essentially a history of an evolving racial consciousness"[2]. What is unique about the growth of the modern African novel is that it has been coeval to a collective intellectual hijacking of African by the Western colonial enterprise. However, the awakening of creative responses to counter the undervaluing of indigenous systems of thought and communication was not a sudden coming into consciousness. Es'kia Mphahlele points out in *African Literature and the Social Enterprise in Process* (1983) that the arrival of Edmund Blyden in Liberia in 1851 marked a crucial stage in the development of modern African thought. Blyden's most important contribution was his promulgation of the theory of the 'African Personality' formulated as one possible means of regaining the African's 'disinherited self'. Consequently, Afro-American literary movements of the early twentieth century played an influential role in the gradual assertion of pride in being black.

The movement towards establishing a common Negro identity gained further momentum in the 1920s when under the influence of the ideology of the 'Black Nationalism' of Marcus Garvey and the Pan-Africanism of Du Bois, the Negritude movement was born. The preoccupation with a 'black affirmation' dominated the literary expression of Francophone poets like David Diop and Leopold Senghor. Others, like Wole Soyinka expressed their lack of concern with the concept of Negritude. Wole Soyinka's remark – does a tiger have to be concerned with its tigritude? – has probably been quoted too often, but it remains a valid point still, concisely summing up the often-expressed views of most African writers, especially the Nigerians, on this subject. This does not, in any way, mean that colonialism left no scars. It most certainly did, and many of those scars can be seen outlined with bitter clarity in the novels of writers like Chinua Achebe, Chimamanda Ngozi Adichie, Ngugi wa Thiong'o, Elleke Boehmer etc. these writers focus on the traditional African society, the effect of Christian influences, and the clash of the western and African values before, during and after the colonial era. Unlike the western novelists, they do not take it upon themselves to paint a particular set as the quintessential villain, eroding their existence. In fact, these writers simply show the society as it was before and after the colonial interference, their native culture with its flaws and advantages and the same for the colonists. While Achebe rues the white man's advent for wiping out villages and trying to destroy native culture and even religion, he also talks about how the Church strove to put an end to the age-old practices such as killing of twins, mutilation of an ogbanje, wife-beating etc. to root out the social evils existing in the traditional set-up. And while there have been several debates on the aesthetic principle of Negritude, it has been generally accepted that the movement served as a springboard for the articulation, and hence growth, of a black consciousness among Anglophone African Writers. Writing began to be marked with a convergence of political and nationalistic thinking and it set the stage for a literature of nation-building.

By the 1950s, the struggle for independence in former British colonies of Ghana, Nigeria and Kenya had begun to grow in strength. Conversely, the literature of the period was marked by a convergence of anti-colonial indignation and nationalist thinking. The first stage of writing of cultural nationalism and racial assertion was governed by the ideological intention of awakening the African consciousness, and a performing of the therapeutic role of healing the wounds and humiliation inflicted by the colonizing process. As Fanon points out in *The Wretched of the Earth*:

The birth of national consciousness in Africa has a strictly contemporaneous connection with the African consciousness.[3]

Cultural nationalist fiction tended to be dominated by a forward-looking optimism. Promises of an egalitarian and classless society had been an integral part of the socialist manifestos of nationalist leaders, and a general sanguinity about the potential of indigenous cultures is reflected in the literary output of the first-generation fiction.

Most first-generation African novelists who were writing in English found themselves in double-bind situation. As product of a colonial system of mission education in English, they had to reassert their own unique African sensibility in a borrowed tongue. Paradoxically, they appropriated the English language as a counter weapon to perform a psychologically affirmative function and to inscribe new meanings. There are innumerable and exciting examples of the creative breaking and re-making of the English language, largely through retention of the stamp of orality. In 1952, Amos Tutuola's *The Palm Wine Drinkard* was the first Nigerian novel to be published by a reputed British company, Faber and Faber. *The Palm Wine Drinkard*, told in the first person, is about an unnamed man who is addicted to palm wine, which is made from the fermented sap of the palm tree and used in ceremonies across Africa. The son of a rich man, the narrator can afford his own tapster (a man who taps the wine tree for sap and then prepares the wine). When the tapster dies, cutting off his supply, the desperate narrator sets off for Dead's Town to try to bring the tapster back. He travels through a world of magic and supernatural beings, surviving various tests and finally gains a magic egg with never-ending palm-wine. Tutuola became a controversial figure in the critical reception of the novel in English for the 'strangeness' of his style and the use of what Dylan Thomas referred to as 'young English'. From a reading of the novel, it can be inferred that the writer holds the narrative together through story-telling, which is an important aspect of folklore. The narrator strikes an immediate rapport with the reader just like a story teller does with his listeners. The sentences are long with a few full stops (breaks) in an attempt to hold the attention of the readers (listeners) which is a much-required element of good story telling. To suggest a natural flow between ideas and incidents, Tutuola makes abundant use of connecting words like 'as', 'so', 'but', 'then' and 'after' in the beginning and within sentences. A case in point is this extract from the novel:

> *So my father gave me a palm-tree farm which was nine miles square and it contained 560,000 palm-trees and this palm-wine tapster was tapping one hundred fifty kegs of palm-wine every morning, but before two o'clock P.M., I would have drunk all of it; after that he would go and tap another 75 kegs in the evening which I would be drinking till morning. So my friends were unaccountable by that time and they were drinking palm-wine with me from morning till a late hour in the night*[4].

In this magic-realistic narrative, Tutuola incorporates Yoruba myth and folklore, and human beings mix freely with the beings from the spiritual world. The early reviewers of the western world, after Dylan Thomas, however, were less kind towards this strange and new kind of writing and consistently described the book as primitive[5], primeval[6], naïve[7], unwilled[8], lazy[9] and barbaric or barbarous[10].

The New York Times Book Review was typical in describing Tutuola as "a true primitive" whose world had "no connection at all with the European rational and Christian traditions", adding that Tutuola was "not a revolutionist of the word...not a surrealist" but an author with an "un-willed style" whose text had "nothing to do with the author's intentions"[11].

The New Yorker took this prejudice to its logical ends, stating that Tutuola was "being taken a great deal too seriously" as he is just a "natural storyteller" with a "lack of inhibition" and an "uncorrupted innocence" whose text was not new to anyone who had been raised on "old fashioned nursery literature"[12].

Given these Western reviews, it is not surprising that the African intellectual, highly influenced by the West, saw the book in negative light, calling it bad for the race, believing that the story showed Nigerians as illiterate and superstitious drunks. They worried that the novel confirmed Europeans' racist "fantastic" concepts of Africa, "a continent of which they are profoundly ignorant"[13]. Some criticized the novel as unoriginal, labeling it as little more than a retelling of Yoruba tales heard in the village square and Tutuola was "merely" a storyteller who "embellished stories for a given audience"[14].

It was only later that the novel began to rise in general estimation. Critics began to value Tutuola's literary style as a unique exploration of the possibilities of African folklore instead of the more typical realist imitation of European novels in African novels. One of the major contributions that Tutuola made was to "kill forever any idea that Africans are the copyists of the cultures of other races"[15].

The lack of resolution in the novel was seen as more authentic, meant to enable group discussion in the same way that African riddles, proverbs and folktales did. The Nigerian critics continue to be divided on its worth, some calling it a work strictly beyond the post-colonial framework, praising its authentic way of writing, while some are not too kind and view the novel as an example of intellectual colonialism, catering to the White man's concept of an illiterate and drunk Africa.

Elechi Amadi is another writer who established himself as a unique figure in African fiction through his first appearance as a novelist, with *The Concubine* in 1966. His attempt to convey the daily life and texture of traditional, pre-colonial African village was appreciated worldwide. He distinguished himself by not offering any explicit contrasts between the traditional world and the one that replaced it. While most novels of his time dealt with the coming of the white man and the effect of that event, Amadi's novel centred on the rural life untouched by any alien influences at all.

In fact, this unique feature is not limited to *The Concubine*. The action of any of his novels like *The Concubine*, 1966 (about the beautiful woman Ihuoma who had been the concubine of the Sea-King in her last life, and thus in her present life spelt doom for her husband and lovers due to the jealousy of her supernatural husband of the past life), *The Great Ponds*, 1976 (about the battle between two village communities over the possession of a pond), *When God Came*, 2011(a science fiction) could have taken place either five years or a century before the colonial intrusion upon the area.

Likewise, the dilemmas that confront and finally destroy his heroes and heroines derive entirely from the beliefs, practices and events of their indigenous culture. It is only in his autobiographical war diary, *Sunset in Biafra*, 1969 and in *Estrangement*, 1986 that he talks about the life and times around him. *Sunset in Biafra* records his personal experiences in the Nigeria-Biafra war. *Estrangement* is set in the backdrop of this war too; though this novel uses this time as the backdrop, yet the plot and characters trace universal themes like love, marriage, jealousy, gender inequality and feminism, instead of revolving around the effects of colonization on the natives of Africa. Amadi's narrative style is compelling, transporting the reader into an authentic African world.

However, the novel that received widespread international acclaim was Chinua Achebe's *Things Fall Apart*. Though Tutuola's novel aroused exceptional worldwide interest, it was this novel, published in 1958, late in the colonial era, that inspired an entire first generation of African novelists to appropriate the English language by incorporating techniques of oral storytelling for a political purpose.

Raised by parents in the Igbo town of Ogidi in Nigeria, Achebe excelled at school and won a scholarship to study medicine, but changed his studies to English Literature at University College (now the University of Ibadan). He became fascinated with world religions and traditional African cultures, and began writing stories as a university student. It was during this time at Ibadan that Achebe began to become critical of European literature about Africa. After reading Joyce Cary's *Mister Johnson* (1939), about a cheerful Nigerian man who, among other things, also works for an abusive British storeowner, he was so disturbed by the book's portrayal of its Nigerian characters as either savages or buffoons that he decided to become a writer. Achebe recognized Cary's dislike for the African protagonist as a sign of the author's cultural ignorance.

Achebe later wrote novels in English that earned him worldwide acclaim. He defended the use of English, a language of colonisers, in

African literature, pointing out the need to answer the colonisers in their own tongue, and to break the myths created about the natives by those foreign writers. He accepted the wide-reaching potential of the English language and used it to tell his own tale of Africa.

Achebe demonstrated his masterly ability to 'Africanize' the English language through the introduction of Igbo words and proverbs into the flow of the text in *Things Fall Apart*. The roots of this writing were grounded in an urgency for self-assertion and the recovery of an 'African' identity in view of the severe colonial negation of the psyche of the black African. Achebe, as he himself professed, did not consider writing as simply a means of entertainment. For him, his novels were supposed to educate and regenerate a sense of nationalism in the youth:

> *The writer cannot expect to be excused from the task of re-education and regeneration that must be done. In fact he should march right in front*[16].

Achebe's novels focus on the traditions of the Igbo society, the effect of Christian influences, and the clash of Western and traditional values during and after the colonial writer. His style relies heavily on the Igbo oral tradition, and combines straightforward narration with representations of folk stories, proverbs and oratory. His writings include his first novel, *Things Fall Apart* (1958), *No Longer at Ease* (1960), *Arrow of God* (1964), *A Man of the People* (1966), *Anthills of Savannah* (1987), and his last *There Was a Country* (2012). He also published a number of short stories, children's books and essay collections.

Achebe, along with writers like Wole Soyinka, John Pepper Clark and T.M. Aluko etc. has successfully managed to raise the literature of this vast continent from the shadowy portrayal done by the European writers like Joseph Conrad and Joyce Cary. Their novels had depicted an Africa that is alarming and beyond redemption. *Heart of Darkness* and *Mister Johnson* showed a debased savage culture and the African writers, through their works have employed that very English language, the legacy of colonialism, to their best advantage. It became a powerful weapon to smash the stereotype and myth regarding the Dark Continent.

A shift in focus from the centre or core to the fringe or periphery is one of the most interesting and significant recent developments in literatures at international and intra-national levels all over the world. In a major showcasing the core to periphery model, unprecedented critical attention is now being focused on New Literatures emanating from marginalized areas like Asia, Africa, Latin America and the Caribbean and these are fast becoming a subject of intense academic interest and scholastic investigation. To begin with, African literature was the stronghold of male writers and critics, leading to a predominance of male oriented modes of creating and critiquing literature. African women writers and their works remained invisible in literary criticism, including academic research for a long time and a serious commitment to literary studies of these writers, both theoretical and critical is a fairly recent phenomenon. The focus now is not only on the male heroes painted by the male writers but also on the real female characters who exhibit their own individuality strength, or stand out even in oppressed and subjugated condition through sheer will and strength of character. They show strength, complexity and diversity of their characters, especially the female characters, through their novels.

In conformity with the shift in core to periphery paradigm, the continuous interrogation and revision of female empowerment in African literature is part of the reality of recent creative works of African women writers like Flora Nwapa, Buchi Emecheta, Ama Ata Aidoo, Bessie Head, Chimamanda Ngozi Adichie etc. who wrote or are writing in the wake of New Literatures in English. Their stories deal with a range of challenging themes including taboo subjects like homosexuality, domestic violence, female circumcision, ageism among others to produce a melting pot of narratives from interesting and informed perspectives.

Their unique contribution to African and World Literature lies in their strong commitment to the representation of women's life stories in order to draw critical attention to the problems of gender and class relations that cut across racial and geographical boundaries. These female writers do their best to highlight the social setup, the patriarchy and suppression of women that has been a part of the African tradition.

Not just this, but they also bring out the inherent strength of women characters who stand strong in the face of the colonizer and fight to retain their individuality. While most of the men in their novels succumb to the external pressures, it is the women who carry the African identity forward.

Flora Nwapa, who is called the mother of modern African literature, is the forerunner to a generation of African women writers. She is also acknowledged as the first African woman novelist to be published in the English language in Britain. She achieved international recognition with her first novel *Efuru* (1966). She is best known for recreating life and traditions from an Igbo woman's point of view.

Ama Ata Aidoo, another major name among the women writers of Africa, has dealt with the tension between Western and African worldviews in her works. Her first novel, *Our Sister Killjoy* (1977) remains one of her most popular works. Many of Aidoo's protagonists are women who defy the stereotypical women's roles of their time. She promoted and supported the work of African women writers extensively.

Buchi Emecheta, also a prominent woman writer from Africa wrote novels, plays, stories for children as well as her autobiography. She wrote more than twenty books, including *Second Class Citizen* (1974), *The Bride Price* (1976), *The Slave Girl* (1977) and *The Joys of Motherhood* (1979). Her themes of child slavery, motherhood, female independence and freedom through education gained recognition from critics and honours. Emecheta once described her stories as the stories of the world where women face the universal problems of poverty and oppression, and the longer they stay, no matter where they have come from originally, the more their problems become identical.

However, most African authoresses prefer to refrain from calling themselves as feminists. Flora Nwapa spoke:

> *I don't think that I am a radical feminist. I don't even accept that I am a feminist. I accept that I am an ordinary woman who is writing about what she knows.*[17]

Buchi Emecheta, another African woman writer, declared in a speech at Georgetown University that:

I have never called myself a feminist. Now if you choose to call me a feminist, that is your business; but I don't subscribe to the feminist idea that all men are brutal and repressive and we must reject them. Some of these men are my brothers and fathers and sons. Am I to reject them too?[18]

The above quotes exemplify the African cultural value, a world where feminism is a Western, un-African concept, and hence, a major section of the African writers is shy of accepting it, no matter what their works say.

Chimamanda Ngozi Adichie, a prominent contemporary authoress from Africa, takes a different stand, however, and acknowledges the question of gender discrimination and the need for feminist thinking. Known across the world for her novels, short stories and non-fiction writings, her works include the novels *Purple Hibiscus* (2003), *Half of a Yellow Sun* (2006), and *Americanah* (2013), the short story collection *The Thing Around Your Neck* (2009), and the book-length essays *We Should All Be Feminists* (2014) and *Dear Ijeawele, or A Feminist Manifesto in Fifteen Suggestions* (2017). Acknowledging the need for feminism to promote gender equality, she has, on multiple occasions, accepted her stand on the matter. In a 2014 interview, Adichie said on feminism and writing that she thinks of herself as a storyteller, but would not mind if someone were to tag her as a feminist writer.

According to her, if we do not address this elephant in the room directly, we would be pretending that women have never been excluded from the mainstream. We would be denying that women have, for centuries, been the target of gender discrimination. She stresses that feminism is not gender specific. Not all men are brutal, not all of them are oppressors. She talks of men she knows who are feminists, who believe in gender-equality, while there are also women who put down other women who ask for an equal status, under the patriarchal idea of male supremacy. She regrets how even little girls are taught 'shame' – to close their legs, to cover themselves, to make them feel guilty for their body, to make them feel guilty for being born a female. Her words bring to mind Okonkwo's chiding to his daughter for not sitting 'like a woman', with legs crossed in *Things Fall Apart*. The problem with such fixed notions of gender, she says, is that they do not accept people for what they are, but constantly tell them how they should be. For her, feminism is not the antonym for misogyny. Feminism is not misandry. Any person, be it a man or a woman, who dares to contest this notion, and believes in equality of all, irrespective of gender, is a feminist:

> *My own definition of a feminist is a man or a woman who says, 'Yes, there's a problem with gender as it is today and we must fix it, we must do better.' All of us, women and men, must do better.*[19]

Although some African writers might be unwilling to address and accept the tag of feminism as it is defined by the West, yet the underlying concept of group action by women, based on common welfare in society, cultural, economic, religious and political matters is indigenous and familiar to a majority of African women. Taking a more upfront line, Ama Ata Aidoo, one of the leading female African writers, states:

> *I should go on to insist that every man and every woman should be a feminist – especially if they believe that Africans should take charge of African land, African wealth, African lives and the burden of African development. It is not possible to advocate independence of African development without also believing that African women must have the best that the environment can offer. For some of us this is the crucial element of feminism.*[20]

Thus, feminism remains a widely debated concept in terms of African writing. Most of the study of African literature has, however, largely been the domain of post-colonial theorists and any other aspects like the social setup, gender studies or human relationships have found lesser space for themselves as subject of in-depth study. Even the most vocal writers, who through their works might appear champions of feminism, remain traditionally, distinctly heterosexual in their personal approach, supportive of motherhood and focused on issues of bread, butter, culture and power.

The rise to global prominence of African literature, and particularly of the African novel, has been seen by many as a vital development in contemporary world culture. African literature has a rich history, especially in the oral tradition. But as far as the written format goes, it's greatly influenced by the colonists. The relationship between oral and written traditions and in particular between oral and modern written literatures is one of great complexity and not a matter of simple evolution. Modern African literatures were born in the educational systems imposed by colonialism, with models drawn from Europe rather than existing African traditions. But the African oral traditions exerted their own influence on these literatures. And thus, most novels, even if talking about the modern man's crisis, walk in the shadows of African past. Be it the pre-colonial stories like *The Concubine* by Elechi Amadi, the colonial usurping like *Things Fall Apart* by Chinua Achebe or the post-colonial *The Bride Price* or *Half of a Yellow Sun* by Chimamanda Ngozi Adichie, dealing with the Civil Wars; all have a sense of dealing with the present times, as well as a longing for the past.

The African continent, being home to thousands of languages and hundreds of varying cultural identities, has rich and diverse traditions. The world's growing focus on this land has helped in shaping the image of Africa as being ethnically and culturally significant in world view. It comes as no surprise that the literature that has emerged from this land of diversities is equally diverse and multifaceted. We see the African writers' powerful connections and love for their respective places of origin, its history, traditions and customs through their works. We see a process of coming to terms with the past, and we see criticism and hope both from those who live on the continent and those whose lives have taken them away from it.

Some of the works attempt to reconcile history and consequence, identity and environment. Some are indicative of a changing Africa, from pre-conial times to colonial and post-colonial one, struggling with democracy and the changes that come with growth. These depictions offer a glimpse into a varied yet connected experience. These stories are personal, in the voice of those who have experienced and inherited them. African literature, rich in its oral tradition, deals with a range of social and cultural issues, from women's rights and feminism to post-war and post-colonial identity, and also dwells much on aspects like social set-up and human relationships, thus providing a wholesome mixture of all genres within itself.

Theme of Love and Marriage in African Literature

The theme of love and marriage in literature is perhaps as old as literature itself. Be it the earliest love ballads or drama, almost all treat love as a recurring theme. Love for a person – parent, sibling or romantic interest; love for one's nation, love for a friend etc., all have found a good place in the novels, since the very beginning. From Homer's Iliad to Shakespeare's *Merchant of Venice*; Jane Austen's *Emma* to Stephanie Meyer's *Twilight*, love has constantly been treated as the moving force across generations and nations, in the different genres of literature. The theme of love has been a recurrent one in the history of literature. Love is an interesting subject in literature because love, unlike other themes, has many twists and turns and many different endings. Love has been present in early works of literature, such as Greek, Roman and Indian mythology, and has continued through Victorian and contemporary times.

Love is unique as it remains a constant even when it spans through different decades, centuries, novels and characters. The basic element of love remains the same. In addition, love is used in literature in a way to compliment other themes associated with inter-personal and social relationships or even patriotism and love for the self. It is useful as it gives common ground to otherwise unrelatable individuals. For example, we are able to identify as much with Aku-nna wondering what her life would have been if her family had not interfered as we have understood the pain of Juliet who is unable to live with her love because of the feud between her family and Romeo's. Many times, literature exhibits love in an unrealistic manner, usually portraying a happy ending, but mostly this is just an exhibit of what the author believes would be in a perfect world. The novels taken under this study however have a very realistic approach to love and none try to draw perfection in an imperfect world.

Amadi explores the power of love in his novel *The Concubine*, yet does not try to make it invincible. Though love wins in spirit due to the indomitable love of Ekwueme and Ihuoma, and the hero comes out as a winner in the eyes of the reader, the reality remains that he did die, and the wrath of the Sea-King won. There is no happy ending here and the novel closes showing the devastated heroine crying over her fate. Emecheta, in *The Bride Price*, too, attempts to show the all-powerful love giving Aku-nna wings to fly out of the shackles of Ibuza but even in her flight, the final chains keep attached and ultimately bring her down; the victory is not complete. The end not absolutely happy. Achebe's portrayal of love in *Things Fall Apart* is multi-faceted, and related intrinsically with the lead character, Okonkwo. His relationship with his wives, children, friends and land form the core of the theme of love in the novel. In a way, his tragedy is also the tragedy of failure in establishing a winning love relationship in most of his life's angles.

Love stories across the world talk of giving oneself unreservedly to another and gaining the whole self or sense of identity back. Love, used both positively and negatively, forms the centre of most mythologies of the world. Happiness and sadness, good and evil, all revolve around the theme of love across cultures. It is no surprise, therefore, that every culture, every mythology has its own god or goddess of love. Be it Kamadeva of Indian mythology, Aphrodite of Greek mythology, Cupid or Venus, the Roman gods of love, each of these gods and goddesses have prominent role in their respective mythologies, encompassing love, beauty, desire, sex, fertility, prosperity and victory.

In fact, like most mythologies of the world, African mythology too has its very own goddess of love in Oshun, often called Yalorde (queen). She was given this title because of her beauty, kindness and open nature. Oshun has skin the colour of cinnamon, radiant black eyes and silky black hair. She is the daughter of Yemaya, the goddess of all waters, and is herself the goddess of freshwater: rivers, lakes and ponds. The people in her kingdom love her dearly because of the care she shows them. She is best known for her kindness, which in African mythology is considered the most important quality that anyone can possess.

Love is something that all human beings desire in life yet it is an undervalued emotion in the worldview that shapes much of the modern ideas. Seldom do we come across a critic assessing a literary piece on the theme of love: especially when studying African literature. The postcolonial theme, the clash of cultures remains the most widely studied theme in African literature. The white man's prejudice and discrimination, the native's struggle to uphold his identity – these seem to have a centerhold on most of the studies. Love and marriage, however, continue to be a constant theme in literature of Africa. Interwoven with social reality and cultural practices of the continent, the novels provide an insight into the socio-historic background of the Africans, their beliefs, myths and tradition, with respect to love and marriage.

The theme of marriage, again, is an age-old one *Pamela, or Virtue Rewarded,* touted as one of the earliest novels in English literature deals with the protagonist's difficulties in life and how her high moral stand is ultimately rewarded with a good marriage. Marriage in literature has been presented in a variety of forms. In many of the novels of late eighteenth century and early nineteenth century, marriage was the goal toward which the story tended and would serve as the perfect ending to redeem the hero or heroine if they needed to be redeemed or rewarded for their virtue. Marriage in fiction reflects the position of marriage in society. As Simone de Beauvoir stated:

> *Marriage is the destiny traditionally offered to women by society. It is still true that most women are married, or have been, or plan to be or suffer from not being.*

The celibate woman is to be explained and defined with reference to marriage, whether she is frustrated, rebellious, or even indifferent in regard to that institution.[21]

Marriage has always been a very different thing for a man as compared to what it means for a woman. Marriage was considered the ultimate social aim of woman, and thus, most novels ended at the altar, with a hope of happily-ever-after. However, a shift in this patriarchal notion began to be visible towards the end of the Victorian era. The unequal treatment of a man and a woman in marriage had long meant a certain imbalance as well as a degree of hypocrisy in this institution. The so-called two halves were never equal. The woman was forced to take up the secondary role, while the man played the superior one – the bread earner, the decision-maker, the owner of the house – the head of the family. The final two decades of the Victorian era witnessed the beginning of a shift in social attitudes regarding gender relations, which was marked by a steady move away from the pattern of patriarchal male supremacy and female dependence towards the modern pattern of gender equality. Spread of education among the women, the revised laws of inheritance and universal suffrage etc. gave a new identity to the women. One, wherein they could be something without dependence on their spouse. The writers now wanted to focus on this newfound liberty, and took this opportunity to write about the falsity and hypocrisy in the institution of marriage.

The Woman Question, raised by Mary Wollstonecraft in her pamphlet, *A Vindication of the Rights of Women* (1792), influenced the mid-Victorian and the late-Victorian feminists. The upper-class women were urged to obtain a proper education and profession in order to make themselves financially independent. Writers growingly criticized the marginalization of women in marriage. Charlotte Bronte, George Elliot, Thomas hardy, Charles Dickens are just some of the notable writers, who based their plot on the theme of marriage. Jane Austen, in fact, has woven all her novels around the theme of marriage. The pressure to marry (and to marry well) forms the focal point of all her plots. Love vs. duty or responsibility, love vs. money etc. are the major conflicts we get to see in her work; in the build up to the marriages in her novels. Some characters married for love, some for convenience, some under family pressure but what continued to be the central focus throughout, was marriage.

Thereafter, novels not only focused on the attainment of the match but rather began to deal with the practical problems dealt to the woman after marriage. The subordination of woman in marriage came to be a central theme. Virginia Woolf's characters like Clarissa Dalloway and Lily Briscoe began to gain widespread popularity and empathy. Their projection of the actual day-to-day sacrifices that women made in order to maintain peace and harmony around them, to keep the male ego afloat, and to keep their marriage sailing was easily relatable to a large number of women, bearing the burden of this social alliance. How these characters had to give up their autonomy and deny their wholeness in order to keep the marital bond strong was something that the readers understood too well. Thomas Hardy showcased how badly it could end for all, if only a woman refused to bow down to the norms of society, like Arabella, and continued to live life on her terms.

Modern novels have treated the theme of love and marriage through the overlapping categories of race, gender, class, ability and sexuality among others. The factors that compel people to remain single or get married form the core of a majority of novels today. For example, Sita, in *Where Shall We Go This Summer?* by Anita Desai, is maladjusted in her marriage and is unable to conform herself to the expectations that the society holds of a married woman. She had been depressed for a long period of time and it took her twenty years to unleash her emotions and break out into a rebel. She feels that her life has been reduced to a procreating machine, with no meaning for herself. She feels herself tossed and driven, like a plaything of obscure forces. Sita seems to exemplify the point Simone de Beauvoir stressed in *The Second Sex*, calling out the negative aspect of a woman's marriage and subsequent pregnancy. As the Other, or more particularly as a wife or a mother, a woman has never been free to define her own possibilities. She is forced to find meaning in the abstract, or, in the patriarchal cultures outside herself. Be it the successful wife or a zealous mother,

her identity depends on these roles, and their success by the standards set by society, again patriarchal, for her to have any chance in this world where the woman is born as a subordinate being. Most of the writers have well understood and painted these complexities in their novels. Marriage and motherhood have been a constant goal for female characters across literatures of the world barring a few exceptions. Even in these exceptions, we witness the explanations required to justify such a thought process where becoming a wife or a mother does not become the primary goal for a female character. On the other hand, single men are strewn over literature of all genre, not requiring any justification, instead seen in the light of greatness and selflessness…or the eccentric; but seldom viewed with pity, as would be the case with the other sex.

African literature projects marriage as an integral part of the social setup. Marriage for the Africans is not just a union of two individuals but also their families. Very much in the lines of the Indian family system, the Africans considered marriage to be an amalgamation of two people, their families, culture and communities. Usually people sought to marry outside their villages so as to establish relations with different societies and communities. The arrangement of marriage and the various ceremonies involved are deeply ingrained in the social system, such that almost everyone takes part in the rituals, and is well aware of the native customs. They help build a strong harmony within the society. As we witness in *Things Fall Apart*, the whole village wears a festive air in celebration of Obierika's daughter's marriage. All the women and children of the neighbourhood gather at his compound to help 'the bride's mother in her difficult but happy task of cooking for a whole village.'[22]

The wedding festivities not only were enjoyed by the immediate family, but an extensive group of relatives and village folk:

> *On the following morning the entire neighbourhood wore a festive air because Okonkwo's friend, Obierika, was celebrating his daughter's uri. It was the day on which her suitor (having already paid the greater part of her bride-price) would bring palm-wine not only to her parents and*

immediate relatives but to the wide and extensive group of kinsmen called umunna. Everybody had been invited—men, women and children.[23]

Marriage is considered one of the most important steps in the life of all human beings on this planet. The Africans view the family institution as the foundation of their society. Its importance lies not only in its being an agent of cultural conditioning of the young people in the society but also in the fact that marriage and procreation, which take place at the family level, make family indispensable for the continuity of the society. Social status and expansion of one's family line were the two major aims for this social union. "Marriage in Africa was the means of ensuring reproduction", explained Dr. Lynne Brydon in the opening remarks of the 2017 Cadbury Conference, an annual event held by the University of Birmingham's Department of African Studies and Anthropology (DASA). Different cultures have different rituals and beliefs about marriage. Love, economic status, religious beliefs, cultural history and social acceptance are just a few reasons that influence individuals marrying across different cultures. The African culture is very diverse and full of tradition based on social norms that have been around for generations. Their social life is patterned around a strong clan and extended family ties. This plays a vital role in the marriage process. The literature of Africa projects various types of marital alliances. Some of them, the most commonly represented ones are:

- *a.* ***Pre-nuptial Relations:*** Among the Hausa and many other tribes like Awok, Borok, Kamuku, Tula, Waje etc. there is a custom known as '*tsaranchi*', by which young unmarried boys and girls live together with the connivance of their parents. A lad may, in this way, sleep constantly with a girl to whom he is betrothed. Or, he may sleep with various girls with a view to making up his mind as to which one he would marry eventually. But if the girl becomes enceinte both the young people are disgraced in the eyes of their society. A great deal of importance is attached to pre-nuptial chastity, especially for girls. The boys, on the other hand, were kind of accepted for their wild ways. For example, in *The Bride Price* we witness the shame that is brought upon Okonkwo's family due to Akunna's self-professed lack of virginity to her captor, but this same captor was sanctioned to court her and play with her body, even without her will. Also, those same people had no reservations as far as their sons' late-night escapades with their girlfriends was concerned. We see Okonkwo and Ngbeke's young sons, Iloba, 20 and Osenekwu,17 happily marching off to meet their girls after dinner:

> *The boys put on their long evening loin cloths and went out of the hut. It was time for them to visit their sweethearts.*[24]

b. **Kinship Marriage**: In Africa, where the patriarchal family is the principal form of social grouping, marriage is regulated by kinship considerations. There are fixed prohibited degrees within which marriage would be incest. Thus, the marriage of any of the cousins, to each other, would be regarded as incest among most of the animistic tribes. But among some of the tribes, the marriage of first cousins would only be discountenanced, while a marriage between far relations is permitted. Among Muslims, however, marriage of first cousins is permitted. But the marriage of cross cousins is considered superior to that of parallel cousins. It would be incest among most of the tribes for half-brothers and half-sisters to marry. Such marriages, though, are not very uncommon among the Yoruba.

c. **Levirate Marriage**: The term levirate is applied to those cases in which a man marries his deceased brother's wife. Levirate marriage is quite common among the African tribes and is intimately connected with the idea of woman as heritable property which can be transferred from one owner to another but must be kept within the family. It is a custom common in many tribes wherein the inherited widow is allowed to redeem her freedom by refunding the bride price which her deceased husband originally paid. This form of marriage also facilitates the acquisition of additional wives and the increase of the family. We witness this kind of marriage in *The Bride Price* by Buchi Emecheta where Ma Blackie is inherited by Okonkwo, her deceased husband's brother. The first hint of this marital alliance can be seen for the first time in this novel when Aku-nna is walking back to Ibuza, her ancestral village, along with her cousin Ogugua. Aku-nna's father, Ezekiel Odia is dead, and having no financial means to support their stay in Lagos city now, her mother, Ma Blackie, is taking her and Nna-nndo, her brother, to the village. Ogugua, a girl of the village, daughter of Okonkwo, Ezekiel Odia's brother, knows well the customs and traditions of her tribe, having lived all her life among them. And so, she tells Aku-nna:

> *"Now we are going to be friends. We shall be like sisters, especially if your mother chooses to be with my father." "Why should my mother choose your father? How come?" Aku-nna asked, puzzled. The two girls had lagged behind, engrossed in their gossip. Ogugua burst out laughing. "You're almost fourteen years old now and you still don't know the customs of our Ibuza people? Your mother is inherited by my father, you see, just as he will inherit everything your father worked for."*[25]

Later we see Ogugua's words turning true in the novel. As per the customs of the tribe, Ma Blackie (Aku-nna's mother) was inherited by Okonkwo and she became his fourth wife. His (Okonkwo's) eyes were already set on his brother's wife, his brother's property, and the bride price that his brother's daughter would fetch him. Thus, in order to ensure that Ma Blackie doesn't say no to his advances, and to secure his right over Aku-nna's future bride price, he decided that she should be allowed to have her way when observing the widow's rites after her first husband's death:

> *"Let her (Ma Blackie) wear the black cotton when she feels like it. Let her have a black headtie too. She was married in church, so why should we let her become infested with lice?" There was a noticeable hush as everyone realized the message behind this pronouncement. Okonkwo Odia wanted his late brother's wife to stay in the family, to be his fourth wife.*[26]

And true enough, after the completion of the mandatory mourning period, Ma Blackie is inherited by her dead husband's brother:

> *Nine months after death of her husband, a hut was built for her next to Oguagua's mother's, and in time it was there that she was visited at night by Okonkwo.*
> *She became his fourth wife.*[27]

d. **Sororate Marriage:** Among some tribes, if a man's wife dies, he is entitled to the refund of the whole or a part of the bride price. It is no doubt with a view to avoiding this refund that we find the custom of marriage with the deceased wife's sister, though the cementing of family ties could also be an object.

e. **Marriage of Slaves:** Slave-marriages were quite common in Africa. Masters could marry off their slaves as they pleased. Thus, a master who had a female slave could give her in marriage to the male slave of a friend, and would obtain both the marriage price and the rights over any children born of such marriage. Or an owner of a female slave could give her as a concubine to a member of his family. In such cases, however, the girl's consent was generally obtained, and if she subsequently bore a child, or even had a miscarriage, she became a free woman. Masters also commonly freed their female slaves in a court of law, and gave them in marriage to free men. Buchi Emecheta, in her novel, *The Slave Girl*, points out:

> *No woman is ever free. To be owned by a man is great honour.*[28]

The Slave Girl is a novel about the sociological concepts of bondage – about the tribe's, the family's and the husband's claims on a woman's selfhood. The protagonist of the novel, Ojebeta Obanje, makes this characteristic final statement towards the end of the novel, accepting totally her subservience to the tribal codes in these words:

> *She was…happy to be submissive, even to accept an occasional beating, because that was what she had been brought up to believe a wife should expect.*[29]

Ojebeta's marriage is fixed with Clifford, the kind-hearted son of Ma Palagada, her mistress:

> *Things seem to be looking up for her when she agrees to marry Clifford, Ma Palagada's son who grows up to be a humane and kind hearted adult, to live as his slave wife, because he sees her not entirely as a slave but as a person.*[30]

Her agreement to marry Clifford is also born out of her understanding that as a slave she has no choice in the matter. However, when Ma Palagada dies, Ojebeta runs away, preferring to face poverty and homelessness on her own rather than continue being a slave-girl in the family which would now be run by her new mistress Victoria, a mean and condescending daughter of Ma Palagoda. Later, her elder brother who had sold her as a slave initially pays eight pounds to Clifford to secure her freedom, to which Clifford gladly agrees. However, even after getting this freedom, Ojebeta is unable to free herself from the shackles of slavery to which a woman is doomed in her lifetime. She is seen submitting her independence to her husband, becoming his property according to the ways of the clan, with no say of her own. The last paragraph of the novel is an epitaph on the powerlessness of a dehumanized woman in a traditional Ibuza society and reads:

> *So as Britain was emerging from war once more victorious and claiming to have stopped the slavery which she had helped to spread in all her black colonies, Ojebeta, now a woman of thirty-five, was changing masters.*[31]

And, on the one hand, where marrying a slave-girl was not unheard of for the upper-class people, subjugating them into the position of a slave-wife, for a girl of a good, respectable family, marrying a slave was taboo. Clifford wanted to marry Obejeta because she is:

> "...*an innocent girl, a girl who would ever look up to him*" *and a slave because* "*his mother had paid for her.*"[32]

Certainly not the most convincing or the best of reasons to get married. But in *The Bride Price* by Buchi Emecheta, we see the whole plot revolving around the reluctance to accept a descendant of a slave as a son-in-law by Okonkwo. Chike is a decent guy, well educated, financially stable and well-positioned in society, yet the fact that his ancestors were slaves is unacceptable to Okonkwo and he refuses Aku-nna's marriage to Chike in spite of the two young people being completely in love with each other. That Aku-nna could fall in love with the descendant of a slave was entirely unthinkable to her family:

> *Iloba cried, his mouth tasting salty. If this was true, it was the greatest insult that could befall a family like theirs, which had never been tainted with the blood of a foreigner, to say nothing of that of the descendants of slaves. "I will kill her if this is true." Okonkwo swore to himself.*[33]

f. ***Polygyny***: Africa is distinguished by the high prevalence of polygynous marriages. Polygyny, or the system by which one man marries more than one woman, is by all the tribes recognized as legitimate; but in practice it is, for biological and economic reasons, the privilege of the wealthy few. While the more important pagan chiefs may have as many as a hundred wives, and the Muslims potentiates may, in addition to their four legitimate wives, keep hundreds of concubines, the poor are compelled by necessity to remain monogamous. It is, therefore, not only the preserve of elite men but is a status to which many men of moderate means aspire at some point in their life span. Madume, in Elechi Amadi's *The Concubine*, is one such poor folk who is counting on the bride price he would be receiving as the time of the marriage of his daughters from his first and till now only wife, Wolu, to marry again:

> *Wolu, Madume's only wife, bore him four daughters – a most annoying thing, despite the dowries he knew he would collect when they got married. But who would bear his name when he died? The thought of*

his elder brother's sons inheriting his houses and lands filled him with dismay. But there was time enough to marry another wife and the problem did not bother him unduly. Moreover, his daughter's marriages would provide him with the money for another wife.[34]

The persistence of polygyny among rural people could be explained through two reasons. Firstly, the African economic system wherein the women and children are largely self-supporting. Much of rural African subsistence is based on the work of women in their gardens; men make only modest contributions. Typically, the lands belong in the name of the men by virtue of their membership in kinship or village units. A man who wishes to add another wife to his household needs to give a share of his land to her for sustenance. But apart from that he practically has nothing else to do for maintaining them, since women, in effect, pay their own way. They produce food and rear their children. There are numerous examples of female farming and the women going to the market to sell their produce to earn their own bread, as well as for the upkeep of their children. The other reason behind the cultural practice of polygamy in Africa is the overriding desire and necessity to have children, especially a male progeny. The concept of divorce is extremely rare in the African society, and hence in polygamy, the first wife is not rejected or put away when the second is taken in.

One might say that, in African traditions, the indissolubility of marriage is conditioned to its fruitfulness. Practically the birth of a child marks the 'consummation' of the marriage. So, if and African woman did not give her husband children, or even failed to give a desired number of children, she was considered to have failed him – and society – in the most serious way possible. And if he chose to consider this marriage null and send her back to her family, society – and the woman herself – would agree. This mentality has been aptly presented in *The Joys of Motherhood* by Buchi Emecheta, in which the protagonist. Nnu Ego's life begins to fall apart after marriage as she is unable to bear children. She was the love child of an influential chief, raised with great care and given in marriage to a worthy man. At sixteen, she is married to Amatokwu, who carried her off ceremoniously in the best of tribal traditions. Her father accepts the normal bride price to show that he gave his blessings to the marriage but he sent his daughter away with lots of wealth, trinkets and beads, along with seven hefty men and seven young girls at her disposal. It was indeed pure display of wealth. But when she does not conceive even after many months of her marriage, her husband takes a new wife, expressing his disappointment in these words:

> "What do you want me to do?" Amatokwu asked. "I am a busy man, I have no time to spend my precious male seed on a woman who is infertile. I have to raise children for my line."[35]

Nnu Ego, who had a very strong desire to become a mother, begins to secretly nurse the new child of Amatokwu's second wife whenever the real mother is preoccupied until eventually from regular stimulations, milk begins to drip from her breasts. However, her husband finds out about this act and beats her and returns her to her father's house.

We witness a similar case in Emecheta's *The Bride Price* wherein, Ma Blackie, the mother of Aku-nna and Nna-nndi, was still subjected to humiliation by her husband Ezekiel Odia, who desired more children:

> *Ma blackie… had a family problem. She was very slow in getting herself pregnant again. Since her husband returned from Burma, when the war ended some five years before, she had not been pregnant like other wives whose husbands had gone abroad to fight Hitler. Her husband, Ezekiel Odia, had sent her to all the native doctors he could afford in Lagos but still no more children… In despair she decided to go to their hometown, Ibuza, to placate their Oboshi river goddess into giving her some babies.*[36]

Ezekiel Odia used to leave no stone unturned to remind Ma Blackie, that as his wife it was her duty to bear him children:

> *She (Aku-nna) has heard over and over again her Ma Blackie and her Nna (father) quarrelling over this great issue of childlessness. Nna would go on and on, talking in that small, sad voice of his, telling Ma, reminding her, that he had had to pay double the normal bride price before he was able to take Ma as his wife. He would work himself up, his little voice whining like a hungry dog's, and then drawing himself up on tiptoe, maybe hoping to add to his stature by so doing, he would remind Ma Blackie that having paid this heavy bride price he had had their marriage sanctified by Anglicanism. And what he has to show for it all – an only son!*[37]

Polygyny and concubinage are the inevitable consequences of the inter-tribal wars that largely prevailed in Africa. Apart from the desire for children, this factor was also quite important in giving rise to polygyny. The male captives were slain or enslaved and the females became the wives or concubines of their captors. The levirate system also facilitates the acquisition of additional wives, and the custom which forbids sexual relation with a wife who is weaning a child is further encouragement to polygyny. In *The Joys of Motherhood* by Emecheta, Nnaife, the second husband of Nnu Ego, is forced by African tradition to inherit his brother's four wives consequent upon his death. This, in spite of the fact that Nnu Ego had bore him nine children by then.

But of course, the strongest incentive of all remains the great desire of the Africans to beget as many children as possible. Children are an economic asset of the first importance and no man can attain a position of real political power unless he has the backing of a large family. Nor does it appear that polygyny is very distasteful to women, for it is commonly the wife who incites the husbands to add to the number of his wives, no doubt with a view to lessening her domestic burdens. And the position of women in African tradition is such that even if the wife might resent the arrival of a rival, all she can do is keep her displeasure to herself.

g. *Polyandry*: Polyandry is the system of marriage in which one woman marries more than one man. How far we may say this is prevalent in Africa depends on the precision with which we define polyandry. In the truest form of polyandry, the wife had simultaneously two or more recognized husbands who share her marital favors. True polyandry is thus to be distinguished from cicisbeism, which is the counterpart of concubinage, i.e., the woman has a male partner in sexual relations, but if children are born to this union the cicisbeo is not the legal father.

In *Things Fall Apart* by Chinua Achebe, a kind of polyandry is witnessed where Ekewefi, Okonkwo's second wife, leaves her first husband to come live with him:

> *There was no festival in all the seasons of the year which gave her as much pleasure as the wrestling match. Many years ago, when she was the village beauty Okonkwo had won her heart by throwing the Cat in the greatest contest within living memory. She did not marry him because he was too poor to pay her bride price. But a few years later she ran away from her husband and came to live with Okonkwo.*[38]

An example of cicisbeism is evident in Buchi Emecheta's *The Joys of Motherhood*. In the novel, Ona is the beautiful daughter of a respected tribal chief who took such great pride in his daughter that he maintained she must never marry:

> *His Ona, a "priceless jewel… was never going to stoop to any man. She was free to have men, however, and if she bore a son, he would take her father's name."*[39]

Ona is depicted as a feminine ideal, very alluring to men, had several lovers, but belonged to none.

b. *Marriage by Purchase*: Purchase is the only marriage recognized by many tribes in Africa, especially the Muslims. Marriage by purchase assumes that the woman is a transferable piece of property. The man buys gifts, or service to her parents, complete rights over the woman and her subsequent progeny. This is shown by the restrictions which are placed on his rights if he fails to make his payments or if they are deficient. Among some tribes the purchase price is recoverable if the girl proves barren, or should the wife die childless. The concept of the woman as the personal property of the husband is further illustrated by the rule that she can be inherited like any other property. We see this sense if inheritance in many African novels. For example, the dialogue of Nnaife to his wife Nnu Ego in *The Joys of Motherhood* throws light on this mentality:

> *Nnaife retorts "Did I not pay your bride price? Am I not your owner? You know, the airs you put on are getting rather boring. I know you are the daughter of Agbadi. Pity he did not marry you himself and keep you by his side forever. If you are going to be my wife, you must accept my work, my way of life. I will not have it any other way."*[40]

Where payments are small the idea of purchase has receded, and many parents refuse to enact a high dowry on the ground that they would accept a nominal amount to keep up the tradition but would not be selling their daughters for a price. Those less scrupulous, however give their daughters to the highest bidder. Sometimes the payments do not cease on marriage. They are continued or not accordingly, as the girl proves herself to be a satisfactory wife.

i. ***Marriage by Exchange***: In marriage by exchange two men agree to exchange their sisters as brides. The girl exchanged may be the man's own sister or a sister in the classificatory sense, i.e., any available female relative. A father might also exchange his daughter to add to the number of his wives. The contract is thus not so much a matter of arrangement between two individuals as between two families, and as in the case of marriage by purchase, the girl is a mere pawn. Under the exchange system the brothers and sisters of one family frequently marry the brothers and sisters of another and their children again intermarry. But among most tribes, care is taken to avoid inbreeding in this way, there being often a definite prohibition against the marriage of first cousins.

j. ***Marriage by Capture***: Women of one tribe were commonly captured in war by men of another, but marriage by capture as a normal mode of mating can only be said to exist to a limited extent. Most of the recorded cases of marriage by capture are those of elopement thinly disguised, for the capture is seldom affected without the girl's consent previously obtained. The seizure and carrying off of the bride, which is often an integral part of the marriage ceremonies (whether the marriage is one of purchase, exchange or elopement), may be a dramatic representation of a system of bride-capture formerly in vogue, but it is more probably symbolic of the captor's superior power and adroitness, and perhaps also as assertion of the patrilocal as against the matrilocal principle. In *The Bride Price*, Emecheta describes the callous ritual in these words:

> *The women, led by Ngbeke with the gong, went around the town crying: "Who has stolen our daughter? Let him inform us!" Gong, gong, gong, gong.... Even as they were doing all this, they knew it was useless. Aku-nna had gone. All the man responsible had to do was cut a curl of her hair – "isinmo"– and she would belong to him for life. Or he could force her into sleeping with him, and if she refused his people would assist him by holding her down until she was disvirgined. And when that had been done, no other person would want to take her anymore.*[41]

If we regard marriage as a contract between two families and not merely between two individuals, then the idea of capture becomes more prominent, and the fact that the girl's consent has been previously obtained or not, is only circumstantial. While in most cases, the girl's consent is sought previous to the whole set-up of capture, there are instances where she's just a non-consenting participant in the whole drama. However, the bride's parents have, in all cases, to be subsequently pacified by gifts. Though once the capture is done, there is not much that the bride's family can do. For none with high social respect would want to take a captured bride. she's as good as gone.

We see a similar case in *The Bride Price*. When Aku-nna is captured by Okoboshi and her family learns of her kidnapping, they all go about looking for her in the night. Okoboshi's family was sure to be found out, thus they waited just enough to break the news themselves to Aku-nna's family. And in the dead of night a few men from Okoboshi's family came to Okonkwo's compound to tell him that his daughter was their's now. There was nothing that he could do now. Even if he fought to get her back, he would not get the bride price he had set his eyes on for so long. Nobody would want to marry a girl who had been captured by another man. For all they knew, he must have already cut her lock of hair or had sex with her, thereby laying his claim on her as per the law of the land. Thus, he had to accept their offer for a formal negotiation, with whatever bride price they offered in the name of custom.

The men from Okoboshi's family brought more gin to dull Okonkwo's pain at his loss, and a minimal amount was agreed upon as the bride price for Aku-nna. After all, she was just like any other girl now. All this modern education did nothing good for any woman. If anything, it had made her arrogant and unprepared for real-life circumstances like this one she had gotten into. Had she got her mind grounded like other village girls, unadulterated by high flying ideas provided by education, she might have been saved. She might have foreseen what was coming and might have run to safety just like other girls in the dance. But caught totally unaware, she was captured and carried away by her captors.

Okonkwo could not control the matter now and thus said yes to the offer brought by Okoboshi's family and drank the token wine (gin) brought by them as a kind of formal offer of marriage. Drinks flowed, and having come to terms with what had transpired, he prayed amid the pieces of kola-nuts scattered on the floor according to the wedding customs of Ibuza. He prayed to the gods that Aku-nna may bear many children.

The importance given to the virgin status of a new bride once again comes to fore when Okonkwo assures his new relatives that Aku-nna had never crossed her line and was as chaste as a bud. They decided to meet the next morning with the proof of Aku-nna's virginity with the bedsheet that would bear proof on this matter to further the proceedings of the marriage negotiations. Okonkwo assured them that his daughter was as chaste as a bud. Nobody had touched her. He asked the groom's family to bring the best quality of palm wine and 'they parted as reasonably happy in-laws, whilst the women slept'.[42]

Thus, whether through consent or not, once the bride is captured, she's married off to the captor, and the rituals are completed, be it of praying to the ancestors, gifts of kolanut, or the payment of bride price.

k. *Marriage by Elopement*: Colloquially, elopement is often used to refer to a marriage conducted in sudden and secretive fashion usually involving a hurried flight away from one's place of residence together with one's beloved with the intention of getting married. Elopement is another regular method of contracting marriage in Africa. Marriage by capture or abduction can also be included in this category when the girls are not carried off against their will, but with their consent, by their lovers.

The young people arrange the night for the elopement, the parents being kept in ignorance. The abductors leave presents of hoes before the hut of the girl's parents, and this is the first announcement the parents receive of their daughter's runaway match. The young pair live a simple secluded life away from their hometown for a while during which time efforts are made to reach out to the girl's parents to seek their approval. If at the end of this period the parents come and greet their daughter and accept a bride price, this is a sign that the marriage is approved and a great feast is held. But if the parents ignore the young couple and refuse the bride price, it is a sign of displeasure, and it is customary that the bride-groom should send the bride back. Sexual relations between runaway couples are taboo until the girl's parents have given a formal consent to the marriage. If the girl in such scenario gets pregnant, the common belief is that she would die in her first childbirth.

We witness a similar situation in *The Bride Price*, where Aku-nna runs away from the house of her abductor Okoboshi, along with her lover Chike. Okonkwo, in the meanwhile had already promised her hand to Okoboshi, also, he would never entertain the idea of being related to a slave's descendant, i.e., Chike. Hence, in spite of all entreaties, he refuses to accept the bride price of Aku-nna from Chike and his father. The poor girl, torn between love and tradition, meets as untimely death while delivering her child, thus proving the myth of the bride price true:

> So it was that Chike and Aku-nna substantiated the traditional superstition they had unknowingly set out to eradicate. Every girl born in Ibuza after Aku-nna's death was told her story, to reinforce the old

> *taboos of the land. If a girl wished to live long and see her children's children, she must accept the husband chosen for her by her people, and the bride price must be paid. If the bride price was not paid, she would never survive the birth of her first child.*[43]

Love and marriage form an integral part of African literature and examples are aplenty of how these twin themes play a defining role in the social set-up of Africa. Having said that, it is also undeniable that both love and marriage, in the African culture, are coated with patriarchy, where gender acts as a significant factor. Marie Linton Umeh surmises that African women, being products of a traditional African culture are quite ineffective in a male dominated world. In her introduction to a collection of essays titled, *Emerging Perspectives on Buchi Emecheta*, Marie Umeh observes that the novels of Buchi Emecheta reflect what Kate Millet calls sexual politics – the patriarchal principle by which all males dominate females and elders dominate the young. Umeh asserts that according to Emecheta, Igbo society embodies the principle of male dominance and female subordination and therefore:

> *Emecheta's women, for the most part, are sacrificed at the altar of a male-oriented society, and men exploit the sex/gender system to maintain male dominance.*[44]

The power of love has been depicted as the ultimate one that not only empowers indivduals to show strength beyond the ordinary, but can also overpower the mightiest of all. In 'The Marriage of Anansewa', by Efua T. Sutherland, we see an almost dead Anansewa rising to life when true love calls her:

Ananse: [Suddenly] Oh, she is waking. Are there such wonders in the world? My child is waking. *[Anansewa stirs]* Does love have such power? Christie open the doors and let everybody in to see the power of amazing love … Love has awakened my child… His love has won victory for us all.[45]

The whole dead act was feigned by Anansewa and her father Ananse, who wanted to avoid her marrying any one of the four chiefs coming to claim her. This elaborate plan was staged to ensure that nobody would counter her marriage with Christie, her true beloved. The feudal system of the society would not have permitted her to choose a commoner over the chiefs, and hence, this is how she went about to claim her lover's right over her. Anansewa declared that it was indeed a special person who could raise his daughter from the dead. None could match his love, and hence, she rightfully belonged to him and no one could contest this.

The themes of love and marriage are worked out frequently in the literary traditions of Africa, within the strictures laid down by society and religion, showing the struggle between the rural and the newly urban, between genders and between generations. The oral tradition is clearly evident in the written works of the novelists, moving beyond ordinary imitation of original narratives to imbibing them into a dynamic text of artistic activity, showcasing the culture and tradition of Africa.

Love and marriage not only make an interesting topic to read, but are actually an integral part of the African life. One of the most elaborate cultural traditions practiced in most of the novels of the three writers taken under this study is the custom of marriage.

John Mbiti in the book *African Religions and Philosophy* relates that marriage is a complex affair with economic and religious aspects which often overlap so firmly that they cannot be separated from one another.

For Africans, marriage is the focus of existence. It is the point where all the members of a given community meet: the departed, the living and those yet to be born. Marriage is a duty, a requirement. He who does not participate in it is a curse to the community, he is a rebel and a law-breaker, he is not only abnormal but "underhuman". Failure to get married under normal circumstances means that the person concerned has rejected society and society rejects him in return.

Thus, in all the three novels taken under this study, we witness the elaborate customs and preparations leading to a marriage. Apart from the bride and the groom and their immediate family, the whole village takes part in the wedding too, presenting the rural culture and solidarity of the African social life. The whole community participates in the marriage rituals to observe and celebrate the initiation of the boy and girl into manhood and womanhood. Love and marriage is not just a personal affair, but a social concern. There are many customs and proprieties attached to courtship and marriage, varying from one society to another. The novels take under this research work throw light on multiple aspects of these relationships in the African society.

Elechi Amadi in *The Concubine*, also talks of love, not just of the mortals, but also of the gods that claim their partners even in this world. His portrayal of the power of love, different hues of love – sacrifice and vengeance, jealousy and rivalry, fatal yet invincible love – all point out the power of pure love that wins even in the face of extreme negativity and imminent death. Also, his description of the elaborate wedding procedures, during Ekwueme and Ahurole's wedding and later during the marriage talks of Ekwueme and Ihuoma, present the importance of love and marriage in African life. The day-to-day texture of traditional, pre-colonial life in African village presented in the novel, shows an authentic picture of the importance of these finer relationships in the African society.

Buchi Emecheta in *The Bride Price* talks of the love relationship between Aku-nna and Chike and then their marriage. The love story of the young couple, interspersed with myth and tradition of Africa, the caste and gender distinctions and disparity, playing with the life and emotions of the young girl forms the basis of the novel. Emecheta presents a world of clashes between the rural and the urban, the traditional and the modern, city education and age-old customs of the village. Aku-nna stands at the crossroads of these clashes and through her story and those of people around her Emecheta spins a web of love, marriage, myth, tradition and rebellion in the small village of Ibuza. Her treatment of love and marriage in the novel is realistic and unedited. The reader gets to witness the power of love along with the drawbacks of standing by love in a society that is still struggling to remove the shackles of outdated customs and rituals. The myth of the bride price, practices like marriage by capture, polygamy and levirate marriage is painted without a gloss, showcasing the ugly reality of the society. Yet Aku-nna's love and efforts to get united with Chike and his constant support for her puts forth a positive note for the future.

Chinua Achebe, in *Things Fall Apart*, talks of love too. Love between husband and wife, love for children and the love for one's land of origin is dealt with in this novel. His depiction of love goes way beyond the man-woman relationship, covering a broad spectrum of different types of love like, parental love, brotherly love, love for a friend, for one's native land, etc. His novel too deals with various aspects of an African marriage. There are multiple references to practices like the bride price, wife beating, polygamy, even polyandry, the freedom of choice of partner etc. The episode of Obierika's daughter's marriage draws the customs and rituals related to marriage in detail. The participation of the whole village in her wedding once again proves the importance of marriage in society, and its treatment as a social event owned by the whole community.

This research work, based on the novels of Elechi Amadi, buchi Emecheta and Chinua Achebe, shall study the representation of love and marriage in African literature as an important and recurrent theme that touches upon other aspects of the society like class division, human relationships, social beliefs, myths, superstition and most importantly, the gender perspectives.

References

1. Thiong'o, Ngugi wa. (1977) *Petals of Blood*. Harare: Zimbabwe Publishing House. p.88.
2. Ivezbaye, Dan (1979) "Issues in the Reassessment of the African Novel" in *African Literature Today*. p.28.
3. Fanon, Frantz (2001) *The Wretched of the Earth*. UK: Penguin Publishers. p.199.
4. Tutuola, Amos (1952) *The Palm-Wine Drinkard*. New York: Grove Press. Print. pp. 191-192.
5. Lindfors, Bernth (1975) *Critical Perspectives on Amos Tutuola*. Three Continents Press. pp. 10,15,22,25,77,91.
6. Lindfors, Bernth (1975) *Critical Perspectives on Amos Tutuola*. Three Continents Press. p. 87.
7. Lindfors, Bernth (1975) *Critical Perspectives on Amos Tutuola*. Three Continents Press. pp.15,18,49.
8. Lindfors, Bernth (1975) *Critical Perspectives on Amos Tutuola*. Three Continents Press. p. 15.
9. Lindfors, Bernth (1975) *Critical Perspectives on Amos Tutuola*. Three Continents Press. p. 21.
10. Lindfors, Bernth (1975) *Critical Perspectives on Amos Tutuola*. Three Continents Press. pp. 18, 21.
11. Rodman, Selden (20 September 1953) "Book Review of The Palm-Wine Drinkard". *New York Times Book Review*.
12. West, Anthony (5 December 1953) "Book Review of The Palm-Wine Drinkard". *New Yorker*.
13. Lindfors, Bernth (1975) Critical Perspectives on Amos Tutuola. Three Continents Press. p. 41.
14. Palmer, Eustace (1978) "Twenty Five Years of Amos Tutuola". *The International Fiction Review*.5 (1). Retrieved 20 January 2015.
15. Lindfors, Bernth (1975) *Critical Perspectives on Amos Tutuola*. Three Continents Press. p. 44.
16. Achebe, Chinua (1975). "The Novelist as a Teacher", *in Morning Yet on Creation Day: Essays*. London: Heinemann African Writers Series. p.72.
17. Ogunyemi, O (1985) *Womanism: The Dynamics of the Contemporary Black Female Novel in English*. Signs, 11, 1. p. 64-80.
18. Mikell, G (1995) *African Feminism: Toward a New Politics of Representation, Feminist Studies*. p. 21.
19. Adichie, Chimamanda Ngozi (2012). *We Should All Be Feminists*. London: Harper Collins Publishers. p.48.
20. Aidoo, A.A. (1998) *African Women Today in Sisterhood Feminisms and Power: From Africa to the Diaspora*, edited by O. Nnaemeka. Trenton, New Jersey:

Africa Wide Press.
21. Beauvoir, Simone de (1949). *The Second Sex*. Vintage Classics p.445.
22. Achebe, Chinua (1958) *Things Fall Apart*. New Delhi: Modern Classics, Penguin India. p.81.
23. Achebe, Chinua (1958) *Things Fall Apart*. New Delhi: Modern Classics, Penguin India. p.81.
24. Emecheta, Buchi (1976) *The Bride Price*. New York: George Brazilier Inc. in. p.80.
25. Emecheta, Buchi (1976) *The Bride Price*. New York: George Brazilier, Inc. p. 64.
26. Emecheta, Buchi (1976). *The Bride Price*, New York: George Brazilier, Inc. p.72.
27. Emecheta, Buchi (1976). *The Bride Price*, New York: George Brazilier, Inc. p.73.
28. Emecheta, Buchi (1977) *The Slave Girl*. New York: George Brazilier, Inc. p.194.
29. Emecheta, Buchi (1977) *The Slave Girl*. New York: George Brazilier, Inc. p.215.
30. Emecheta, Buchi (1977) *The Slave Girl*. New York: George Brazilier, Inc. p.140.
31. Emecheta, Buchi (1977) *The Slave Girl*. New York: George Brazilier, Inc. p.222.
32. Emecheta, Buchi (1977) *The Slave Girl*. New York: George Brazilier, Inc. p.145.
33. Emecheta, Buchi (1979). *The Bride Price*, New York: George Brazilier, Inc. p.79.
34. Amadi, Elechi (1966). *The Concubine*. London: Heinemann African Writers Series. p.4.
35. Emecheta, Buchi (1979). *The Joys of Motherhood*. New York: George Brazilier, Inc. p.32.
36. Emecheta, Buchi (1979). *The Bride Price*. New York: George Brazilier, Inc. p.8.
37. Emecheta, Buchi (1979). *The Bride Price*. New York: George Brazilier, Inc. p.9.
38. Achebe, Chinua (1958). *Things Fall Apart*. New Delhi: Modern Classics, Penguin India. p.29.
39. Emecheta, Buchi (1979). *The Joys of Motherhood*. New York: George Brazilier, Inc. p.12.
40. Emecheta, Buchi (1979). *The Joys of Motherhood*. New York: George Brazilier, Inc. pp. 48-49.
41. Emecheta, Buchi (1976). *The Bride Price*. New York: George Brazilier, Inc. p. 132.
42. Emecheta, Buchi (1976). *The Bride Price*. New York: George Brazilier, Inc. p. 133.
43. Emecheta, Buchi (1976). *The Bride Price*. New York: George Brazilier, Inc. p. 168.
44. Umeh, Marie Linton. (1996) *Emerging Perspectives on Buchi Emecheta*. Trenton, NJ: Africa World Press Inc. p. 24.
45. Sutherland, Efua T. (1975). *The Marriage of Anansewa*. Essex, UK: Longman group Ltd. Act Four, pp. 80-81.

Chapter - II

The Concubine

The Concubine by Elechi Amadi is a unique mixture of myth and cultural construct intertwined with human relationships in a pre-colonized Africa, where the supernatural interference in the mortal world set the course of the lives of the people. This chapter shall aim at studying love as a predominant theme in the novel. Love is presented as a personal pursuit, several times crossing the rules set by the gods and the society. In fact, if anything, the gods and the society mostly work against the fulfillment of love in the novel. We shall analyze Amadi's depiction of love as a predominant force, the greatest of strengths that can pose a challenge even to the supernatural forces surrounding Ihuoma's life. Amadi in his first novel also highlights some major aspects of the Igbo marriage. The major customs and rituals related to the African marriage in Igbo tribe have been shown in a realistic light, making it possible to analyse various practices related to it, like the settlement of marriage by the elders (many a time without the children's consent), child-marriage, marriage negotiations, bride price, marriage guide appointement, the bane of widowhood, widow remarriage, etc.

The Concubine, Elechi Amadi's first novel, published in 1966, is considered as his crowning achievement. The title of the book,

The Concubine, is symbolic as its meaning is revealed to the readers only in the closing chapters of the novel. It becomes clear that, "The Concubine" is none other than the beautiful Ihuoma, and that too, not of any ordinary mortal, but of the "Sea-King". At the beginning of the novel, we get introduced to Ihuoma as married to Emenike, who soon succumbs to 'lock-chest'. Next in line to die is Madume, the villainous neighbor who has an eye on Ihuoma and her property. He gets into an argument with her after she refuses his proposal for marriage and when he tries to assault her, a spitting cobra makes him blind. He later dies in a miserable condition. Ekwueme is another young man who tries to woo Ihuoma after Emenike's death. Ihuoma likes him too and later falls in love with him and they agree to get married. But by now it becomes clear that a power stronger than that of a human is behind Ihuoma. It is upto the mortal Ekwueme to prove his love for Ihuoma where he is ready to draw the wrath of the supernatural beings, but not to give up his love for her. The power of love has been depicted in its truest form, enabling an ordinary man to rise against the gods, and winning aesthetically in the eyes of the reader despite his certain defeat in the literal sense.

The story is a tale of a young woman Ihuoma, who belongs to Nigeria's ethnic Igbo tribe. Amadi makes an effort to depict the African traditional way of life in its totality through the tale of Ihuoma. The religious, social, cultural and even economic practices concerning the day-to-day life of the native African is presented in the novel. A number of rural villages and their cultural practices are mentioned by the author, all of which aid in building the African authenticity of the novel. Like Amadi's other books, it centres on traditional values in African society.

The plot of the novel revolves around the main character – Ihuoma, a beautiful and equally attractive lady who draws the admiration of all and sundry, not only for her beauty but also for the graceful way in which she conducts herself in everything that she does. Ihuoma, the unmistakably beautiful woman of the village is admired by others in the novel, both physically and morally. Her grace and poise prove irresistible for Ekwueme who falls madly in love with her. Though his love for her grows daily by leaps and bounds as is very much visible to all around them, his parents frown at the idea of his marrying a woman whose womb has born another man's children. Ihuoma too refuses to accept his love or show her own love for him fearing that the society might make fun of them and shun them for such an alliance. Also, Ekwueme had been engaged to Ahurole, another girl from her village who was like a sister to her (coming from the same village). Breaking off this match would again be not acceptable to society. Later, Amadi talks of the biggest hurdle in the love story of Ihuoma and Ahurole, which goes way beyond the normal societal norms. This hurdle comes in the form of Ihuoma's past life.

Her situation in life involves her past life, when she was said to be the wife of the mythical Sea-King deity. This gives her great status in the present, but portends doom for any mortal man who seeks to marry her. As the the novel develops, Ihuoma is wed and widowed more than once, as a result of the wrath of the Sea-King toward those who would try to usurp his bride. This wrath of the Sea-King is indicative of the general understanding of the wife as being primarily the husband's property. Just like a man guards his property. Th mythical god guards his wife, not allowing anyone else to own her even in the mortal world that she is now a part of.

In the novel, Ihuoma whose beauty attracts all men and women in the village of Omokachi and Omigwe, maintains a very compassionate, rational behavior, intelligence and social decorum in her day-to-day life. Her good name spans beyond her own villages (of her birth and marriage) even to the neighbouring village of Chiolu. As a woman, she is a model of perfect beauty as the narrator attests by narrating that she was a pretty woman, and probably that is why she was married off so early. She was quite young and had not lost her charm inspite of bearing three children. If anything, it could be said that her age added to her beauty, making her ant-hill complexion glow even more and her features more rounded and smoother. Her smile, with the narrow gap in the upper row of her white teeth was disarming. At the time this novel is set in, a gap in the teeth was fashionable. Ihuoma's beauty was natural, and the other women of the village envied her, yet respected her for her classy demeanour.

Her beauty was the scale of all women who wanted to be considered beautiful. It is no surprise, therefore, that her husband was thought lucky and all men desired her. That she was beautiful was generally accepted. But the way she carried herself added to her charisma. Everybody envied her. And everybody loved her. In truth, she she was aware of her own beauty and loved to gaze at herself in the mirror. That she was beautiful she had no doubt, but that did not make her arrogant.

She was sympathetic, kind, gentle and reserved. It was her husband's boast that in the six years of their marriage she had never had any serious quarrel with another woman. She was not good at invectives and other women talked much faster than she did. The fact that she would be outdone in a verbal exchange perhaps partly retained her from coming into open verbal conflict with her neighbours. Gradually she accepted her drawbacks and acquired the capacity to bear any stinging remark of some neighbour without answering. This increased her prestige among the womenfolk and even the most quarrelsome and garrulous among them was reluctant to be unpleasant to her. Love begets love and this was true in the case of Ihuoma. Amadi shows her mild nature when she is not able to behave rudely with Wolu after Emenike's death even though she wanted to. Wolu was Madume's wife. It was generally believed that it was Madume's fight with Emenike which had later brought forth his demise. Any other woman would not have had the strength to bear a visit from the wife of her husband's murderer. But Ihuoma did not only receive Wolu, but also refrained from saying anything rude to her. Ihuoma was not the kind of woman who engaged in quarrels. She was, in fact, the problem-solver, the agony aunt – the woman who found herself settling quarrels and offering advice even to older women.

For the village people, these characteristics of Ihuoma place her on the pedestal of the tribal and communal center of exemplary womanhood and motherhood. As a result, all the men in the village admire her and most of them desire her. Most men, like Madume, envy her husband Emenike who married her at a young age. When the novel opens, the couple behaves like a perfect family blessed by the gods with three children. Theirs is a home full of love and laughter, where the wife and the husband engage in a happy banter and the children run about playing without a care in the world, until tragedy strikes.

The Concubine has its setting in the rural Nigeria and the author makes an effort to depict the African traditional way of life in its totality; its religious, social, cultural and even economic practices. The New Statesman, in its book review of *The Concubine*, declared it as:

> *A highly sophisticated measured treatment of … the fatal loves of a woman in an Eastern Nigerian village. Written in a grave and simple style, it… reveals its author as a fine writer ruminating on a past already turning into a legend.*[1]

Elechi Amadi's novel, *The Concubine*, differs from most Nigerian novel in its setting, for it takes place entirely in a pre-colonial era. No European administrators or missionaries enter to disrupt the lives of these native people in the villages. The tribal system is still stable and capable of coping with its own disasters in its own way. Amadi tells the story wholly from the inside, never attempting to give a contemporary interpretation to the event, but adhering meticulously to the concepts and life-view held by the people within the novel. For example, in the beginning of the novel, when Emenike indulges in a fatal fight with Madume, the author does not once claim the latter to be cold-hearted murderer, as could be seen from a modernistic judicial point of view. Instead, he refers to it as Emenike's misfortune as was seen by the villagers at that time:

> *… when later Emenike married Ihouma, and (Madume) blamed him wholly for his loss of the girl he wanted. It was very easy for him to pick quarrels with Emenike, because many events called for a degree of intimacy between the villagers… But Emenike was not afraid of him. He knew he could hold his own against him any day given a fair chance. But a man's god must be away on a journey on the day of an important fight*

and that may make all the difference. This was clearly what had happened in the last fight between Madume and Emenike.[2]

This method gives the novel an unfaltering authenticity, which in turn helps to extend the novel's meaning beyond any one culture, for Amadi's theme is man's struggle with fate itself, his perpetual attempt to placate and therefore to control his gods.

A beautiful young woman, Ihuoma, is the central character of the novel, yet the novel is not as much about her, as about the effect she has on the three men, who involve themselves, at various times, with her life. This effect is always an unintentional one, for Ihuoma, although far from being a passive woman, never attempts to influence or dominate others. In fact, she is the epitome of beauty, virtue and propriety. She accepts her beauty calmly, but she does not use it as a weapon. She is surprised at the devotion she inspires, but it is not until nearly the end of the novel that either the reader or Ihuoma herself begins to suspect anything sinister in her attractiveness.

Ihuoma's plight involves her past life, when she was said to be the wife of the mythical Sea-King deity. This gives her great status in the present. Though unknown to herself or anyone around her, her past life's beauty is reflected in this life as well, and this draws everyone close to her. Men and women, all admire her. While this good-natured beauty gives her a high position in the eyes of villagers, it also portends doom for any mortal man who seeks to marry her. As the novel progresses, Ihuoma is wed and widowed twice as a result of the wrath of the Sea-King toward those who would usurp his bride. The Sea-King also brought about Madume's death who had tried to propose to Ihuoma and then misbehaved with her upon her refusal.

Amadi, in the novel, has treated the theme of the supernatural as the major framework regulating the lives, actions and the behavioral patterns of the characters. Ihuoma, who in her previous birth, was a beloved concubine of the Sea-King, is doomed to be loved by men, but whosoever shall try to woo her, would also be incurring the wrath of her supernatural lover, the Sea-King. The position of the Sea-King in the life of Ihuoma is reflected by the great dibia Anyika thus:

> *Ihuoma belongs to the sea. When she was in the spirit world, she was the wife of the Sea-King, the ruling spirit of the sea. Against the advice of her husband, she sought the company of human beings and was incarnated. The Sea-King was very angry but because he loved her best of all his wives, he did not destroy her immediately she was born. He decided to humour her and let her live her normal earthly span and come back to him. However, because of his great love for her, he is terribly jealous, and tries to destroy any man who makes love to her.*[3]

When the novel begins, Ihuoma is shown living happily with her husband Emenike, and their three children, until one day he is drawn unavoidably into a fight with his neighbor Madume, who claims a piece of land which rightfully belongs to Emenike. In their wrestling bout, Emenike falls on a jagged tree stump and badly hurts his side. After a time, he appears to recover and goes with other men of the village to the forest shrine of Amadioha, god of thunder. There, in the eyes of the shrine's priest, Emenike reads his own death. When he dies shortly after, the villagers attribute it to the internal damage done in his fight with Madume.

The themes of love and marriage are both explored in the initial pages of the novel. Love, since time immemorial has been a recurring theme in literature across the world. It is the most profound emotion experienced by man. Whether platonic or romantic, fleeting or lifelong, love has the power to nurture meaningful relationships, shatter our hearts, teach important lessons, and change lives forever. Amadi, in his novel, has delved into these aspects of love, yet again, proving the everlasting power of love. Love defies all boundaries by appearing across all genres, age groups, and periods in history.

Amadi's treatment of love in *The Concubine* makes the story acutely heartfelt and memorable regardless of the outcome. Ihuoma's love for her husband and the tragedy that strikes her upon his death has been poignantly portrayed. Thereafter, her journey to overcome her traumatic experience to forge her own identity and to help make a life for herself and her children, going on to fall in love once again with Ekwueme is beautifully presented by Amadi. The selfless love exhibited by Ihuoma, contrasted by the vindictive love of Ahurole – both toward Ekwueme – present the extremities of love. Ihuoma, in her denial of Ekwueme's proposal, exhibits her true love for Ekwueme, thinking about his and his family's credibility and well-being in the society before her own happiness. On the other hand, Ahurole does not think twice before administering love-potion (a near death-potion) to her husband to win over his love and sway him away from his true love, Ihuoma. She is least bothered about the possible side effects inspite of the dibia's warning and does not even pause to bear the responsibility of her actions after Ekwueme's mental condition worsens due to her potion. Her love proves to be shallow and more of adamance than genuine feeling. Her running away from the madman she had created proves her falsity. Love really is a complex theme to examine. Based on the novel taken under this study, there are some elements that can be pointed out with ease, as defining love.

Firstly, love and its challenges are major themes that run through the pages of *The Concubine*. Highlighting love as a theme often indicates that characters will experience challenges in their relationship that they must overcome. For Ekwueme and Ihuoma, this means rising above the social obstacles and overcoming the supernatural forces working against their union. While the first seems relatively easy that they were able to manage, the supernatural forces come out as a force to reckon with. However, the power of love is such that the couple comes out as a winner even in the face of imminent defeat. Ekwueme continues to love Ihuoma despite unreturned affection for the most part of the novel, and Ihuoma unleashes her repressed emotions once she accepts that the society would not judge her negatively for associating with Ekwueme. When he is in real need of her in his illness, she never even thinks of turning away, say what people may.

Secondly, mirrors of love or, in this case, mirror relationships come across as an excellent technique for showing love at work. While Ihuoma and Ekwueme's love is deep and pure, Ekwueme's and Ahurole's relationship suffers due to absence of love. The constant bickering of Madume and Wolu is also a contrast to the mutually respectful relationship shared by Nnadi and his wife, Mgbachi.

Thirdly, the theme of love as a feeling that can make us utter fools runs through the novel in the character of Ekwueme. Blinded by his love for Ihuoma, he has no care for the world and does not even shy from declaring his love for Ihuoma and his intention to break up his long-standing engagement in front of his father. In his madness too, he appears the perfect fool for Ihuoma, jumping like a monkey here and there, listening only to her. It was only her sight and her voice that could calm him.

Fourthly, romantic love is not the only kind of love that is explored in the novel. Amadi presents various other kinds of love – between parent and child, between friends, between neighbours, etc. Ihuoma's love for her children motivates her to work day and night to ensure their filled bellies and happy faces even when their father had died. She was not willing to accept Ekwueme's proposal fearing that after he tired of her, her children from her first marriage would seem like a burden to him. Ihuoma's mother's love for her makes her try and convince Ihuoma for a second marriage. She is quick to assess Ekwueme's feelings for her daughter and asks her to consider it without thinking about social propriety. Once again, Ekwueme's parents love him a lot and thus at first are unwilling to let him invite the scorn of the society by not going through with his childhood engagement. Yet again, it is their love for him that makes them gladly accept Ihuoma even after the warning of Anyika regarding the Sea-King and his possessiveness for Ihuoma. Ihuoma's treatment of her friends, family and neighbours (even Wolu, whose husband was rumoured to have a hand in the death of her first husband Emenike), touches upon the qualities of kindness, compassion and forgiveness, all of which are platonic forms of love.

Along with the theme of love, Amadi examines the theme of marriage, along with the themes of friendship, desire and rivalry. This thematic web makes sense since love is often connected to these topics in real life. Love in literature is not just about happy love, and happily-ever-after. This novel, taken under this research work highlights the various aspects associated with love. And marriage works as a major theme in the novel, closely connected with love.

Amadi intertwines the theme of love with marriage in his novel. Various aspects of an African marriage are shown. The dominance of man in the man-wife relationship, as well as the different customs associated with marriage are mentioned in detail to depict the reality of African marriage system. The villages of Omokachi and Omigwe, shown closely in the novel, exhibit a strong patriarchal system as husbands control and dominate the house. Their wives are subservient and steadfast in attending to their needs. Amadi explores this equation right from the initial pages through the character of Madume. He was in his early thirties, and by no means a very successful man. His compound was small with only two houses in it. In fact, he was so lazy that he did not care for more houses as more houses would mean more thatching in the rainy season and he hated to exert himself.

The subjugated position of a wife in the African society is portrayed through Wolu, Madume's wife, who was tired of her husband's lazy ways, but could not do much to anger him in a society where wife-beating was an accepted norm. Eileen Krige, in *Essays on African Marriage in Southern Africa*:

> *Wives were subordinate members of their marital household. Husbands and sisters, but not wives entertained visitors. Although wives sometimes attacked their husbands when angry; wife-beating was frequent and socially acceptable.*[4]

Wolu, as the wife of Madume, was no exception. Amadi writes:

> *His wife (Wolu) always complained of a leaking roof, and had threatened on occasion to thatch the house herself, to shame him before the village. When she discovered half*

a dozen canes in her husband's bedroom, she thought differently of the matter.[5]

The tradition of polygamy, the desire for a male child, and the hankering after bride-price – some constant features of African marriage are also dealt with, while showing Madume's character. Wolu, his wife had bore him four daughters, which was quite annoying for him. The desire for a male child constantly played in his mind. He was inherently a greedy man. Not once did the thought of the bride price he would acquire from his daughters' marriage leave his mind, yet the patriarchal society that he lived in made him also wish for a male heir who would carry his name after his death. Daughters could bring dowry but had no right of inheritance. For that a male heir was required. The thought of his elder brother's son inheriting his houses and lands filed him with dismay. But that was the law of the land. Property went to next in line male heir. He could do nothing about it, except pray for a son of his own. Also, he planned on getting another wife who could bear him a son, but for that he needed to pay a bride price. So he had in his mind, planned to get his daughters' bride prices which would provide him money to pay for another wife for himself. He believed that he was quite young and had lots of time to get a male child over the years. Moreover, he believed that 'his daughters' marriages would provide him with the money for another wife'.[6]

Madume's attraction towards Ihuoma and a kind of one-sided love for her is another factor that shapes his mean character. His dislike for Emenike, Ihuoma's husband, stemmed from his jealousy. Emenike was a good-looking, friendly young man, considered by the old men, as an ideal. He was good-looking, well-formed and a favorite with the girls. Madume had hopes of marrying Ihuoma, but she and her parents chose Emenike over him:

Perhaps Madume's hatred for Emenike might not have been so great if only the latter had not snatched Ihuoma from him. Madume had high hopes of marrying Ihuoma, the the most desirable girl in Omigwe village. Neither

> *Ihuoma nor her parents had been keen on the match, but Madume, overlooked this fact when later Emenike married Ihuoma and blamed him wholly for the loss of the girl he wanted.*[7]

This theme of love and jealousy is a constant motif in the novel. Be it here, in the case of Madume, or later in the case of Ahurole and Ekwueme or Ihuoma and the Sea-King.

In the novel, after Emenike's sudden and tragic death, Madume represses his feelings of responsibility over Emenike's death and once more attempts to take back the disputed piece of land, this time by threatening Ihuoma, who is trying to work the farm and keep her family together. Wives in Africa are not restricted to the chores within the house, but also work on the farm and sell their products in the market:

> *As wives, women's access to garden lands and livestock for their use depended mainly on their husbands, who allocated productive means and their products to each wife for the use of her house (mother and her children) and by inheritance of their own children.*[8]

Paradoxically, Madume also hopes to take Ihuoma as his second wife. Ihuoma stands up to his threats, and when he makes advances to her, she rejects him sharply. In fury, Madume chops down some of her plantains, and in the process encounters a spitting cobra. With the snake's venom in his eyes, Madume calls for the dibia, or the medicine man, Anyika, but he refuses to treat him saying that the event was clearly an act of the gods:

> *Madume became blind through a spitting cobra and eventually hanged himself. Many thought his death was the result of an unfortunate accident, a just reward for his "big-eye". I must say I had the same views at the time. But it is now very clear, Madume's real trouble began after he had assaulted Ihuoma while she was harvesting plantains.*

> *Added to this was the fact that he had a secret desire to make Ihuoma his lover or may be marry her. All this was too much for the Sea-King and he himself assumed the form of a serpent and dealt with his rival… just before Emenike died I detected some water spirits among the throng that eventually liquidated him. When Madume came to me for divinations once, I also stumbled on these water spirits.*[9]

In the divination, Anyika receives some intimations of the presence of Sea-God, but he, like the other villagers, interprets Madume's misfortune as a punishment for violating Ihuoma's land. Madume goes blind and unable to bear his helplessness, hangs himself.

The theme of love progresses in the novel through Ekwueme. A young bachelor, Ekwueme, finds himself more and more drawn toward Ihuoma, and the novel traces the course of their slow and turbulent courtship. Ihuoma is also attracted by him, but keeps on refusing him until almost the end, partly because she cannot forget her dead husband, and partly because Ekwueme has been engaged since childhood to a girl in a nearby village, Omigwe, to which even Ihuoma belonged. Ihuoma feels that she, a widow with the responsibility of her children, would be a burden for a young man like Ekwueme, who might soon grow tired of her. Also, she feels that, as he was betrothed to another girl, it would be an offence to the whole community if she were to marry Ekwueme instead:

> *'Ekwe listen, the woman began, 'you know very well I like you'. How can I deny it? You like me too; otherwise you would not want to marry me. But you need a young maiden who would obey you and give you the first fruits of her womb. Do not cheat yourself. I am too old for you. You would soon grow tired of me. My children would be a constant burden on you. No Ekwe, I do not want to spoil your life. Since your childhood you have been engaged to Ahurole. She is young, well-behaved and beautiful. Go*

and marry her instead. Ekwueme was moved and felt his love grow even stronger for this woman.[10]

Marriage in Africa is a very integral part of life – both, at the individual's level as well as the level of community. Thus, it is but natural that the parents be highly concerned with the marriage of their children as it is, in a way, the focus of existence of their lives. The parents consider it their duty to settle their chidren's match. They openly discuss and arrange marriages of their children, not always waiting for the agreement of those very children whose lives they are set on deciding. The choice of partner and arrangement of the chidren's marriage is a primary concern of the parents in African society. Thus in the novel we see the great influence exerted by Ekwueme's parents over him regarding his marriage to Ahurole.

Ekwueme was just a little boy, and Ahurole an infant, when their parents had decided to get them married when the right time would arrive, that is, when they would be old enough for marriage. Their opinion is the last thing their parents seek. The custom demanded that once the match was set, even if in the womb, the children had to wait till maturity to start a relationship. And when the time comes the parents of the groom have to inform the bride's parents that they are ready to initiate formal talks for marriage. The importance of the parents is not difficult to deduce seeing Ekwueme's situation in the novel. He has to abide by his parent's word even though he himself is least happy about it. Amadi talks about the period of marriage negotiations, rituals attached and the customs performed to forge familiarity between the family of the newlywed and of the village, once again emphasizing the role of marriage in community life.

Another aspect of the African tradition is introduced in the novel through the marriage of Ekwueme and Ahurole. Their's was a match arranged in childhood. It was a practice not very common, yet not unheard of in the rural African settings. Girls at the time of their birth, or very early childhood were promised in marriage to the boy of their parents' choice though the actual ceremony did not take place until she came of age to understand the meaning of marriage, most commonly, the time of puberty, yet, such arrangements ensured that she was the property of her husband's family. In care of her parents only till the right time came for the marriage ceremony:

> *Ahurole was engaged to Ekwueme when she was eight days old. Ekwueme was then about five years old. The initial ceremony was simple. Ekwueme's father, Wigwe, merely put some kola nuts and the shoots of young palm wine saplings into the vessel from which Ahurole drank. Thereafter he kept an eye on her casually. As both children grew, they were made to understand their position. Nothing was done beyond this until the children were of age. Indeed, all it meant practically was that no other suitors would bother Ahurole's father. All marriages were not contracted in this way, but when they were, they flattered the parents of the girl. Clearly, only the baby-girls of the trusted parents could be engaged in this way.*[11]

Thus, Ahurole's parents, Wagbara and Wonuma, were justly proud of their daughter's engagement. For years they had exercised extra care and vigilance over her as she was now someone else's property, in their care.

Negotiations might well have started two years back when Ahurole had become mature enough for marriage, but Wagbara said he was not in a hurry for his daughter's marriage. This implied two things. Firstly, that he was not too keen on his daughter's bride price, which meant he was well off and not in a hurry to obtain the sum he would be given by the groom's family upon the settlement of the wedding date. Secondly, it implied that he was quite sure of his good influence over his daughter and did not fear her stepping out of the social boundaries.

But now that she had grown up, time had come at last for formal negotiations. Ahurole had grown up quite some time back, and most of her contemporaries were not only married, but also had children. As mentioned above, these formal negotiations might well have started two years back but Wagbara was not in a hurry to marry off his daughter.

Which meant, that he was quite well off himself and thus not too keen on acquiring his daughter's bride price; also, it showed his confidence in his daughter's upbringing. He was sure of his good influence on his daughter and thus confident that she would not go astray. African society as discussed before, laid a great emphasis on the virginity of the unmarried girls. Olayinka Koso Thomas points out:

> *Virginity in all traditional African societies, is a prerequisite for marriage. It is highly valued and its preservation reflects the moral quality of the girl's family. A guarantee and proof of virginity before marriage establishes paternity and ensures the inheritance right of the new born after consummation of the marriage. Proof of virginity is usually an integral part of the marriage transaction.*[12]

The days that followed were full of wine and gifts. The groom and his family visited the bride's house for about six months till the final agreement of the bride price. Ahurole's uncle was appointed the guide for marriage, one who would help to bring down the bride price settlement and also would introduce the two parties in marriage. He would tell the groom who the relations were and what their importance was in the family and society so that they could be paid respect accordingly by him. After six months the bride price was settled. The entire family of Ekwueme rejoiced and hurried to bring Ahurole to his village. They feared that Ekwueme might rebel against them and insist on marrying Ihuoma. It was their duty, according to his parents, to guide their children through to a proper marriage.

And Ekwueme too, though reluctant to marry Ahurole, followed his parents' advice and went ahead with the arranged marriage as he did not want his parents to have their words fall empty. The African culture was an oral culture and much importance was given to the words. If a man said he would do something he would… there was no signed document required. The society stood as witness and jury as well as the police in such matters. A man who did not keep his word was shunned by all. Thus Emenike, though very much in love with Ihuoma, still agreed to get married to Ahurole as he did not see any point in continuing with his adamant love when Ihuoma herself had refused his proposal and his not marrying Ahurole could get his parents into trouble.

He did not wish to see his family getting into problems with the villagers, nor did he want to be ostracized for defying the tradition and breaking a childhood engagement, even if his heart still beat for Ihuoma. After a lot of cajoling on the part of his parents, and a straight denial of his marriage proposal by Ihuoma in front of his father, Ekwueme finally allows himself to be persuaded into the arranged marriage. But this marriage does not delete Ihuoma from his memory. If anything, Ahurole's petulant behavior only magnifies the calm and composed goodness of Ihuoma in his mind and he rues his fate more and more. While his family wanted him to ignore her faults and accept her as she was, Ekwueme for the first time realized how difficult married life could be, because try as much as he did, he was unable to overlook her faults. On the other hand, Ahurole too, did little to invoke love for herself in his heart. She continued to exhibit her childish and cranky behavior and this pushed him further away. However, Ekwueme's family tried their best to promote their relationship.

When Ahurole was brought to Ekwueme's house, there were lots of celebrations and warm welcome of the bride. The family, intent on proving Ekwueme's decision of marrying her correct, magnified her virtues and ignored her flaws. Ekwueme's mother paid extra attention to ensure tthat her daughter-in-law felt at home in the new house. Her positive leadership of the compound brings to light her power as a mother-in-law to influence the household. This aspect of the African marriage is highlighted by Amadi when he notes the control that the mother-in-law exercises on the household of her son and his wife through the character of Adaku. Eileen Krige and Jack Krige, in *The Realm of a Rain-Queen: A Study of the Patterns of Lovedu Society* (1943) have noted:

> *Wives worked under the direction of their husband's mother, and in the early years of wifehood, cooked and stamped grain at her hearth and cultivated for her. It was the mother-in-law who gave the wife permission to*

attend work and social events. With age and the arrival of new wives, a wife gained her own hearth and increasing independence of her mother-in-law.[13]

Similarly, after the wedding in the initial months, Ekwueme and Ahurole ate from their mother's kitchen, as the rest of the family, but by and by, they got their own hearth established. Amadi talks of Adaku giving Ahurole the place and permission to start her own kitchen after a few months of her marriage thereby showing her approval of her daughter-in-law as an able wife and keeper of the house. This was considered quite a feat for the new bride in the African tradition:

> *For the first few months Ahurole and her husband ate from the same plot with the rest of the family. Later she was ceremoniously installed in her own hearth. Then Ekwe felt he was truly married and played the man at every possible opportunity. He cut down on frivolous talk as much as possible and his dancing.*[14]

While Adaku's decision to give Ahurole her own separate hearth was more of her effort to establish Ahurole's competence in the eyes of Ekwueme, the reality remained that Ahurole was perhaps not even ready for marriage, leave alone taking the responsibility of the house and kitchen. Ekwueme's young wife, Ahurole, is given to sulking and tears and Ekwueme does not know how to handle her and is basically not willing to try. Ahurole's immaturity and emotional outbursts disappoint him and he is drawn further away in his heart from this arranged marriage and the wife forced upon him. The stark contrast between his ill-tempered wife, and the calm and matured woman that Ihuoma was, draws him more and more towards the latter. He begins dropping by Ihuoma's compound and talking to her.

Ekwueme is a trapper, but his chief interest lies in singing and flute-playing. He is gentle, has never been sufficiently certain of himself, and has been too dependent upon his mother, even into his adulthood. Ihuoma, very much like his mother, is his ideal woman, for she combines physical beauty with the reassuring and the maternal qualities he longed for. He wished his wife would have the same qualities, but is highly let down by her sulking, petulant behavior. His desire for Ihuoma increases every time Ahurole exhibits her childish ill-tempered behavior.

> The only woman he ever liked apart from his mother was Ihuoma. She was so understanding, motherly and beautiful. Ahurole was beautiful. He hoped she would be understanding and – perhaps motherly as well.[15]

When he had agreed to marry according to his parents' wishes, he had thought to himself that perhaps this was what lay in store for him and he would try to make the best of it. He had always looked down upon people who got into fights with their spouses and had often thought of not becoming like them. However, all his hopes come crashing down when Ahurole proves to be nothing more than a spoilt child, ready to cry at the slightest provocation. This kind of childish behavior tests his patience and he feel himself tied up with her against his will. He feels like running away from her, crying for no reason, and finds solace in the company of Ihuoma. When his wife discovers he has been seeing Ihuoma, however, she is enraged. Her jealousy and insecurities stem up from her love and possessiveness for her husband. Alongwith the help of her mother, and in spite of the warning of Anyika, the medicine man of the village, she sets about administering love potion to her husband. Anyika, an experienced and gifted medicine man had tried his best to discourage her from taking such a drastic step:

> 'But it won't harm him', Ahurole put in. 'In the long run it might, my daughter. I am sure you have seen active and intelligent men suddenly become passive, stupid and dependent. That is what a love potion can do. So go and settle your differences with your husband peacefully. If you insist, then you must go somewhere else.'[16]

But the mother-daughter duo does not pay heed to Anyika's advice and decide to take the matter in their own hands. Wonuma, Ahurole's mother declares that since they are not being given the love potion in Omokachi, she would go to Chiolu to fetch it. There she obtains the required drug from another medicine man. Ahurole, cleverly administers it to her husband, least suspecting what this all could lead to.

Ahurole, blinded with jealousy and determined to win the love and affection of her husband, administers the love potion to Ekwueme, to bring him back. The drug is the one that her mother obtained from the dibia, a medicine man from another village, for Anyika, the local medicine man, refused to take part in the business. Ekwueme, after taking the drug falls ill. He has convulsions, and nearly insane, he runs away into the forest. Far from bringing him closer, it takes him away from even himself as he begins to lose his mind. Ahurole in terror at what she has done returns to her parents' village.

Amadi, describes fascinatingly the episode of Ekwueme's illness, for the drug has the effect of reversing his personality. He viciously resists the attempts of his friends to get him to go back home. Where he was once docile towards authority, he now pours out vituperation upon the elders. And where he was once reserved and shy in his expression of love towards Ihuoma, he now declares that he will not come down from the tree where he has ensconced himself unless Ihuoma appears. Ihuoma agrees to come, although she is understandably embarrassed by the scene. When Anyika, the dibia, has administered an antidote to the drug that poisoned the young man, Ekwueme recovers and is painfully ashamed of his actions when he was under the influence of the drug.

Ihuoma continues to see him while he is convalescing, and gradually realizes that she is in love with him. The growth of this relationship is portrayed with moving gentleness, for both Ekwueme and Ihuoma are almost afraid to believe in their own happiness. The love they project is of the simplest and most honest kind. The two decide to get married and their families gladly extend their consent. As is their African custom, after the death of the husband, the wife becomes the responsibility of the dead husband's brother. So Ekwueme seeks permission from Nnadi, Ihuoma's brother-in-law, to marry her. He had no objections and gladly gave his consent provided Emenike's compound was not allowed to fall to pieces.

Another marital custom showed in the novel is the practice of returning the bride price in case a marriage breaks down. Since Ahurole had been solely responsible for her husband's illness and instead of helping him through with it, she had run away to her parents' house, her marriage was as good as over. Not only was she blamed for her rash act that almost drove her husband mad, but her parents were also ashamed of her deed and her father, Wagbara, full of guilt, offered to return the bride price, when Ekwueme's marriage talks with Ihuoma started:

> *Ekwueme's parents were eager too for the marriage. Wagbara was told to return the bride price on Ahurole's behalf. He did so promptly and offered to refund even the money spent on drinks. Wigwe was touched. He said he would not take it. 'Wigwe, I am ashamed of the whole business', Wagbara said while refunding the bride price, 'but there is nothing we can do about it. Your son has expressed a strong desire to break off the marriage, and who can blame him? But whenever you come to Omigwe, do not pass by my compound with your face averted. You will always be welcome here. Marriage relationships are never completely severed.*[17]

At this point when the two have decided to marry and when their respective families have accepted it, a terrifying obstacle appears. Anyika was one person who did not approve of the marriage. He announces that his divinations have told him something which makes the marriage – or any other marriage for Ihuoma – impossible.

> 'The marriage will not work out well.'
> 'Why?' Wigwe asked.
> 'Spirits, strong spirits.'
> 'They are against the marriage?'
> 'Yes'…

> ...'look at her', Anyika went on, 'have you seen anyone quite so right in everything, almost perfect? I tell you only a sea-goddess – for that is precisely what she is – can be all that.'
> Wigwe nodded his head slowly and solemnly.
> 'Do you mean to say', he said between clenched teeth, 'that this girl was never meant to get married?' 'Under the circumstances, no.'
> 'She was to die untouched by men?'
> 'Well she could be someone's concubine. Her Sea-King husband can be persuaded to put up with that after highly involved rites. But as a wife she is completely ruled out.'[18]

Anyika says that there are a few women like Ihuoma in the world, who actually belong to the spirit world. But just like Ihuoma was cursed to a worldly life, for some fault of hers by the Sea-King, so are the others. Yet being born in this world does not sever their ties with the spirit world and the supernatural beings constantly try and steer the course of their lives. Anyika declares that it is death to marry them and they leave behind 'a harrowing string of dead husbands.' They are usually very beautiful but followed by their invisible husbands of the spirit world. Whenever a mortal makes advances towards such a woman, the spirit world unleashes all its powers to make such alliances fatal. Ihuoma, beloved of the village, is also the beloved of the Sea-King, and the god will kill any man who seeks to marry her. She could be a concubine, but never a wife. They think of Emenike, her first husband who died a considerable time after he had appeared to recover from his wound, as if he were fated to die. They also recall Madume, so strangely encountering the snake immediately after he had told Ihuoma he wanted to marry her.

At first Ekwueme can hardly believe the dibia, but smitten with love for Ihuoma, he says he will marry Ihuoma even if it is true:

> 'Dede, I do not know whether you believe this or not. It does not matter. One this is clear, I shall marry Ihuoma.

> *She is a human being and if marrying a woman like her is a fatal mistake, I am prepared to make it. If I am her husband for a day before my death my soul will go singing happily to the spirit world. There also I shall be prepared to dare the wrath of four hundred Sea-Kings for her sake."*[19]

Ihuoma herself does not know whether the revelation about her is true of not. If it is, she has been totally unaware of it. Old Anyika swears that nothing can be done, so in the timeless manner of humans, Ekwueme and his father seek the advice of another dibia. This one claims that the Sea-King can be bound and rendered harmless, with the proper rituals and sacrifices. But can a man bind the gods?

The concluding pages of the novel are a counterpoint, with the happiness of Ihuoma and Ekwueme raising and recurring, but always in the background there is the anxiety, the sense of having to get the sacrifice prepared quickly, the apprehensions about the ritual which will have to be performed from a boat on the river, the domain of the Sea-King, rather than the province of men, land. Ekwueme who cannot swim and who by now is certain that the Sea-King will appear does not make a secret of his fear. But in spite of his fear, he stands tall like a man, ready to fight for his love even in the face of assured defeat and death. However, he goes along with the planned sacrifice along with his parents under the guidance of Agwoturumbe, the new dibia they are in consult with now.

Another feature of African tradition with respect to a widow remarriage is revealed in the negotiations following the marriage arrangement of Ihuoma and Ekwueme. As she was no more a responsibility of her parents, but belonged to her deceased husband's family that had paid her bride price, it was her brother-in-law, Nnadi who had the right to give her away in marriage now:

> *Marriage proceedings in respect of a widow were not protracted.*
> *The main thing was the payment of the bride price to the family of the deceased husband. As this could not*

> *be done until after the sacrifice, there was little else to do. Wines were tendered and drunk and gifts exchanged.*[20]

When nearly every paraphernalia for the sacrifice is ready, Ekwueme sends Ihuoma's young son to shoot a lizard with his bow, for this is the last thing necessary for the sacrifice. Ekwueme steps outside the hut door just as the boy shoots at a lizard. The arrow which has a barbed point, hit the upper part of Ekwueme's belly, wounding him fatally. Ihuoma is left devastated, wishing for her own death.

The enigma remains. Amadi wisely refrains from pulling out a last-minute alternative explanation. The built-up of the novel has been slow and extremely careful. The first accident, and Emenike's death, is thought by the villagers mainly to have been a simple accident. The manner of Madume's death has more significance attached to it. Finally, after Anyika's revelation about Ihuoma, the death of Ekwueme has a kind of reverberance, a tragic inevitability. Ekwueme is bound to try to evade his fate, and he is also bound to fail, for he will encounter it in a form quite other than he anticipated.

The view of the gods, as it appears in the novel, has been held deliberately within the framework of the society about which Amadi is writing. The novel treats the theme of supernatural love as a major force regulating the life, actions and the behavioral pattern of the characters. The role of the supernatural is predestined on the character of Ihuoma who does not really belong to this world. The death of her husband and suitors are linked to the sea god who, because of his love for her, does not want to see anyone going near her.

Although Amadi presents his characters in depth, with motivations which are always comprehensible, he does not seek to provide psychological alternatives to the interpretation of the central conflict, which is between men and their fate as controlled by their deities. The gods are gods only – neither good nor evil, but merely powerful. In this particular novel, it is the sea god who controls and runs the lives of the people involved with Ihuoma.

Ekwueme in spite of warning of Anyika, and his decision to marry Ihuoma in the face of all odds, did not really seek death. In fact, he was doing all in his power to evade his imminent fate. He had, ironically, himself asked Ihuoma's son to shoot a lizard for the sacrifice to appease the Sea-King. The boy simply fired his arrow along the nearest wall, as Ekwueme advised him to do, in order to knock off any lizard perched there. Ekwueme did not know that the arrow would be shot at the precise moment he would be getting up to meet the dibia. It was fate undoubtedly that caught him unawares, bringing along his death.

It is the same with earlier deaths. Emenike did not seek the fight with Madume, and when he read his death in the priest's eyes, he felt a shuddering curiosity but no wish to die. Madume might have been his own cause of accident if the accident had been of a different nature, but he could scarcely have anticipated, even subconsciously, the presence of a spitting cobra. It is therefore evident that all the affairs in the novel are controlled by the sea god. Ihuoma, the wife-incarnate of the Sea-King cannot take a husband or a lover due to the supernatural hold on her life. The Sea-King would have ordinarily killed her and brought her back to his realm, but he does not do so because of his love for her. But it is the same love that also does not tolerate another man in her life. In as much as this, the sea god did not want anybody to have an affair with her. The three men in her life – Emenike, Madume and Ekwueme – all meet their unfortunate ends as a result of the sea god's interference. The sea god has no mercy on anyone that tries to woo Ihuoma, though re-incarnated and now a human, who is controlled by the Sea-King who is still very possessive of her and jealous of anybody who looks to come near her.

In *The Concubine*, Amadi's principal statement remains an undeniably tragic one. Through the theme of love and marriage of Ihuoma and Emenike and Ekwueme, the age-old conflict of man with his gods, his awe of them and at the same time his proud attempts to bind them, to make them do his will is explored.

The influence of myth and the supernatural on human lives is a constant motif in the novel, intertwined with the multi-angular love story of Ihuoma, the Sea-King and her lovers, especially, Ekwueme. Supernatural forces are evidently seen to have an upper hand on human relationships and control the course that such relationships take. The myth of Ihuoma's re-incarnation shapes the lives of all around her. Speaking of the importance of myth in African tradition, and shaping its history, Stanley Macebuh remarked:

> ...*myth is an attempt to reveal the primal foundations of African culture, and therefore the history.*[21]

Hardly anyone writing about African myths has shown the profound understanding of their meaning and communal significance as Wole Soyinka. In his collection of essays, *Myth, Literature and the African World*, he tries to elicit the African self-apprehended world in myth and literature. A significant passage in '*The Fourth Stage*' quoted by Soyinka in *Who's Afraid of Elesin Oba?* explains this point:

> *Yoruba myth is a recurrent exercise in the experience of disintegration and this is significant for the seeming distancing of will among a people whose mores, culture and metaphysics are based on apparent resignation and acceptance but which are experienced in depth, a statement of man's penetrating insight into the final resolution of things and the constant evidence of harmony.*[22]

The supernatural and mythic control is evidenced in the novel where the Sea-King has a hold on Ihuoma's life and eliminates all who try to win or succeed in winning her love. In line with the theme on the role of divinities in human lives is the theme of superstition. Superstitions were common in traditional African society and are seen in the novel when community members consult mediums before undertaking various quests. Marriage engagements in the novel have superstitious connotations. For example, when initially Ekwueme, unwilling to divulge the real reason behind his disinterest to marry Ahurole was putting it off on flimsy grouds, his mother Adaku, grows suspicious of a bewitching of her boy:

> *What had come over Ekwe? Someone must be involved.*
> *He must have been bewitched.*[23]

Later, again, we see the dibia, Agwoturumbe expressly instructing Wigwe, Ekwueme's father, that the bride price should not be paid for Ihuoma until the Sea-King had been appeased through the sacrifice:

> *'When will you be ready?' (for the sacrifice)*
> *'Eight days', Wigwe replied. 'Meanwhile can we go on with the marriage negotiations?'*
> *'Yes, but the bride price should not be paid until the sacrifices have been offered, to be on the safe side.'*[24]

The theme of love continues to work as the central motif in the novel. Emphasis is on how strong love is. The author depicts love posing a challenge to the supernatural forces surrounding Ihuoma's life. Ihuoma, the almost flawless embodiment of Omokachi's ideal of propriety and grace, a goddess-human who, unknown to her and the villagers, is fated to be the wife of the Sea-King only, as she had been before the birth. Re-incarnated into the Omokachi community, she becomes a death snare for men; the bait to lure those with amorous intentions to a deadly rivalry with the Sea-King, in which, but obviously, the mortals are destined to lose.

The theme of rivalry and jealousy, working in tandem with love is not only limited to the cosmic forces. Ahurole, who is married to Ekwueme, also takes drastic measures to win over her husband, who is attracted to Ihuoma. As her marriage with Ekwueme is devoid of love, Ahurole feels distanced from her husband and decides to administer a love potion to him, as per her mother's advice. However, the 'medicine' has a negative effect and instead of falling head over heels in love with his wife, Ekwueme becomes unstable and is drawn further towards Ihuoma. He recovers from his illness only after being granted the permission to marry Ihuoma.

The story explores man's potential to manipulate his or her destiny and pursuit of love versus the decree of the mystical cosmos employed through folklore, tradition and superstition. The mortal's love is explored through the husband and suitors of Ihuoma while the supernatural forces take the form of the Sea-King. The novel contains an acute awareness of fate's ironies, for the exact moment when we think the prize is within our grasp, the gods cut the thread.

But, in spite of the supernatural influence, the power of love remains undefeated. Ekwueme dies, not as a victim, but as a hero. Although Amadi's view of life is not an optimistic one, it is not a passively fatalistic one either. Ekwueme may be doomed by his love for Ihuoma, but he is not defeated by the gods. He does not become less than he is. Despite his previous timidity and his present fear, he declares that he will marry Ihuoma even if she is the beloved of the Sea-King. He does not want to get into a battle with the gods, but when he is forced into this role, he does not draw back. He goes on, only too aware of his vulnerable humanity, but stronger within himself than he has ever managed to be before. Such is the power of love. The victory, with Ekwueme's death, does not entirely belong to the gods.

Along with the theme of love, the African marriage system is represented throughout the novel through various cultural norms and rituals. Right from the beginning of the novel, wherein Madume exhibits his dominance over his wife showing the reality of African marriage and the secondary position of the wife, to the gender inequality exhibited through the conversations between Ekwueme's parents, where the father's word is supreme, each instance shows the disparity in power between man and wife in wedlock. Every time a wife speaks something that the husband does not agree with, she is forced into silence and the husband's opinion is made her voice too.

The practice of polygamy is discussed over and over again through the novel, highlighting the African custom of a man keeping more than one wife. Madume's plan to marry Ihuoma is an example of this tradition. He feels that as Ihuoma was a widow now, she would be glad to accept his advances, and the piece of land that Emenike had claimed from him, with the support of the villagers, would come back to him. His determination to 'make passes at Ihuoma and to marry her if possibe'[25], though he had his wife already in Wolu, depicts the acceptability of multiple wives for a husband in the society. Moreover, his asking his own wife to take his message of proposal to Ihuoma, and her lacking courage to outrightly deny this favour although she knew that Ihuoma would never accept such a thing shows the subjugated position of a wife. Wolu was very much aware that her husband did not deserve a woman like Ihuoma, but she still could not say as much to his face.

The casual reference to multiple wives is made at several places in the novel. For example, when Ihuoma is discussing the preparations for her husband's burial rites with her brother-in-law Nnnadi and his wife Mgbachi, they all agree upon the enormity of the task that lay before Ihuoma. Emenike's second burial rites called for a lot of preparation to host the large number of guests that were expected. Mgbachi agrees upon the intensity of the work at hand recalling the efforts put in by her father's wives when he had died:

> *'I remember when my father died six, no seven, years ago. My mother and the three other wives nearly collapsed under the strain of the rites.'*[26]

The marriage settlement of children by their parents is another feature of the African society. The match is set by the parents and the children have little power to break against it. Ahurole's marriage with Ekwueme was settled when she was merely eight days old, and he was about five years old. All her growing up years she was raised with no choice of a suitor, a lover or a husband. Her fate was sealed. It can only be imagined how she must have felt after marriage when she must have realized her husband's apathy towards her, and his interest in another woman. Blinded with rage and desire she did what she could best think of, that is, administering a love potion to Ekwueme. Sadly, it reacted and made him lose his mental balance for a while. Scared of punishment, and devoid of any real feelings for this relationship, she fled to her parents, the place she knew she'd be safe. Ahurole's earlier banter with her brother also highlights the secondary position of a girl in her parents' house. He points out how she'd soon be going to her husband's place and thus, would leave all rights here behind her. He also states nonchalantly how he hoped her husband woukd beat her, thus showing the ease with which wife-beating was acceptable in the society by one and all:

> *'Look here, Ahurole, don't take undue advantage of your seniority.*
> *I have had enough.'*
> *'Will you slap me?'*
> *'I won't but I sincerely hope your husband will give you a sound beating first thing when you get to his house.'*[27]

On the other hand, Ekwueme's frustration is also understandable – to be tied down by a promise made by other people on his behalf was clearly not his choice. But then, the society that he lived in would never allow him to break his father's word. When his father hears from him that he wants to marry Ihuoma and not Ahurole, he clearly tells him that he was being a fool in harbouring such thoughts. Ekwueme had been a very fine person till now, liked and respected by all in and around their village. But calling off an almost twenty-year-old engagement would certainly dislodge him from his position in the society. No one would ever support him in this:

> *'Listen my son, you must not be like the caterpillar that holds fast to tree branches when small but loses its grip and falls to its death when much older. So far you have shown all signs of growing into a sensible young man.*
> *If at this critical stage you turn into a fool, it will be most unfortunate… Be sensible. Tomorrow I am going to start negotiations on Ahurole. I have informed her parents and relations. Everything is ready. We can't go back. I tell you it is almost an abomination to break off an engagement like this. It is unheard of. No one would ever side with you.'*[28]

What Wigwe said was once again stressed upon by Ihuoma herself. She too refused to marry Ekwueme, citing the social constraints. She was a widow with three children. She could not even imagine becoming the wife of young Ekwueme, that too when he had been in such a long-standing engagement with another girl. She knew that their society would never accept it, and she would also be ridiculed if they got a hint. Her good name would be spoiled forever:

> *'I am a woman,' she said meditatively, 'and a woman's good name can disappear overnight. What you propose can bring nothing but shame to me and regrets to you.'*[29]

Elechi Amadi takes up the issue of widowhood and widow remarriage in his novel too. The various rituals and disadvantages for a woman associated with widowhood have been portrayed through Ihuoma's life after her husband Emenike's death. A woman who loses her husband to death has a very difficult life ahead. Amadi talks of the hardships of a widow through the life Ihuoma had to lead after Emenike's death. A widow has to take care of her husband's farm and compound to ensure it is not run down by weeds. Also, she needs to fend all alone for herself and her children (if any). Talking about the difficulties of a woman who has lost her husband, Amadi points out that 'only roofs of widows may leak during the rains'. However, Ihuoma was saved such discomfort by the timely help of her brother-in-law Nnadi and his friends Wodu Wakiri and Ekwueme. Still her life is not easy with Emenike gone. She has three children, and thus can barely afford to sit through the mourning period. She works on the farm, and also looks after her husband's compound. As a widow she also had to make all preparations for her husband's burial rites after his death, and once again after a year of his death. These rites involved preparing an extension to the reception hall to host the vast number of guests that would be arriving, and to prepare lavish food and drinks for everyone too. Each day she worked in the farm and also prepared for these rites as 'she knew it was her duty and that the more efficiently she discharged it the more honour she would accord her departed husband.'[30]

Elechi Amadi deals with the issue of widow remarriage in a sensitive manner, talking about the beauty and goodness of Ihuoma, yet the society's perception of her ineligibility to become Ekwueme's wife just because she was a widow. Having the responsibility of her children upon her, it is quite difficult to imagine that someone would want to marry her and take on the additional burden. No such considerations would have been allowed in case of a widower. Before Ekwueme's discovery of his love for Ihuoma, his sympathy for her echoes the general thoughts of the people regarding a young widow:

> *It was too bad that such a young girl should languish in protracted widowhood. But, as yet, there was nothing that could be done about it.*[31]

Widowhood was no less than a curse for a woman. Not only did it affect her emotionally and economically, but even in the physical world, the smallest of pleasures was taken away from her as if to stress that the wife had no right to outlive her husband. Amadi pens down the very short episode of Ihuoma's pride over her looks very beautifully to bring out the brutality of the customs associated with widowhood. Ihuoma was not at all vain, yet she knew that she was beautiful, and took pleasure in this realization.

> *She wondered what it was like to be ugly...she wanted to gaze at herself. That she was beautiful, she had no doubt, but that did not make her arrogant. She was sympathetic, gentle, and reserved.*[32]

She was a beautiful woman who loved to sing and dance. But the untimely death of her husband had taken not just conjugal happiness away from her but had reduced her to barely a remnant of what she had been. The same oduma tune that had made her sing and dance now reduced her to tears.

One evening, about one month after Emenike's death, an oduma dance was held in the village arena. Being a widow, whose husband had died recently, she lay crying in her bed all through the night of the dance. The widow was not only shunned from activities of enjoyment, but her general way of life was also dictated to change.

She had to get her hair shorn, could not eat properly, and could not even wear a new dress for long. Ihuoma had to dress simply in sackcloth for a year after her husband's death. The women were so conditioned that a life without husband was supposed to be a life devoid of any happiness at all. Over and over, we see Ihuoma ruing her fate, cursing her looks, and unwilling to do anything that she used to do earlier – like laugh, dance, sing, dress well etc. as she had no one to admire her with her husband dead. It did not matter that the villagers still thought her young and beautiful; for her, life had finished with Emenike:

> *All through the night of the dance Ihuoma lay tossing on her bed. The gentle night breeze brought the oduma music clearly to her. She had no enthusiasm for it now and listened out of sheer habit…Ihuoma felt she could never be the same again. Her hair was closely shaven according to tradition; she looked emaciated; her cheek-bones showed and her voice was husky and uncertain; her dress was untidy.*[33]

This dehumanizing of widows is something that many novelists have pointed out in their novels, leading the reader to wonder if being born a woman is a crime in Africa, because there are no such rituals for a widower. Why should there always be widow's rites and not widower's rites? Alongwith Amadi's portarayal of Ihuoma in *The Concubine*, this theme of widowhood is recurrent in many African pieces by prominent authors such as Isidore Okpewho in *The Last Duty*, Mariam Ba in *So Long a Letter*, Bayo Adebowale in *Lonely Days* among others. In all of them, the maltreatment and psychological trauma that a widow goes through in the name of custom and tradition is poignantly illustrated.

Widowhood is a harsh reality for as long as people are born, they are going to die. Widows are found in every community but in Africa, the experience of the widow is such that women dread to be widows.

In Africa, widows go through a lot of hardship that stems from the society, the husband's family and from tradition. The treatment that women receive in their time of grief and loss shows the plight of women and widows, specially, in some communities of Africa. The novels like *The Concubine* and *So Long a Letter* look at the issue of widowhood in Africa and show how gender and its attendant problems impede on the woman's social standing and general development in society. For example, Ihuoma had to sell most of her yam plots as a woman was not expected to cultivate yam, the king of crops, as it was considered primarily a male domain. Her character shows how an African woman handles widowhood and how the African society sees a widow.

Gender and feminism, as a recognized phenomenon today makes it almost impossible for one to address any issue whether in politics, economy, philosophy, literature or any other field without a specific reference to call for gender equality. Elaine Showalter, talking about gender, called it a crucial determinant in the production, circulation and consumption of literary discourse. One can, of course, apply the principles in the analysis of widowhood. Gender disparity can be witnessed in the difference in the place of a widow and a widower in the society.

In many cultures, prejudices against women are in fact deep-rooted. Widowhood practices are among the prejudies that have constantly impinged on the dignity and rights of women in different cultures in Africa. The BBC English Dictionary (I) has defined widowhood as the state of being a widow or widower. In most cultures in Africa however, widowhood practices have become the exclusive preserve for widows with accompanying elaborate guiding regulations, and not for widowers for whom the culture or tradition has prescribed little or no mourning rights.

Unarguably, every marriage ultimately ends with the death of either of the man or woman, or even both, that is, not taking into account the system of divorce which still doesn't exist in most cultures traditionally. However, the death of a spouse may be the extreme of life's crisis as this severs most of the deepest emotional bonds established in a lifetime. Ironically though, the toll of the death of a husband tends to be more overwhelming on the woman than on the man when he loses his wife. This is because the woman is mostly traumatized and disorganized by such development on account of the harrowing experiences that await her as couched in widowhood rites.

These rites are sets of expectations regarding the actions and behavior of the widow; including actions by others towards the widow; as well as the rituals performed by or on behalf of the widow from the time of the death of her husband. These widowhood practices have not only dehumanized and subjugated women who are widows to unimaginable predicaments, but also tragi-institutionalized their plights in various African cultures. '*Di bu ugwu nwanyi*', which translates to 'husband constitutes honour and dignity to womanhood', is a popular traditional expression among the Igbo society of the south east of Nigeria. The very moment a woman loses her her husband, she automatically loses her prized dignity, that intangible but observable status that the society accords to married women. Also, most cultures in Africa place husbands as gods in their wives' lives. This apparent divinity that the culture ascribes to the husband necessitates the performance of certain rites and rituals when he dies.

The widow, who might have enjoyed every amount of freedom and goodwill while her husband lived, suddenly turns incommunicado as the death of her husband heralds a period of imprisonment and hostility for her. Her movements become restricted throughout the mourning period and culture forces her to eat bare minimum, tasteless food just enough to somehow survive. Thus, we see Ihuoma losing much of the roundness of her face during her period of mourning. She is not expected to be happy or laugh, chat or play with people in this period as she is supposed to be unclean and abominable till she performs the last rites of the husband that spans over a year. She is to observe strict discipline in her life, devoid of any kind of enjoyment and she is mandated to continually cry and wail for her deceased husband. She is subjected to wearing mourning clothes throughout her mourning period thus making her readily identifiable as widow and therefore stigmatized. She also faces the further humiliation of her hair shaven off. All these customs mark her out as an outcast in the normal society of men as a creature at war with the world beyond until she frees herself by fulfilling all widowhood rites.

Amadi focuses on the plight and suffering of widows in terms of their social, economic, psychological and cultural rights violation in Africa. Ihuoma represents the widows in African society as silent victims who suffer cruel and dehumanizing cultural and ritual practices as a mourning process for their dead spouses. Just like Amadi has painted the sufferings of Ihuoma after her husband's death, Mariam Ba in *So Long a Letter* portrays the plight and suffering of widows in their social, economic and psychological state using the character of Ramatuolaye's experience. Ba looks at the situation of widows as silent victims, and also delineates the oppressive structures that give rise to oppressive traditions and cultural practices that work against the women who become widows.

Ihuoma belonged to the Igbo land where widows are subjected to numerous hardships. A widow is somehow believed to be responsible for her husband's death, and thus there are various rituals devised for them to perform penance of sorts. In an attempt to absolve them of guilt, they are shaved, kept in dark rooms for days with little or nothing to eat. Sometimes they are made to sleep in the same room with their husband's corpse and the water used in bathing the dead man is given to the woman to drink. Any attempt by the widow to contest this is met with stiff resistance and and name-calling. The factors influencing widows' lives, the options available to them and the multiplicity of interests that affect their behavior, have all been analysed in various texts of African literature. This analysis, very much like in Ihuoma's case of the oduma dance, shows how the widow feels out of place and neglected after her husband's death. She could only listen to the music and cry rather than go and join them in the village dance.

Amadi's portrayal of Ihuoma's hardships faced as a widow is a reflection of the construction of widowhood in the traditional Igbo society where the demise of the husband makes his wife culpable. Her experiences capture social realities about widowhood in Igbo culture with the stance that widows are repressed and oppressed through various customs in the African Igbo society, turning widowhood into a traumatic experience that every married woman dreads. This state of affairs, occasioned by the death of a spouse leads to loss of spousal intimacy and protection. When Ihuoma is assaulted by Madume on the disputed plantation, she is quick to call for help and cry out that he would not have mustered such lecherous courage had her husband been alive to protect her. The husband is not just the keeper of his wife, but also her guard and protector according to tradition.

Though a widow had to fight hard for her sustenance and work harder for the upkeep of her children, yet she was viewed as a dependent and not as a contributor. Inspite of working hard on her farms, her yams were taken away. Though she was considered fit enough to cultivate and sell her produce in the market yet she had to depend upon the men in the family (in this case, her brother-in-law Nnadi), to have her roof mended. Very little attention is paid to the widow's economic role as she is viewed only under the glass of sympathy and as a dependant. Widows, like Ihuoma, are more worried about what people might think of them rather than their own discomfort due to the endless customs associated with widowhood. They would never raise their voice against the inhuman treatment, fearing what their kins may say or think about them and their outspoken nature if they dared to show dissent. So, they remain silent and hide behind their masks and wear smiling faces even in the face of hardship and deprivation.

Widowhood, throughout Africa, if one may point out, is a period of hardship and deprivation as it includes varying degrees of physical seclusion for ritual purification. Inspite of the second-hand treatment given to the widows, in reality, after the death of the husbands, these women take on double responsibility. A widow often takes an even larger role in her family's welfare. Like Ihuoma worked double hard for the maintenance of Emenike's children, farm and compound.

Alongwith the theme of widowhood, Elechi Amadi also raises the issue of widow remarriage. While a general acceptance of a widow's remarriage is quite clear through the conversations between the characters in the novel, yet for her to become the first wife of a young man is something that is frowned upon. Madume feels that he has a good chance at getting Ihuoma as his second wife as she is a widow with three children, and would definitely accept his offer. Though he is proven wrong through Ihuoma's straight rejection and later dies due to supernatural interference, the fact remains that nobody would have minded a widow's marriage to a man already having a wife or even more. On the other hand, the strong case presented by Ekwueme's parents – Wigwe and Adaku, and Ihuoma herself, against her marriage to him shows the society's deep-rooted gender bias and an individual's fear to go against the set norms. Ihuoma's reluctance to accept Ekwueme's proposal, and his family's distress at the chances of defilement of the tradition of betrothal due to their son's blind love for a widow, both, present a very sad picture of the situation. The parents of Ekwueme were not just alarmed at the prospect of breaking off of his engagement to Ahurole, what also troubled them was his desire to get married to a woman who was a widow, and had the responsibility of her children and her dead husband's compound on her. According to Ihuoma, Ekwueme deserved 'a young maiden' who would give him 'the first fruits of her womb'[34]. She feels that he would soon grow tired of her and her children with Emenike would be a constant burden on him. The same concern is expressed later by his mother and father in different conversations, both trying to dissuade him from falling in love with Ihuoma:

> *I do not say there is anything wrong with Ihuoma. She is a good young woman, but nevertheless a wrong choice for you. She has three children. She is looking after her late husband's compound. Her allegiance to you would take second place. Remember that a hen cannot scratch for food with her two legs simultaneously. Be sensible.*[35]

These words of Wigwe simply echo the general opinion about a widow and her remarriage. Ihuoma too had expressed the same line of thought when turning down Ekwueme's proposal. She was sure that Ekwueme would soon tire of her and begin to find her children a bother. Also, as the widow of Emenike, she was not ready to leave his compound:

> '*Not so, Ekwe, I shall not leave my husband's compound. I intend to stay here and bring up his children. It should never be said that his compound was overrun with weeds.*'[36]

Adaku, Ekwueme's mother opined the same when talking to her husband. She had always liked Ihuoma too, but the thought of her as a prospective bride for her son was unacceptable because she had been married once and had children to care for. She tells her son:

> '*Ekwe, do you realize that she has three children and that she is too old for you to marry.*'
> '*I am older than she is.*'
> '*I know, but she is too old for you to marry.*'
> '*She is young enough.*'
> '*Who will maintain her children?*'[37]

The insistence of all these three people, namely Ihuoma, Wigwe and Adaku, on Ekwueme to go through with his engagement to Ahurole, and get married to her, is also related to another important aspect of an African marriage that is the expected virginity of the bride, especially if she is to become the first wife of a man. For a young eligible bachelor like Ekwueme to take on a non-virgin as his first wife was absolutely unthinkable. A great deal of importance is attached to pre-nuptial chastity, especially for girls. The pride in virginity of girls before marriage and the extreme importance attached to its preservance till marriage is a primary concern that runs through the African novels in general, and is visible in this one too. Ahurole's parents prided themselves upon their good upbringing of their daughter and thus were in no hurry to wed her off inspite of the arrangement made in her childhood. When Ekwueme's father starts the marriage negotiation, Wagbara expresses his delight alongwith not being in a hurry to settle for an early date, thereby expressing his disinterest in acquiring a heavy bride price, once again drawing attention of the reader to another important aspect of African marriage, which is, the bride price.

The bride price is the payment made by the groom's side to the bride's family seeking their permission to take their daughter in marriage. Generally, the bride price is paid to the father of the bride, and in his absence to the next father-like figure in the family. The groom's family paid multiple visits to the bride's home, with kegs of palm wine and kola-nuts, in each visit the bride price was negotiated, and once the amount was settled, a date was fixed, and on that day, the groom and his family came with the village elders for the formal presentation of wine.

The customs related to the wedding have been shown in detail through the wedding ceremony of Ahurole and Ekwueme. After the initial days of negotiations, the big day was the day of formal presentation of wine. On this day Wigwe came accompanied by several village elders, Ekwueme and his friends, and relations, all dressed in their fine wrappers. They all came singing to Wagbara's compound carrying expensive wine. This part of the wedding was the most important as the groom's family brings along the final settlement of the bride price along with wine, and is well received with good food and drinks by the bride's family. Traditionally, the bride is supposed to return with the groom's family to his home for four days and thereafter would return to her parents' place. Later, the groom would come to receive her and she would move permanently to his house, which would now be her house too.

Another unique feature of an African marriage comes to fore during the initiation of marriage negotiations of Ahurole and Ekwueme. Wigwe, Ekwueme's father asks Wagbara (Ahurole's father) as to who would be his guide during the negotiations; and Wagbara introduces his younger brother Nwenike as the guide for the groom's side. Nwenike was Ahurole's uncle and had always regarded her as his own daughter. Amadi, through this episode tells us about the very important role of a guide in African wedding:

> *In a marriage a guide is a very important fellow. He introduces the prospective bridegroom (or his representative) to important relations of the bride. He gives him a good idea as to their order of importance. More important still*

> *he fights tooth and nail to slash down the bride price. Although related to the bride, he is expected to side with the bridegroom in all things. The choice of a guide makes all the difference in marriage proceedings.*[38]

Elechi Amadi demonstrates the African way of life and its customs related to matrimony through his novel and also presents the communal bond and harmony present in the pre-colonized society. Life in Omokachi and Omigwe is filled with deep love and respect between the villagers. Though not related by blood, they care about one another like family. They stand by each other in times of anguish, joy and sorrow. For example, we see the whole village turning up to welcome Ekwueme and his family when they come to take Ahurole with them:

> *Wagbara with the help of his neighbours prepared a great feast for his guests and made sure that nothing was lacking.*
> *Not that he could not do it alone, but the neighbours could not bear to see him having all the fun of entertaining. Ahurole was their child too. They could not stay back on a great occasion like this.* [39]

The custom of giving away the daughter in marriage is not unique to Africa, and thus Amadi's treatment of the subject is quite universal. The fact that Ahurole could not stay long at her husband's place and returned to her parents' after the unfortunate episode of the 'love potion' prompted Wagbara to offer the return of her bride price to Wigwe. Thus, symbolizing that the girl belongs to the husband's family till her death if her bride price is not repaid. Later we notice this understanding once again when Ekwueme seeks Nnadi's (Emenike's brother) permission to marry Ihuoma and not her parents'. Nnadi, being the inheritor of his brother's property after his death, had also inherited the guardianship of Ihuoma in the absence of her husband. The African tradition also allows for the brother of the deceased to take the latter's wife as his own. Though Nnadi does not marry Ihuoma, he continues to be her guardian in every other aspect – be it thatching her roof (primarily a husband's duty), checking in to see her late visitors (as in the case of Wigwe and Ekwueme) or permitting her remarriage (to Ekwueme).

Amadi, in *The Concubine*, presents love and marriage in its traditional boundary and yet the inclusion of the supernatural makes it a transcending phenomenon. These twin concerns, being universal in nature, are presented in duality – as being blind to convention (like Ekwueme's love for Ihuoma) and also bound by tradition (as Ihuoma's feelings for Ekwueme that she manages to keep in restrains for a long time). Ihuoma does not give in to her love for Ekwueme inspite of her own mother's encouragement. She keeps pushing him away till she sees that he really needed her during his illness. Even later, she accepts him only after being sure that his parents and society would not object to their marriage. Such was the way things worked in this world. The village life of Omokachi was noted for its tradition. Decorum and propriety were the hallmarks of their rural society. They lived by the rules and excessive and fanatical feelings over anything was frowned upon. Also, any person exhibiting extreme feelings for anything was called crazy. Anyone who could not control his feelings was regarded as being unduly influenced by his *agwu*. Anyika, the village medicine man, often confirmed this, as in the case of Ahurole. Unable to take hold of her anger and jealousy against Ihuoma, and determined to win the love of her husband at all costs, she had administered a love potion to her husband Ekwueme, that had resulted in his losing his mental balance. It was after much effort and care of his family, Anyika and Ihuoma, that he was able to get back to his normal self.

Talking about the sublime concept of love in the Omokachi village, Amadi says that Ahurole's attitude to get Ekwueme's love at all costs was something that could not be supported by the people ever. For in her land, a woman deliberately scheming to land a man was unheard of. It was precisely for this reason that Ihuoma had discouraged Ekwueme's advances and proposal to her. As a widow and mother of three children, she knew well that if she reciprocated Ekwueme's love in public, she would be the villain in their eyes. Ekwueme's mother had already set her mind on the belief that Ihuoma must have bewitched her son. She saw no other reason why he would want to break off his engagement to Ahurole and pursue Ihuoma. Yet later we witness Ekwueme's love winning over every hurdle. Ahurole loses him and his family's support due to her own impatience and folly. Ihuoma stood by him during his worst hour, thereby earning trust and respect of his family and society. Once Ahurole was gone, there was no reason left for Ihuoma to continue denying her feelings for Ekwueme and she agrees to get married to him. In the world of Amadi's novel, "even love and sex were put in their proper place…Love was love and never failed."[40]

Ihuoma exhibits patience in her love for Ekwueme, proving that true love never fails to materialize into a proper relationship. Ekwueme too, abided by the rules of the society and married the girl his parents had selected for him. It was a series of events no less than the workings of destiny that ruled in his favour and he was able to stand a chance at marrying Ihuoma after all. Amadi justifies Ihuoma's earlier stand for Ekwueme, where she had repressed her feelings for him by citing the psychology of the people of Omokachi in matters of love and marriage:

> *If a woman could not marry one man she could always marry another. A woman deliberately scheming to land a man was unheard of.*
>
> *True, she might encourage him, but this encouragement was a subtle reflex action, a legacy of her prehistoric ancestors. A mature man's love was sincere, deep and stable and therefore easy to reciprocate, difficult to turn down. That was why it was possible for a girl to marry a man without formal courtship.*[41]

This was the world of Ihuoma and she stayed true to her type. Inspite of holding love for Ekwueme in her heart, she never encouraged him consciously. Yet the power of Ekwueme's love turned the events in such a manner that no marriage, no widowhood, nor any kind of social propriety could stop them to acknowledge their love finally for each other; and the people of their family and village also supported them wholeheartedly. Ihuoma and Ekwueme, once sure of their love for each other, and empowered with the support of their family and society, get ready to marry inspite of the fact that they never had had any formal courtship.

The element of the supernatural, introduced toward the end of the novel does not only scare and surprise but also makes the reader root for Ekwueme. Though pitted to fall against the Sea-King, his imminent defeat looks like a victory still. His refusal to back down from his love makes him a hero in the true sense. Inspite of his death, the power of love remains undefeated. Ekwueme dies, not as a victim, but as a hero.

Elechi Amadi, in his debut novel, has managed to portray a society still ruled by traditional gods, supernatural elements and supersitions, preparing a beautiful blend of interpersonal relationships in the backdrop of the rural African life. His portrayal of love is that of an emotion that outweighs every other feeling on earth and even beyond. The desire to connect with another human being is a basic drive. Therefore, the theme of love in literature is perhaps as old as literature itself. Amadi, too, has tried to capture love, mercurial and difficult. Love can be grand or tragic, but it is always compelling. And marriage comes across as the ultimate unifying agent, on the basis of which societies and empires are based. The depiction of love and the state of marriage in the villages of Omogachi and Omigwe show the interpersonal relationships created and sustained on the foundation of love and marriage in the society. Amadi offers a view into the human relationships that such a society creates. The theme of love and marriage that runs through the pages of this novel possesses timelessness as well as universality.

References

1. Amadi, Elechi. (1966). *Book Review of The Concubine*. UK: The New Statesman.
2. Amadi, Elechi. (1966). *The Concubine*. London: Heinemann African Writers Series. p.5.
3. *ibid*, p.195.
4. Krige, Eileen. (1981*). Essays on African Marriage in Southern Africa*. Cape Town: Juta Publishers. p.71.
5. *ibid*, p.4.
6. *ibid*, p.4.
7. *ibid*, p.5.
8. Krige, Eileen. (1978). *Social System and Tradition in South Africa: Essays in honour of Eileen Krige*. (Written in collaboration with William John Argyle and Eleanor Preston Whyte). London: Oxford Universiy Press. p72.
9. *ibid*, p.195.
10. *ibid*, p.91.
11. *ibid*, p.99.
12. Koso Thomas, Olayinka. (1987). *The Circumcision of Women: A Strategy for Eradication*. London and New Jersey: Zed Books Ltd. p.9.
13. Krige, Eileen and Krige, Jack. (1943). *The Realm of a Rain-Queen: A Study of the Patterns of Lovedu Society*. London: Oxford University Press. p.71.
14. *ibid*, p.130.
15. *ibid*, p.132.
16. *ibid*, p.159.
17. *ibid*, p.193.
18. *ibid*, pp.194-196
19. *ibid*, p.197.
20. *ibid*, p.200.
21. Macebuh, Stanley. (1980). *Poetics and the Mythic Imagination*. United States of America: Three Continents Press. p.201.
22. Soyinka, Wole. (1988). *Who's Afraid of Elesin Oba? Art, Dialoge and Outrage: Essays on Literature and Culture*. Ibadan: New Horn Press. (Dialogue 28). p.121.
23. *ibid*, p.104.
24. *ibid*, p.200.
25. *ibid*, p.54.
26. *ibid*, p.31.
27. *ibid*, p.98.
28. *ibid*, p.107.
29. *ibid*, p.92.
30. *ibid*, p.30.
31. *ibid*, p.24.

32. *ibid*, p.11.
33. *ibid*, p.28.
34. *ibid*, p.91.
35. *ibid*, p.107.
36. *ibid*, p.92.
37. *ibid*, p.105.
38. *ibid*, p.121.
39. *ibid*, p.123.
40. *ibid*, p.123.

Chapter - III

The Bride Price

Buchi Emecheta's *The Bride Price* illustrates the collective power of tribal and social imperative customs and traditions that come to play when a woman refuses to comply to the marriage arrangements of the family:

> … *because each ant would be lost if it did not follow the footsteps of those in front, those who have gone on that very path before.*[1]

The novel is a particularly strong representation of the collective solidarity, with the voice of the tribe or the voices of the sub-groups of the tribe, chanting the codes of conduct like a Greek chorus. In this novel, her own age group, the mothers, the aunts, the fathers and the male elders, and the dibias provide tribal folklore in the form of stories, maxims, proverbs, rituals and taboos that accompany Aku-nna as she evolves from girlhood to womanhood. These accumulate in her mind as a great and implacable collective subconscious that she cannot get rid of. *The Bride Price* is as much an acknowledgement of the power of this tribal super-ego, as it is a diatribe against the old ways. A modern educated woman Aku-nna rebels against the hypocrisy and injustice towards women inherent in tradition, but she cannot fight the strength of her deeply entrenched and internalized Igbo customs; she cannot root them out of her own heart and mind, nor from the hearts and minds of the people.

The Bride Price interconnects the myth, marriage and literature of Africa. In the novel, Emecheta deals not only with the subordinate role that the female is forced to acquire in a marriage, and the society, but also the hypocrisy of the whole setup where on one hand, a daughter is claimed to be the father's wealth and the most prized possession and on the other hand, she is just an asset waiting to be liquidated in the name of bride price.

The clash of cultures remains the most widely studied theme in African literature. The white man's prejudice and discrimination, the native's struggle to uphold his identity – these seem to have a centrehold on the most of the studies. What is often ignored is the fact that this genre also deals extensively with myth and superstition, which find a very prominent role in oral tradition as well as written texts. The African literature is woven through myth and superstition that hold not just the past but also determine the say of the future. This novel explores the theme of love and marriage through the role of myth in the life of Aku-nna, a young bride who is constantly haunted by the fear of an early death during childbirth as her bride price was not paid. The psychological turmoil she undergoes with this constant apprehension, and her ultimate death fulfilling this myth points to the very sad state of African custom where traditions are valued more than human life.

African literature has most commonly been viewed as a literature of identity. In the post-colonial light, especially literary critics as well as readers have long been pre-occupied with the native tradition versus the colonists' idea of civilization. What, however, has remained a constant motif in the African literature, is the stronghold of myth. The critics, though accepting myth as a common topic, have continuously viewed it as a remnant of the past rather than a force that moves the present. Wole Soyinka, a seminal writer in African literature discussed the absurdity of viewing all African writings as a culture clash. In the Author's Note prefacing the text of '*Death and the King's Horsemen*', he inserts a very important message for his readers:

> *The bane of themes of this genre is that they are no sooner employed creatively that they acquire the facile tag of 'clash of cultures', a prejudicial label which, quite apart from its frequent misapplication, presupposes a potential equality in every given situation of an alien culture and the indigenous, in the soil of the latter.*[2]

Buchi Emecheta, in her novel, *The Bride Price*, traces the traditional superstition through the lives of Aku-nna and Chike, the young lovers who try to defy the age-old customs only to be defeated by fate. In the treatment of the whole novel, love, marriage and myth form an integral part. It is the myth of the bride price that sets the action in motion and finally draws the sad conclusion. The myth stated that if a girl got married against the will of her parents and her bride price was not paid, or the parents refused to accept her bride price, she would eternally be doomed to live without the blessings of her parents. And in such a scenario, if she consummated her marriage and got pregnant without her bride price being paid, she was fated to die during her first childbirth. The bride price is a tradition integral to the African society. According to April A. Gordon :

> *Bride wealth in Africa is a custom that requires a transfer of goods and services from the male's family to the bride's family or to the bride. It does not mean selling daughters, rather, it indicates the high value attached to the women in African societies. It is considered that girls will bring wealth to the husband's family, so the girl's family must be compensated for the loss of their daughter. In fact, African women often work together to arrange suitable marriages and to maximize the bride wealth.*[3]

As girls are viewed as assets, it is viewed that due to this custom, somehow girls are getting more opportunities for education. We see in *The Bride Price* that Okonkwo agrees to Aku-nna's school education with this view that she would fetch him a higher bride price if she were educated, which would make her a more prized commodity among the general uneducated people of Ibuza.

> *"Aku-nna and Oguagua will get married at about the same time.*
>
> *Their bride prices will come to me. You see the trend today, that the educated girls fetch more money... Aku-nna had to be allowed to stay in school so that she could be married to a rich man, from one of those newly prosperous families springing up like mushrooms mushrooms all over Ibuza.*[4]

While the greed of a higher bride price encouraged education of girls, it cannot be denied that this custom reduced the institution of marriage into commercial proposition.

It also encouraged polygamy in the sense that a chief or a wealthy man could afford to pay for a number of wives as against a large number of poor men who could hardly acquire price for a single bride. The higher the number of wives, the more affluent a man was considered to be. For example, Okonkwo already had three wives when he married the widow of his brother, and Aku-nna's mother, Ma Blackie, thus making her his fourth wife.

Another aspect of the bride price was that with its payment, the wife became the property of her husband, which also gave him unlimited powers to treat her as a beast. Women are seen to be fit only for production and reproduction. In fact, in most African societies, especially in rural areas it is considered that education of a girl is a waste of resources, as she will get married after all. On the other hand, girls are valuable only because they bring wealth to the family in the form of the bride price, which is paid to the girl's family. This legitimated her as the husband's wife and property, at her husband's death, the wife can be passed to the brother, who can marry her to keep her in the family, and not having to pay back her bride price. These old conservative customs serve only to reinforce that a woman is nothing more than a piece of property. Emecheta in her novel, uses this practice of bride price to literally, as well as, symbolically, represent women's submission to man in marriage in African culture.

The novel works very much like a fairy tale romance where the child Aku-nna disobeys her parents, the tribe, to end up marrying her lover, Chike, the teacher whom Aku-nna loves. He represents the radical who wants to change and modernize things, but as an Osu, or a slave descendent, he is doubly damned: he is respected as a teacher, but the age-old taboo against the Osu slave cult prohibits him from entering into the clan, so that both his politics and his birth exclude him from the mainstream community. Aku-nna is the proverbial innocent child in the fairy tale, who must choose, learn and suffer the consequences.

The narrative development traces Aku-nna's growth from girlhood to womanhood, the evaluation of her personality and her awareness of the institutions, the rituals, the traditions and the values inherent in the community code. At thirteen, after her father's death in a modern big city, Lagos, Aku-nna and her brother Nna-nndo return with their mother, Ma Blackie, to the rural village of Ibuza to live with her uncle Okunkwo, who claims the family as a rightful legal inheritance from his dead brother. Aku-nna falls in love with her rural village school teacher, Chike Ofulue, but their relationship is forbidden by tribal taboos because he comes from a family of Osu, an ostracized slave cult dedicated to the gods. As soon as she attains puberty, Aku-nna is abducted by her jealous suitor, Okoboshi, who, according to an ancient tribal custom, can claim a wife by kidnapping her and burying a lock of her hair, allowing the woman's family no choice but to oblige by exacting a minimal bride price. In a dramatic turn of events, Chike rescues Aku-nna from Okoboshi and his family. Both love each other very deeply and elope to another village Ughelli, their union doubly dangerous, first in defiance of the taboo against an alliance between slave and free families, and second, as a challenge to the old curse that any woman who marries without her family's approval and whose bride price has not been paid, will die in childbirth. To quote:

> *If a girl wished to live long and see her children's children, she must accept the husband chosen for her by her people, and the bride price must be paid. If the bride price was not paid, she would never survive the birth of her first child.*[5]

Uncle Okonkwo refuses to accept either the bride price or the marriage to Chike, an Osu. In the end Aku-nna dies in childbirth thereby fulfilling the tribal curse.

As the novel opens, we meet Aku-nna, the protagonist, who is 'fitting' the key into the keyhole, a phase and act metaphorically suggestive of the fact that she, at the formative age of thirteen, is aware of the forms and fitting in. She and her eleven old year brother, Nna-nndo, have been entrusted with the domestic responsibilities of the house. Their mother is in Ibuza to undergo treatment for fertility, from a medicine man to placate their Oboshi river goddess into giving her some babies. Aku-nna fully realizes the seriousness of her mother's problem because many a time she had heard other women of the neighbourhood and some of them living in the same compound, making songs of Ma Blackie's childlessness. She had heard her parents quarelling over this great issue of childlessness. Nna would go on and on, talking in his small and sad voice, telling Ma, reminding her, that he had paid double the normal bride price to marry her. He had taken great efforts and also spent a lot to get their marriage sanctified by Anglicanism. But even after all the efforts and expenditure, all he had to show from this marriage was a single son. The Africans valued the number of sons just like the number of wives and houses and cattle etc. For Aku-nna's father, his marriage was as good as a failure if he did not beget multiple male children from it. The deep-rooted gender discrimination in the society is apparent through this conversation between Ma Blackie and Ezekiel Odia, just a prelude to other diiscriminations like class and caste that play an important part in Aku-nna's love story with Chike.

In the African society, marriage was merely a means to procure children, especially male. If a wife failed to deliver a male child, in fact, a number of boys, she was considered a failure as a woman, as a wife. The husband, if not satisfied with her ability to bear him sufficient number of children, could also send her back to her parents or take in another wife.

Aku-nna could clearly see her place in this scheme of things. She knew well, that as a girl, she was too insignificant a being to be regarded as a blessing to this unfortunate marriage. Not only was she a girl, but also 'much too thin' for the approval of her parents. Also, she was very susceptible to diseases. So much so that if anyone were to fall ill down the lane, she was sure to catch that illness. Her parents refer to her as an "ogbanje"-a living dead. Her mother often chides her by asking Aku-nna to make up her mind if she is going to live or die. It often seems so, that the only thing her parents look forward to, in respect to Aku-nna, is the bride price that her future husband would be paying for her.

The only commodity value female children bring to the family is the bride price. Aku-nna was not only expected to follow the customs of her community but even her name was a constant reminder of what she owed to her father:

> *He had named her Aku-nna meaning literally "father's wealth", knowing that the only consolation he could count on from her would be her bride price. To him this was something to look forward to.*
>
> *Aku-nna on her part was determined not to let her father down. She was going to marry well, a rich man of whom her father would approve and who would be able to afford an expensive bride price.*[6]

Aku-nna's father had named her such, literally meaning "father's wealth", and on her part, the girl even as a young child was a determined not to disappoint her father. She imagines an ideal future where she will marry well, a rich man, who would win the approval of her father, and would also be easily able to afford a handsome bride price. She imagines that she will have her marriage first of all solemnized by the beautiful goddess of Ibuza, then the Christians will sing her a wedding march, then her father Nna will call up the spirits of her great, great grandparents to guide her, then after all that, she would leave her father's house.

These plans however fall haywire with the untimely death of Ezekial Odia, Aku-nna's father. Ma Blackie, her mother follows the traditional custom and agrees to be the fourth wife of Okonkwo, her late husband's brother. With her own mother getting too busy in Okonkwo's house politics and her younger brother Nna-nndo engaged in his own wild ways, Aku-nna finds a friend and sympathizer in Chike, her young teacher at school. The two fall in love and decide to hide it till she completes her school fearing that her family would stop her education and marry her off to some lad of their choice if they got to know of her affair. Never in their dreams even would they allow the marriage of their daughter to a descendent of a slave. But as the old saying goes, love, like fire, cannot be hidden for long and people get talking.

Emecheta, through her novel, informs us about the traditional African society where marriage intertwines with myth. Various customs of the African society establish the secondary role of the women, and the novel shows those customs ensuring that the wife remains a mere property of her father and his family. While the ownership keeps changing, these traditional customs never allow a woman to be the master of her own life. Aku-nna goes through her various fundamental roles in the society as daughter, as prospective bride as a member of her age group and as wife and through life's various basic experiences: puberty, courtship, marriage, childbirth and death – all this, while she is caught between the two conflicting forces of communal will and her own need for independent choices and identity.

Aku-nna's fairy tale version of her future as a woman in a traditional African society is deconstructed as the narrative develops with increasing menace, beginning with her father's illness and subsequent death. She is alarmed when she learns he is going to the hospital because in a patriarchal set-up as head of the family, he is special. Aku-nna believed that there was a kind of bond between her and her father, which did not exist between her and her mother. She loved and respected her father as he was the sole provider of the house. And also, because she felt some kind of a connect with his subdued whiny voice, reminding her of her own frailties as opposed to the loud and strong personality of her mother. She firmly believed that her father cared fror her in his own way too, much more than he showed in front of the people, because the custom did not allow for a close bond to exist between a father and a daughter, for was she not only a girl? A girl belonged to her father today as his daughter, and tomorrow, before his very eyes, would go to another man in marriage.

Girls are considered as someone else's property, and thus fathers are wary of showing too much love for them. Though she never had a chance to talk about these things with her father, now that he was gone and these two uncles stood before her, she was feeling very frightened for the well-being of her father. She wondered why her father had not told her about the foot or his health. She felt betrayed in a way, yet put on a bold face to take hold of her emotions. She did not want anyone to know how scared she was for her father.

Unknown to Ma Blackie and children of Odia family, Ezekiel, the father, is dying. It is his farewell to his children (as the mother, at this time, is visiting the country village of Ibuza) that sets the rest of the events in motion. In their culture, a woman without a husband is unable, we are told, to take care of herself or her children. The translation of Aku-nna's brother's name, Nna-nndo, reminds Aku-nna of this fact. His name means "father is the shelter." In Nigerian culture, a mother is only a woman, incapable of handling the responsibility of her family without the husband. A fatherless family is a family without a head – a non-existing family. The death of Nna forms the first harsh sign to Aku-nna that her imagined future is a naïve fantasy. She tells herself:

> *Aku-nna said to herself. It is not that we have no father any more, we have no parents any more. Did not our father rightly call you Nna-nndo, meaning "Father is*

the shelter"? So not only have we lost a father, we have lost our life, our shelter!"

Emecheta, in an author's aside in the voice of a storyteller, comments harshly on the secondary status of women in the African society:

> *It is so even today in Nigeria: when you have lost your father, you have lost your parents. Your mother is only a woman and women are supposed to be boneless. A fatherless family is a family without a head, a family without shelter, a family without parents, in fact a non-existing family. Such traditions do not change very much.*[8]

Emecheta dramatizes the influence of the collective tribal conscience at Nna's funeral, in the voices of the aunts. During the mourning period, before the funeral, Aku-nna having cried and cried, according to the family's expectations, until her throat was parched and sore, listens as her aunts Uzo and Matilda discuss her own future; Uzo advises in what sounds like an indictment on Aku-nna's total erasure as a person:

> *"Can't you see that you have no father any more? You are an orphan now and you have to learn to take care of whatever clothes you have. Nobody's going to buy you any more, until you marry. Then you husband will take care of you."*[9]

The role of the husband as the caretaker, the provider, has been emphasized over and over again in the novels of Africa, pointing out the superior, God-like existence of the 'first sex' in a marriage. The man is supreme – the giver, the provider, and women are left upon his mercy in the social structure. When Aku-nna's father meets his untimely death, the aunts are less bothered about Nna-nndo's future as he is a male but are all sympathetic towards the imminent fate of the girl. Since the girl's education was of little value in their society the women in their neighborhood were quite sure that she would be married off soon in the absence of a father, in order to pay for her brother's education from her bride price:

> "The pity of it all," put in Auntie Matilda, "is that they will marry her off very quickly in order to get enough money to pay Nna-nndo's school fees."[10]

About her prospects in the marriage market, Uzo says:

> "Oh, that should not be difficult. She is not ugly, and not a crying beauty either, but she is soft, quiet and intelligent. She will gladden the heart of an educated man, you mark my words. Most girls from Lagos are very quickly married away to rich and educated men because of their smooth bodies and their schooling", explained Uzo.[11]

The aunts are well aware of the travails of being a woman in Africa, be it Lagos, or elsewhere. Though they themselves had suffered much from the way their tradition shaped their destiny, they have accepted all of it and could not even think of any other way of life for any other girl. Perhaps they meant to console Aku-nna by sharing their own plight as a woman but they ended up making her feel all the more desolate and unconvinced about her future.

Aunt Matilda expresses her disappointement in having to lead the kind of life her generation had by default. Being a woman entailed bearing not just children, but also the beatings of the husband, working harder than their bodies allowed for the sustenance of the family and still not having and option to turn back and go the safe haven of their parental home. Talking about the hardships the rural women had to face, she says that it was not possible for the girls brought up in the village to have smooth bodies. They would have to fend for themselves there, go to the forest to pick up wood, help the mother with the hearth, and run other chores. Girls brought up in city had no idea of all this and thus could revel in their smooth bodies. Aku-nna, brought up in the city Lagos had no inkling about the difficulties of rural life. Aunt

Matilda gives a vivid glimpse of rural life when she reminisces the kind of work they had to do back in the village. She says that the children born in Lagos would never know what it is to uproot a strong cassava from parched and dry earth, unwilling to give up her produce. And after all the exertion of uprooting the plant the shock to find a large snake curled at the top of the plant watching them and their work. She calls the girls nowadays lucky for having an easy life. They had everything brought to them on plate. She exhibits the conditioning of women in this regard saying that this was the fate of women like them and they had to bear their burden, and learn to accept it. There was nothing really that they could do about it.

The novel underlines the psychological hold that myth and tradition have on the minds of African people and the consequent adherence to the old ways. Emecheta depicts the tribal rituals of Nna's funeral, its amalgamation of the tribal sense of propriety along with the Christian or western sense. Ezekiel was buried as he lived in a conflict of two cultures. Emecheta relates the burial practices and beliefs of the traditional culture, which have been infiltrated by the belief in heaven and hell as preached by the African ministers. Fearful of offending any of the gods, the Igbo people follow the ceremonial dictates of both cultures. Aku-nna is initiated into the significance of community traditions through such rituals and others that follow. The death of her father, which illustrates the rituals of mourning and burial, also preludes the custom of transferring the widow Ma Blackie and the family to the surviving brother of the deceased, who then can exercise his rights of inheritance – a practice which confirms a woman's status as a mere possession instead of a person and makes her feel totally helpless in a world where she has no control over the worlds where she has no control over the rules that shape her life and destiny.

Ma Blackie, Ezekiel's widow and Aku-nna's mother, discovers her husband dead on her return to Lagos. She had left Lagos to visit her homeland, Ibuza, in hopes of regaining fertility and to give Ezekiel third child. But now that she is left a widow. She is well aware that without an earning man in the family, she cannot afford to remain in Lagos and bring up her children there in the absence of their father. Thus, she prepares her children for their return to Ibuza.

The condition of a woman as being socially seen incapable of raising her kids up without a father is highly ironical considering the fact that in the African society women were working as hard as men to make the ends meet. For example, the women who the children saw, trotting towards the market place, on their way to Ibuza:

> *They were carrying a heavy pile of damp cassava pulp, all tied with banana skins onto baskets; many of the baskets were not very big, but with the heaps of dripping cassava pulp piled high on them they ended up looking like skyscrapers. Akpu, as the cassava pulp was called locally, was a very heavy foodstuff made from the roots of the cassava plant-so heavy was it that the necks of the poor women carriers (who were sweating profusely although the heat of the early sun was still moderate) were compressed to half their normal sizes.*[12]

In spite of carrying equal, if not more, responsibilities of handling the household, women had inferior status in the society and were considered insufficient to rear their children on their own. While in reality, men hardly concerned themselves with the problem of fetching for their children because they were more of a symbolic kind of the household where others strove to take care of him. The men did earn, no doubt, but that was it. They rarely bothered about any other problem after giving whatever fixed amount they had to give to their wives, with other matters. Okonkwo was no different. In Ibuza, an agrarian village of the Igbo people, a man's status was measured by the number of wives he could keep. Okunkwo already had three wives, but he, by virtue of his brother's death, inherits and eventually marries Ma Blackie, thus making her his fourth wife. He does this while looking forward to the bride price that Aku-nna would bring him. Since he was going to be the father now, he could lay claim to her bride price that would come along at the time of her marriage. Okonkwo, being as ambitious man, covets the title of Obi, which he can acquire if he has sufficient money. Such titles could be bought in the land. These titles elevated the social standing of a man and people used to look up to them, especially in the matters of community. Their advice was sought, and respects were paid on special occasion. Once again, the disparity between a man and woman belonging to the Igbo society is quite evident from this, that while a man's status was measured by his title, a woman's standing came from her virtue of being the 'wife'. Thus, there was a constant struggle and competition amonth the wives to become the favorite of their husband such that they could enjoy more privileges. E. Krige writes that 'wives were subordinate members of their marital household.'[13]

Women were seen as fit only for production and reproduction. They worked in the fields and reared the children. Yet they were considered inferior to the men in social standing. The men 'owned' them as they owned fields and cattle. The women, however, seem to be seldom complaining of this arrangement. After all they were never forced, but had their own choice in the matter, however little the scope of an alternative be. For example, Okonkwo's daughter from his first wife, tells Aku-nna that she would be like a sister to her if her mother chose to be with her father :

> "…Now we are going to be friends. We shall be like sisters, especially if your mother chooses to be with my father."
> "Why would any mother choose your father? How come?"
> Aku-nna asked, puzzled. The two girls had lagged behind, engrossed in their gossip. Oguagua burst out laughing.
> "You're almost fourteen years old now and you still don't know the customs of out Ibuza people? Your mother is inherited by my father, you see, just as he will inherit everything your father worked for…"[14]

The position of a woman in marriage, that of a property, was not something you questioned. It was as easily and naturally accepted by all as the rising of the sun in the east and the setting in the west. You just did not question it. It existed. That's all. Chimamanda Ngozi Adichie in her essay *We Should All Be Feminists* writes :

> "*We are all social being. We internalize ideas from out socialization.*
> *Even the language we use illustrates this. The language of marriage is often a language of ownership, not a language of partnership...*
> *We teach females that in relationships, compromises is what a woman is more likely to do.*"[15]

When Aku-nna cries in consternation exclaiming, as if in a physical pain-how can her mother fit into that type of life? – we are able to hear the futility of her question, for adjust, Ma Blackie would have to, no matter what her will. The woman in that society had no say in the shaping of their own lives. The rules of the tribe dictated their life and destiny. So deep was the fear of these rules that we see Aku-nna and Chike trying to hide something as natural as menstruation just so that she not be married off before the completion of her education. This is one significant ritual that initiates Aku-nna into the tribal mindset and marks her fate as a woman – her coming of age and the attendant fertility ceremonies. For her as an Igbo girl, the first menstrual cycle means she must submit to certain outrageous courtship customs, entertaining prospective grooms with kola nuts and palm-wine and allowing them to fondle her, to squeeze her breasts and then finally to get married to the suitors of her uncle's choice for his mercenary advantage.

Aku-nna and Chike's relationship comes like a fresh breath of life in an otherwise sordid traditional setup. Their love, young and pure, provides the much-required confidence and a feeling of self-worth to Aku-nna. For in the death of Ezekiel Odia, she had not only lost a father, but she had also lost a mother.

> *Ma Blackie found herself so immersed in the Okonkwo*
> *family politics, and in making ends meet, that she seldom*
> *had time to ask how the world was with her daughter.*[16]

Aku-nna was told over and over again how fortunate she was to be allowed schooling even after the death of her father. The parents were both lost to her, and so was her brother as he was busy in his own wild ways of boyhood. In such times she began to retract more and more into herself. She barely spoke her mind to anyone or behaved in a fashion suitable to her age. The loneliness she felt within in this new environment in the place of her origin, made her spirits low. In such times, it was Chile's kind attention that helped her gain confidence.

> *...girl... who was without a father and still able to*
> *continue her schooling. There were few girls who were so*
> *fortunate. This knowledge drove Aku-nna more and more*
> *into herself until, indeed rather than in words, Chike*
> *Ofulue told her that she was valued, treasured and loved.*[17]

Aku-nna, who would soon be fifteen, was intelligent and a promising beauty, and hence, many eyes were set on her in Ibuza. On top of her personal appearance, her mild and docile ways, her education, which was quite rare among girls of her community, made her very much desired. And thus, it was no wonder that all were waiting for her coming of age. According to the Igbo custom, a girl could receive suitors once she started menstruation as it meant that she was no more a girl, but a woman ready for marriage. The beginning of the menstrual cycle indicated that the girl would have to submit to the courtship customs of the land. These customs, by all means outrageous, brought down the girl to the status of a doll, which the boys could play with in mirth. The prospective grooms would keep offering their love through kola-nuts and palm wine and would also treat her body like a plaything. And thus, Chike and Aku-nna decide to hide the fact that the girl had started her periods, at least till she had passed her exam as they feared that her education would be stopped mid-way if her family came to know of her puberty and married her off to the highest bidder immediately. In fact, it was during this decision making that Chike first realized his unbending love for Aku-nna, and she saw her undying devotion to him.

> *He came closer to her, not caring whether they were seen or not.*
> *He wanted to marry this girl, even if it meant breaking all the laws of Ibuza. As he held her to his clammy chest, her body shook, from fear and from something else inside her which she could not name.*[18]

Would Romeo have been as adamant to have Juliet if the Capulets and the Montagues had not opposed their union? Would they not have considered their love just a passing phase had it not been flamed by the fuel of rebellion? Well, this is a debate that's been going on for years and years about the human psyche. How we tend to be more inclined towards the forbidden fruit. Such was the case with Chike and Aku-nna. Had they been left alone; their fling might have been just that – a fling. But the resistance made their will stronger. Even when Chike had himself not realized that he loved her, his father began to sermonize him against spoiling the girl. And Aku-nna grew more defiant in her mind with every hint at Chike's status in the society as Osu, the descendant of a slave.

Chike was a handsome young man and though women knew that he came from an "Osu" family, a slave family, they pretended not to see it. They could not be any less bothered by his origin because though the descendant of a slave, this date, his family owned the highest posts and biggest cars in the city. He had slept with most of the local girls in his late teens and in fact, now, looked down upon most of them. Though he still had a few mistresses among the younger wives of many old chiefs, his conscience did not bother him on that front, for these wives were still very young yet tied to ageing husbands, just because they had paid a hefty amount to their fathers as the bride price. These old men were just concerned with having a number of spouses and prided themselves on providing enough yam to fill their bellies. If they had any idea that their young girl wives needed more than just food to satisfy them, they were not talking. Instead, they turned a blind eye to their affairs outside marriage to young boys of their own age. In Ibuza, every young man was entitled to his fun. And if a girl was ever caught, all the blame went to her. Nobody cared to question the boy involved.

The blame was always placed on the girls in case their affair was found out. A girl who had had affairs before marriage or indulged in pre-marital adventures and sex was never respected by the people in her new home. She was shunned by the society too. Every person in the village would know about her past, especially if she was unfortunate enough to be married to an egocentric man. Loss of virginity of the wife would be absolutely unacceptable to him if it was not to him, no matter how many girls he might have had physical relations with. There were men who would go about raping girls, even young virgins of thirteen and fourteen; but these very men would still expect the women they married to be as chaste as flower buds.

And the men, for their part, would rather let their wives' affairs stay under the wraps rather than admit to the fact that their young wives were not satisfied by their husbands and thus had to take lovers from outside. Such was the society in which Chike and Aku-nna lived. And hence, when their growing friendship and fondness for each other reached their people, they were apprehensive about it. Chike's father well aware of his indulgencies, had never tried to curb him, but this time it was different. Aku-nna was different.

Chike's father called him specially to talk about the rumours he had heard about his affair with Aku-nna. He cautioned him that he had been to school with Ezekiel Odia, who was his junior in school. He would not like that a son of his should bring shame on Ezekiel Odia's only daughter. The senior Ofulue, with his years of experience had immediately understood Chike's desire for Aku-nna seeing the way he was looking at her in the church. In fact, he said, everybody had noticed this. Love cannot be hidden and thus he knew that Chike held a soft heart for her. But also aware of his son's ways, he begged him not to spoil the girl.

Chike was quite taken aback as he had thought he had succeeded in keeping his feelings under lock and key. He had hoped that the people would not notice his desire for her and that he had regarded Aku-nna as just another pupil. He had been so cautious to keep his feelings under the wraps that he had not even spoken to the girl outside his lessons. His father's words made him anxious but he had to say something to his father, if only to put his mind at rest. He thought hard and then confessed that he did care for her. His voice choked with emotion when he told his father that she seemed so alone and yet so beautiful, almost like an angel. But he loved her so much that she was like an angel to him, way above normal human girls, so how could he spoil an angel? He assured his father that his feelings for Aku-nna were absolutely genuine and true and that he would never, even in his dreams, do anything that could harm her.

The young man was so distressed at his father's suggestions that he might do something to spoil the girl that he had no idea how he even survived the night. For his father who had all along maintained that he would not sponsor his children's higher education, that they'd have to work hard and get their own scholarships, was even ready to pay for his university course just to send him away from Ibuza. His father just wanted him out of town because he thought he was getting involved with Aku-nna.

Ngbeke, Okunkwo's first wife, was also of the same opinion. She too believed that there was something up between Chike and Aku-nna. When she hears her sons discussing with glee the prospects of Aku-nna marrying a rich man and raising the entire Odia family from poverty to wealth, she reprimands them and asks them not to build castles in the air as for all they knew, Aku-nna could end up marrying the 'son of a slave who teaches her at school.' When her children express their distress at this suggestion, she is quick to point out that:

> "There is no smoke without fire, my children. I hope it is only rumour. But even if it is, it is best to nip it in the bud."[19]

As Ngbeke had said, there was never smoke without fire, and she wasn't wrong in any way. The young teacher was definitely attracted by his meek pupil who was so different from other feisty village girls:

> *Chike was falling in love with his fifteen-year-old pupil without knowing it; even had it occurred to him what was happening he was powerless to stop the process. He had never seen a girl so dependent, so unsure of herself, so afraid of her own people.*[20]

The damsel in distress looks at Chike as the quintessential Prince Charming, who does not disappoint. Through his caring, and soft words, he is soon able to etch a special place for himself in her heart. He becomes her go-to person when she had no one else left, for her mother was busy in her pwn household politics of the wives and her brother in his own wild ways. Chike Ofulue's kindness told her that she was 'valued, treasured and loved.'

Very soon Chike and Aku-nna became friends and confidantes, and in the eyes of rumour-mongers, lovers. They might as well have left each other alone, but for the interference of their families. As they say:

> *It is said that stolen water is sweet. Maybe Chike would have outgrown Aku-nna and maybe she would have come to regard anything there might be between them as mere childish infatuation, if the adults had just left them alone.*[21]

Aku-nna and Chike were drawn to each other because of this reverse psychology that came into play through their families' opposition to their speculated match. For Aku-nna, it was a series of 'don'ts'. Like she must not get herself mixed with that teacher, 'don't do this, don't do that.' It was all dont's; such that for her, such caution became a matter of everyday trivia, she stopped caring about. Likewise, Chike also got irritated with his father's uncalled for sermons regarding the girl, and began to see her in a different light. Just like the temptation of the forbidden fruit, the prospect of their love and union began to form a very appealing future prospect for the two.

While Chike felt most disturbed after his father's warnings and had perhaps begun to have an idea of his feelings towards Aku-nna, he was as sure as he could be when he held her in his arms when he found that she had started her periods for the first time. She, on her part, had always felt safe and comfortable with him around; when Chike speaks of helping her pass the exams even if that was the last thing he'd do before leaving Ibuza, she is most disturbed:

> *He noticed that her tears had stopped; he felt she needed reassurance, so he said aloud: "I shall help you pass that examination. If it is the last thing I do before I leave this horrible town."*
>
> *"Leave it? Where are you going?" The disappointment and expectancy in her voice was such that it was transparent to him that she cared.*[22]

Aku-nna was chilled to the core even at the thought of his going away. From the very first glimpse she had caught of him on his new bicycle, while entering this alien native land of hers, she had not once stopped thinking of him. She constantly dreamt of him with open eyes. His voice was enough to send her into a happy frenzy. His look, his voice, his touch, all assured her that all would be well. He was like water in this parched land. His sympathy was the only joy she had in this sea of apathy. She loved him, of course, but could she tell this to him straight-out without appearing cheap and badly brought up? Somewhere deep down, conscious of her family's weak financial status, she also felt that the world might judge her negatively if she expressed herself; people might say that she was just attracted by the high houses and cars his family had. But she had no idea how she could convince then that Chike was the only person who brought some warmth in her otherwise lonely life. It is paradoxical, that these same people, who would not shy from acknowledging Chike's financial superiority, would also disapprove of the match citing his 'Osu lineage'. But again, the mere thought of his leaving the town, his leaving her, was heartbreaking:

> *But if he left, left her alone in this town, she would be heartbroken.*
> *She would be lost, like the ants without their tracks.*[23]

We witness Aku-nna's dilemma, where on one hand she is incapacitated by her love for Chike, she could not help but love him, and on the other hand, her fear of the culture and tradition of the society was holding her back from expressing her feelings. We see the quintessential question popping up in her mind as she wonders what people would say. Would anybody stand by her? The kind of marriages she had witnessed till date made her even more unsure:

> *If she disobeyed her mother and uncle, and if in future Chike became nasty and started to beat her-as most Ibuza men seemed to beat their women-then nobody would put in a kind word for her.*[24]

Such thoughts trouble the young girl, and with no clear path in front of her, and no friend to share her pain, she feels lonely. In her loneliness, Chike brings the hope for a better future when he professes his love for her and promises her a life of happiness with him. He tells her that he would make sure that from this day on she should cry only out of happiness and not sadness. He promises her a lifetime of joy with him and also assures her that her happiness mattered the most for him and he would do everything in his power to ensure that she stayed happy.

These words were no less than an affirmation of his feelings for her, Chike's love for Aku-nna. Looking at her, this sad lonely girl. Chike was filled with a sense of protectiveness he had never felt for anyone before. When she starts her first menstruation all of a sudden, between this conversation, he is filled with a sudden urge to be by her, come what may:

> *He came closer to her, not caring whether they were seen or not.*
>
> *He wanted to marry this girl even if it meant breaking all the laws of Ibuza.*[25]

As they stood, Chike holding Aku-nna in a tight hug, they both realized their love for each other. They never wanted to let go of each other:

> *It seemed that they stood there for a long time. He did not want her to go, and she herself did not want to go.*[26]

With the realization of their love for each other, another realization that dawns upon the couple is that in their society, a menstruating girl was considered of marriageable age, and she might now be not even allowed to continue her schooling, and instead, might be married off to the highest bidder of her bride price to satisfy her uncle's greed. Her first menstrual cycle meant that she must now submit to those outrageous Igbo courtship customs, she'd have to entertain prospective grooms with kola-nuts and palm-wine, allowing them to fondle her, to squeeze her breasts and then finally to get married to the suitor of her uncle's choice for his mercenary advantage. They feared that their love might be nipped right here, in the bud, and Aku-nna's life would be traded off for her bride price. Thus, they decide to hide the news of her menstruation from the world. We see a lover's concern in Chike's decision and the way he managed to convince Aku-nna to do what's best for her disregarding the cultural norms. The understanding and care he exhibits for her, expresses his love for her better that any words could ever have. She was filled with a joy she had never known before on hearing him speak of her as his own:

> *"Akum …can you keep quiet about this? Don't tell anyone yet, not till after the exam."*
>
> *Her confusion was giving way to a kind of mild joy, especially as she noticed that Chike had called her Akum,*

meaning "my wealth." She did not mind belonging to him and being his wealth; she would like to be owned by a man like Chike.[27]

Aku-nna, helped by her teacher-lover Chike, successfully hides her first two periods by using the sanitary napkins that he brings for her. But on an outing for firewood with twelve of her age-mates, the third menstrual cycle comes and, with the traditional customs and myth deeply rooted in her psyche, she is forced to confess the onset of periods to her friends rather than hiding it and crossing the river and becoming a leper for the rest of her life. The Igbo community believed that a girl on her periods was unclean and not supposed to cross the river or a stream as that would bring on the wrath of the river goddess. Meanwhile the secret that she and Chike had shared up till now had brought them even closer. They used to spend whatever time they could find, together, talking about everything that she had never shared with anyone else. On the very evening that Aku-nna had first menstrual signaling her coming of age according to their custom, Chike had come to her room with medicines, pads, etc., and even a book to explain it all to her.

The Igbo custom allowed boys to come to the girls' huts for night games. They would play with girls' breasts, squeeze them till they hurt, and the girl was supposed to try as much as possible to 'ward them off and not to be bad tempered about it':

So long as it was done inside the hut where an adult was near, and so long as the girl did not let the boy go too far, it was not frowned on.[28]

Such games were an accepted form of play in the Igbo society. these young suitors expressed their love to their chosen girls in the rough manner some girls did eventually marry their early sweethearts, but in most cases, the boys were too young to afford the bride price or just not yet ready for the marriage, hence these flings ended just with time. Most of the times these boys just stood by and watched their first loves married off to men old enough to be their fathers, just because these men were wealthy and paid a good price for the girls. But Chike was different, and when he begins his play with Aku-nna they both know that it's not going to end in another light-hearted fling:

> *He sat beside her on the couch and put his arms close round her... he touched her breasts, the way a suitor might, not the way the rough boys squeezed them just for fun... he held her like that and asked her what she thought they should do.*
> *'Tell my people that you want to marry me,' she said, her voice faint and whispery.*[29]

Aku-nna's simple but sincere reply fills Chike with excitement and a sense of foreboding. Being well aware of the world they belong to, he states that their people would never allow their union. While he can barely control his love for her, he also realizes its futility and asks if she had not heard that his ancestors were slaves and had never been born on this land? Did she think of their relationship as a joke? Aku-nna, on her part, had no idea where her new-found determination stemmed from. All her life she had stayed the meek and docile one, but now, her love for this man gave her a new spirit and strength she had never known before. Her certainty puts all doubts to rest:

> *She covered his mouth with her hand, not knowing where the boldness which was working inside her came from. "there is no other person for me in this world, Chike. I don't even know anyone else-I always say the wrong thing, do the wrong thing.*
> *You are the only person I know who I am not afraid of.*[30]

When Aku-nna professed her love, Chike was so overwhelmed that he did not know what else he could say or do and started "kissing her the way Europeans did in films". Aku-nna, on her part, did not really enjoy this experience, but we see, once again, the age-old gender roles come into play when she does not express her displeasure, but instead submits to Chike's advances, because she had "read in old copies of True Romances that kissing was meant to do something to a girl". Theirs is a typical love story where the damsel-in-distress, that is, Aku-nna falls for the prince charming, that is, Chike, who is supposed to save her from her sad and lonely life and take her to some joyful land of the dreams. Like all typical heroines of love stories, she wants to be the all-giving angel, who would never care for the ways of the world and shy away from making her hero feel special:

> *Aku-nna knew one was supposed to like being kissed but she did not know how to enjoy it. She had read in old copies of "True Romances" that kissing was meant to do something to a girl. Well, it had done nothing for her, but she let him have his play. All she wanted was to make him happy, to make him realize that his being an outcast did not matter to her.* [31]

Her love for Chike is evident in her happy acceptance of his love, and even though there played a doubt in her young mind regarding the way he was expressing his love, she makes sure that she does not react in a way he might find hurtful. She was bothered by his kisses as she had read somewhere that kissing caused tuberculosis, but she did not have the heart to stop him and ask about it. She saw no point in it as she had already been kissed enough by him to leave her breathless, also she was so full of love for him that she did not care. His passion for her, filled her with ecstasy and the young lovers reveled in each other's arms:

> *"You will always be mine ", he said into her ear.*[32]

Chike's voice, thick with emotion, left no doubt in Aku-nna's mind, that with him, her future lay. Not all the warnings of the family or society could separate them now.

Chike and Aku-nna used to meet every market day at Asaba, where she used to go to sell her plantains. Chike used to dump her stack in the river and give her the money for it, so that they could utilize the time she would have to sit in the market, to spend together. The two of them had discovered a secluded quiet place by the river bank, where they sat, doing nothing, just talking their hearts out, or listening to each other's silences. As virginity of girls was highly prized in their culture, and for Chike, she was not just a love interest but something apart, something pure that he did not want to pollute, he used to stop himself from going too far after a few gentle caresses. Aku-nna understood his love for her thus, was beginning to respond to his unspoken wishes. Theirs was a love both Chike and Aku-nna prized. They took out time to spend with each other away from the glare of the villagers. Though Chike desired her yet he was careful to not go too far. He understood her mind and refrained from doing anything that could shock or spoil her. At the same time Aku-nna too had begun to realize that though Chike might talk endlessly in the classroom, as that was his job being a teacher, but when he was by himself with her, he preferred silence. Sometimes they listened to the music of the river and the noises coming from the nearby bushes but mostly they reveled in their togetherness in silence, simply listening to their hearts. Emecheta's description of these dates is no less than the quintessential romance stories of the western world and she presents the sublimity in the love of the young couple beautifully.

Chike had made up his mind that he would not leave for any university without Aku-nna, and had declared as much to his father, who kept on warning him against getting into a relationship with Aku-nna. Ofulue, Chike's father, tried his best to make his son understand their social status. That in spite of all the money they had, they'd always remain 'Osu', or slave descendants in the eyes of Ibuza people, and they would never ever forget or forgive if an Osu took away their daughter. But all such warning fell on deaf ears:

> *That Chike was a man who for the first time in his life had fallen uncontrollably in love was plain to see.*[33]

Seeing that Chike's love could not be shaken, Ofulue agrees to accept it and asks his son about his plan. Chike tells his father that he was head over heels in love with Aku-nna and was sure that she loved him equally. And he was well aware of the difficulties and non-acceptance they'd have to face in this town, and hence, had already planned to move to another town, Ughelli. He had chosen the town of Ughelli, only about a hundred miles away because he had a lot of friends living there already, and without the support of family, which was expected if they eloped, he believed it would be a good call to find a place near his friends at least. Many of his college friends from Urhobo owned small mud houses with zinc roofs there and he could see himself with Aku-nna living there, owning perhaps their first home together in Ughelli. He knew the world they lived in, and there was no way that Aku-nna's family would accept him, an osu, as her husband. They would have to elope, and there was no other way. He was so much in love with Aku-nna that he could not be happy with any other woman an he was certain that there was no man but himself in Aku-nna's heart and mind.

Chike is well aware of his father's worth in the society and that in spite of being an Osu, he had earned respect for himself, but apologizes for being such a son who might bring shame to his father. His actions might give the people a chance to point finger at them. Yet, he had no control over his feelings:

> *He apologized for being such an impossible son, but what was he to do?*
> *"I dream about the girl – I see her in everything, in the stream, I see her smile when I am riding alone, I hear her small voice when birds sing."*[34]

Chike's romantic words for Aku-nna convinces his father that there's nothing he can do, except help the love birds. And so, he asks Chike to keep hope and inform him as soon as Aku-nna starts menstruation as that would mean she's ready for marriage. He urges his son to keep on his guard regarding the girl so that she has no stain on her character. Also, that if they were the first to ask her hand for marriage, they might as well be granted their wish. He, however, is strict in pointing out that in their society, a girl had to stay a virgin till marriage to command respect from the people and thus Chike should always take care around her:

> *"There is one thing I beg of you. Whatever you do, don't spoil that girl-don't disvirgin her before you are sure she will be your wife.*
> *There is no worse fate for any woman in this town than that of one who arrives at her husband's couch polluted."*
> *"Noone is having her but me", Chike insisted.*
> *"And you are not stealing her either. We may be descended from an Osu woman, but I like to do things in the proper manner. Tell me when she becomes a woman, then we shall go and speak to her people."*[35]

There was no need for his father's cautioning, as Chike knew already how dangerous the territory of his love was. He had told Aku-nna of his discussion with his father, and that he approved of her. She was happy with the prospect of his parents coming formally to ask for her in the proper way, thought she wasn't unaware of the difficulties that lay in between. But now that her third menstruation cycle had started all of a sudden, when she was out collecting wood with her girlfriends, she was not sure what she should do. If she hid her periods, she would have to cross the stream to get back to her house along with the girls. If they saw what she was hiding, she might be ostracized forever. If she told them, they'd all know that she was no longer a child who knew nothing; but a young woman on the verge of parenthood. The news of her puberty would travel as fast as the winds, and everything might go out of control. On second thoughts, even if she attempted to hide this circumstance from the girls, and was successful in it, how would she hide it from the river god who would certainly know the truth? Would the god, or whoever owned the river forgive her for crossing it even when she knew she was unclean? Or would she be condemned as an outcast leper for the rest of her life? We witness her dependency on Chike, her love in this moment as well:

> *Her thoughts were in a turmoil of indecision about what to do next. Her closeness with Chike had crystallized and was now so established that she could not make a decision without wanting to know his opinion.*[36]

But the fact remained that Chike was not present on that farm and Aku-nna had to decide for herself. As she does not want to break the community code, she lets her friends discover her state, who are all overjoyed at this new development. For them, their friend had come of age, and was now a woman, just like them.

News of Aku-nna's puberty travels fast in Ibuza, which is also described as a town where people did not need newspapers and radio as local media. People talked. As fast as the news of Aku-nna moved in the town, the tongues also started talking about Chike, who had been seen looking at the girl with desirous eyes:

> *He stood there watching her unmoved, hearing no other sound, though his nerves bayed like hounds at the moon... He saw her only as she was in that moment... She looked at him appealing, then quickly began to stare at the ground, aware that they were now being shamelessly watched as they were surrounded by human silence.*[37]

As Chike looked at Aku-nna, he was so overcome with love that nothing else mattered to him. A young lover's romantic fantasy is illustrated through his day dream. He has no care in the world or of the society as his senses are totally bewitched by his love for the girl. Chike showed no sign of any awareness that he was being watched by the people around him. His consciousness was enveloped by his gaze on Aku-nna. He showed no signs of being conscious of the scrutiny. He had eyes only for his love and he realized that the girl he saw now was very different from the girl he had first seen entering Ibuza. Aku-nna had grown up into a beautiful young woman and it was only the laws of the land that stopped him from picking her up right then and there and taking her away into a world of his own away from the cares of society. He wanted to run up the hills of Atakpo with her where nobody could see them for many, many years; a place where they would be all by themselves like the savages of old times, he hunting for food and she waiting at their home to receive his love and give him hers. There would be no social botheration nor the worry of culture, tradition and family.

Chike's dream is no different from the classic dream of the lovers, exhibited time and again through romances in the literature and the movies. But the Igbo society was not yet ready to let his dream materialize. He himself realized that they were all fantasies of his anxious mind. For he was well aware of the harsh reality of their situation. But this one moment was enough to fuel the rumour-mongers. The details of the amorous happenings on the spread, like wildfire, and reached the families even before the girls.

> *The news of the happenings on the farm had preceded the girl's home as had speculation that Chike Ofulue, the son of a slave, had looked at the daughter of a free-born Ibuza citizen with desirous eyes.*[38]

Once again, we bear witness to the importance attached to the bride price in the way Okonkwo welcomes Aku-nna home. For hadn't he waited all these years for this very day?

> *He stood there in the fading light eyeing her as one would a precious statue, inwardly congratulating himself on his luck in having had the opportunity to marry her mother. Now the entire bride price would come to him.*[39]

The fact that Ma Blackie was carrying his child made him even surer that he'd get whatever he asked, for the woman had been craving a child for years. Now that she was pregnant with his child, she shouldn't possibly refuse him anything, not even her daughter's bride price. At the same time, he was also concerned about the news about Chike that he had heard, and Okonkwo, as one belonging to one of the reputed, old families of Ibuza, did not wish to have his family name slurred by some erratic act of youth. Hence, he warns Aku-nna to understand her place, to know her limits. In the authoritative voice of Okonkwo, we hear the age-old opposition to love that dares to cross social norms :

> *"Aku-nna, Chike Ofulue is only a friend. You must remember that.*
> *Now that you have grown, that friendship must gradually die. But die it must."*[40]

Okonkwo, through this strict warning was making sure that Aku-nna understood his authority and that she should never dare to cross him :

> *He was telling her, not in so many words, that she could never escape. She was trapped in the intricate web of Ibuza tradition.*
> *She must either obey or bring shame and destruction on her people.*[41]

While Aku-nna's heart wrenched at the thought of bringing any kind of negativity on her family, the thought of staying away from Chike was absolutely unbearable. In order to justify her feelings for Chike, she began to reason that Okonkwo must also have loved once, and thus, would see her point. She thought that the joy her 'father' had exhibited on her becoming a woman, must have stemmed from his understanding of its emotional implications. She feels that the way Okonkwo had come to meet her with a fowl for a gift, just proved that he was a human with a heart, not just an authoritative heartless voice :

> *…and it seemed to prove to her that these men, these elders did have feelings for some of the women they married. Okonkwo must know how she was going to feel. His life could not have been entirely loveless; he must have cared for some woman once, and been loved and cared for in return, otherwise he would surely not have come himself to congratulate Aku-nna on becoming a woman.*[42]

Okonkwo might have this soft streak somewhere within, but he was definitely not showing it to Aku-nna. For him, his name, untainted reputation and the expected bride price, were all too important to give up for a girl's silly love affair.

According to Igbo customs, Aku-nna is eligible for a legal customary marriage when she begins to menstruate because puberty must be reached before marriage. But Chike's overture is so different from the traditions, but humiliating way in which a man can quickly 'own' a wife in Igbo society, that it drives Aku-nna even closer to her love. While the rest of the boys were least concerned about hurting her or not, on her emotions in their rough play, Chike's sensitivity and restraint further won her heart. Chike unlike the usual men around him, did not treat Aku-nna as a mere possession, but he saw her as an equal human being. This was a welcome change from the general norm in the society where the female was barely given the treatment of a human. Her consent, her opinion, her choice mattered the least. Those that could buy her out, used to offer a good bride price, and those that couldn't simply captured and cut her hair or raped her. Emecheta describes the callous ritual in these words :

> *In Ibuza a young girl must be prepared for anything to happen. Some youth who had no money to pay for the bride might sneak out of the bush to cut a curl from a girl's head so that she would belong to him for life and never be able to return to her parents:because he has given her the everlasting haircut, he would be able to treat her as he liked, and no other man would ever touch her.*[43]

By now Aku-nna was well aware of the society's expectations from her, and though she was ready to give in to some extent, her heart, ready to entertain young men, now that she was officially a 'woman', whether she liked it or not, she would try her best to save herself for her true love. With this determination, she welcomes the young suitors into her mother's hut, but wearing a blouse as she did not want anyone other than Chike to see her.

> *She debated within herself whether to wear a blouse or not, and finally decided to put on one… she would keep her body hidden so that he alone could look at her.*[44]

Aku-nna's pain and fear at the thought of losing Chike wells up in her eyes over and over again in the form of tears. Most of the boys, who came to court her, either did not notice, or simply ignored, as they weren't completely unaware of the reason, but unwilling to admit that a 'slave' could be their rival. Aku-nna is so full of dread because of these happenings that she'd prefer death to living without Chike:

> *Her heart ached and tears began to well up in her eyes again, This time because it looks as if she was going to be trapped into a marriage that she was helpless to prevent. God, please kill me instead, she prayed, rather than let this be happening to me. Her mind ached for Chike, and so did her body.*[45]

Aku-nna and Chike's love story, already in a turmoil due to the social bindations, finds another nemesis in Okoboshi. Okoboshi, the son of an Ibuza chief, had his eyes set on Aku-nna. While he wanted to own her, make him his wife, he was angered with her visible preference for Chike. On the very first night of Aku-nna's declared womanhood, when all the boys had gathered to court her, Chike had beaten him, flat to the ground for what he saw as misbehaving with Aku-nna. The blow was too much to digest for Okoboshi, the only son of his mother, who 'had been brought up to think the whole world belonged to him by right.' And thus, full of hate and rage, at Aku-nna's apparent rejection, Okoboshi kidnaps her. Aku-nna, helpless at the hands of her kidnappers, wonders if she'd ever get to see her love again.

> *What was a girl to do in a predicament of this sort?... So, this was supposed to be the end of her dreams... After everything, she was nothing but a common native girl kidnapped into being a bride.*[46]

Chike, who had wanted nothing more than to take Aku-nna away from the disrespectful and insulting environment she lived in, especially after her love for Chike was made public, felt like he'd die on realizing the ultimate dishonor his girl would be now subjected to. He felt sick to the core and did not even mind weeping into his father's chest.

On the other hand, Aku-nna's family, on the realization of her forced capture, were full of rage, and swearing to have their revenge. All of Okonkwo's sons swore that they would kidnap and cut locks of hair from the heads of all girls belonging to the family responsible for this deed. Ma Blackie went in a state of shock, while Nna-nndo, after crying for a while, ran to the only friend he could trust on not to harm his sister, i.e., Chike. And Chike had vowed that he would get her back at any cost. Though Ma Blackie and Nna-nndo wondered how Chike would do it, they knew that he would. Even while the family was mourning the stealing of their daughter, they knew that she must, by now, be lost forever to them :

> *Even as they were doing all these, they knew it was useless.*
>
> *Aku-nna had gone. All the man responsible had to do was cut a curl of her hair-"isinno"- and she would belong to him for life. Or he could force her into sleeping with him and if she refused his people would assist him by holding her down until she was disvirgined. And when that had been done, no other person would want to take her anymore.*[47]

The Igbo customs of marriage are highlighted through the portrayal of Aku-nna's marriage talks. The girl who was earlier supposed to be given away in traditional marriage where the groom and his family would ask for her hand and Okonkwo would have given his blessings to the family of her choice, getting a hefty bride price in return, was all overturned by this unexpected development of his daughter's capture. Okoboshi Obidi's family sent three male members in the middle of the night to disclose to Okonkwo that his step-daughter Aku-nna was lying peaceably on the mud couch specially prepared for her and her husband, Okoboshi. There was nothing really that Okonkwo could do now. He had no choice but to accept the gin and kola-nut that they had brought and agree to the minimum bride price they settled upon.

It is highly ironical that the same people who saw nothing wrong in forcing a girl into marriage, lay such high value on the virginity of the girl. For them, the act of a male captor was justified, but the girl having lost her virginity before marriage was a shame. Okonkwo, himself a part of this cultural mindset, assured the Obidis that his daughter was as intact as a closed flower. Nobody had touched her. For there was no bigger shame for a family, be it the girls or the groom's, to have his bride brought disvirgined to his marital bed.

Aku-nna, too shocked to completely process the proceedings around her in her new 'home', was filled with anger and self-pity while all around her, the Obidis continued performing various marriage rituals for the new bride. The women, all took in the 'half-conscious and half clothed' girl and admired her smooth skin. The senior Obidi poured chalk, the symbol of fertility, on her breasts and prayed to his ancestors that Aku-nna may use them to feed many children she would give birth to, for Okoboshi. Okoboshi's family – his mother and sisters – tried their best to make Aku-nna comfortable and also accepting of the plight she was thrown in now. Her 'new' family, on the other hand were least bothered about her thoughts or even her physical state and they went on welcoming her and praying that she would give them many sons and daughters. Their apathy for her condition reflects the general attitude toward girls in their society, where even if a girl was captured and married by force, she was expected to concede and happily bear children for her captor as that was what girls, in their eyes, were born to do.

Aku-nna was taken into a room where the mud couch had been colorfully painted, and on the other side she saw a wooden bed, spread with a white sheet, edged with red checked patterns. On the center of the bed was placed a white towel, which stood for another important ritual among the Igbos. This towel was supposed to be a virginity test to check if the hymen broke on the marriage bed or the girl had already lost her purity :

That was to be one of the presents her mother would receive in the morning, stained with the blood she was going to shed on being disvirgined.[48]

Aku-nna was well aware of the Igbo value associated with virginity. No man would ever dream of marrying a disvirgined girl as his first wife especially. Such a girl was not accepted with respect by anyone she knew. She realized that any attempt to run out of this room would be a failure. If the need be, others would come inside and hold her down to help Okoboshi take her, citing his limp as an excuse to not hurt his pride; but there would not be an escape – she knew. So, she, in a dramatic move, subverts Okoboshi's raw male aggression by a clever female strategy. His attempts at kidnapping and forcing her into wifehood are thwarted when she frustrates his attack to disvirgin her and to consummate his lust. The terrified male is caught in his own male-created taboos when he tried to force her onto bed and begins to untie his lappa; Aku-nna, in her last-ditch attempt to save herself, declares that she was no virgin, and in fact, had given herself to the very son of a slave, Chike, who Okoboshi looked down upon:

> *Then she laughed, like a mad woman…*
> *"Look at you," she sneered, laughing mockingly all the time.*
> *"Look at you, and shame on you, Okoboshi, the son of Obidi!*
> *You say your father is a chief-dog chief, that is what he is, if the best he can manage to steal for his son is a girl who has been taught, what men taste like by a slave."*[49]

Shocked and frustrated, Okoboshi leaves her and Aku-nna is saved from the impending indignity of forcible possession at the hands of Okoboshi and his family who think:

> *She had brought shame on all the people who had been unfortunate enough to come into contact with her. She was*

> *nothing but a common slut, fit to be kicked around and spat upon by slaves, because in her last incarnation she had been a slave water-carrier, only good enough to be gorillas for them to sleep with. She was not a human being but a curse to all human beings.*[50]

It is so ironical that capturing a girl and marrying her without her consent was acceptable, but not her coming to such a husband's bed disvirgined. So much so, that even her own family, who had been mourning her loss and trying to come to terms with her abduction and the sudden falling apart of their plans regarding her bride price, are not willing to accept her back when they hear of it that their daughter was not a virgin.

Okoboshi spits on her face in disgust and declares that he would not touch her, but still won't let her go. He would marry her and keep her in his compound as a slave to serve on other girls he would marry by his own choice. Apparently, he could not be less bothered about Aku-nna because he never wanted to marry her in the first place. It was his father's plan to get even with his old enemy Ofulue, Chike's father; and in order to torture him emotionally, he had got Aku-nna captured for marriage to his son. But now that she was a self-declared promiscuous girl, he wanted never to touch her, but would show her place by making her fetch and carry for his subsequent wives.

The irony of Okoboshi's perception and the strength of Emecheta's attack against female indignity is reinforced by our superior knowledge of the victim's purity. Okoboshi's callous treatment for Aku-nna and his lack of affection for her is in sharp contrast to Chike's humane and gentle, nurturing approach, providing her emotional and physical support as she matures into a woman. Chike not only acts as her lover and teacher, becoming her only source of emotional stability and educational emancipation, but he also fulfils those nurturing maternal roles which Ma Blackie in her undue involvement with her second husband Okonkwo's family, tended to neglect. Aku-nna, lying in captivity, wonders like most young lovers:

How simple our lives would have been but for the interference of our parents.[51]

Aku-nna has to face various kinds of atrocities – mental and physical abuse to punish her for her supposed impurity. But she knows she has to take it all in silence to save herself from an even worse fate of becoming the wife of Okoboshi in the real sense. For now, 'she allowed herself to shed a few tears into the silent stream' as she noticed that even her own family and friends had forsaken her. She wondered if Chike would reject her too in this shameful hour? Would he believe in her – her love and purity – or he would look away like Obiajube, her friend, who now felt disgraced by her acquaintance. She knew in her heart that she had done nothing wrong and was absolutely pure for her love. In fact, Okoboshi had also not performed the formal ritual of cutting a lock of her hair, so sure he was, first of possessing her, and then of her immorality. But where could she go? She knew that for all practical purposes, her own lie had made her an outcaste among her own people and they'd never accpept her now – would Chike be a part of them too?

> *Would Chike reject her too in her shameful hour? Okoboshi had not bothered to cut off a lock of her hair because it was not worth cutting; she could run away if she wanted, but to where? Her uncle would surely kill her on sight and she could not count on her mother who would not be permitted to make any decision.*[52]

While Aku-nna's mother-in-law still hopes that the newlyweds would reconcile and live a happy married life in future after the dust settles down over these events, Aku-nna knows that all this was too much for her. She would not survive such abuse and insults for long. Emecheta makes it clear throughout the novel that no amount of education or intellectual maturity can erase or dilute the power of tribal influence totally and no recognition of injustices or open rebellion permits total "psychic escape". The laws of the land were so ingrained into the minds of the people that there was no real escape possible:

> *But if she was forced to live with these people for long, she would soon die, for that was the intention behind all the taboos and customs. Anyone who contravened them was better dead. If you tried to hang on to life, you would gradually be helped towards death by psychological pressures. And when you were dead, people would ask: did we not say so? Nobody goes against the laws of the land and survives.*[53]

In this moment of despair, Aku-nna gets a new lease of life through her brother Nna-nndo who comes to meet her and assures her he knew the lies that were spread about her character were just lies. Not only that, he also brought her a letter from Chike that reassured her that he still loved her and that she should be prepared to run away at his signal.

Events move quickly and the young couple plan to realize their fantasies of escape. The couple elope, marry and settle down but the marriage remains traditionally unrecognized. Uncle Okonkwo does not accept bride price from Chike's father and Aku-nna herself is unable to rise above the limitations of the traditions against which she had rebelled initially. Her nightmares of hallucinations about the consequences of the unpaid bride price become real enough. Although they have good jobs and a lovely home in Ughelli and Chike protects her through a continuous reinforcement of his love and tenderness, social traditions are so deeply rooted in Aku-nna's mind that she is finally destroyed by her own fears and a sense of alienation from the tribe. Aku-nna thus becomes the victim of the society-inflicted punishment, ostracization by her family and friends, and her own inability to enjoy total physical and psychological revolt against stultifying conventions. Just as she had earlier felt the strength of the taboo about crossing the river during menstruation, she now feels very strongly that if the bride price is not paid, she will die. Her death is, as if, a self-fulfilling prophecy.

Aku-nna and Chike's love story had meets its climactic point when Chike appears out of the bush to take her away from the Obidis. Her love for him – absolutely blind and trusting – reaches its zenith when she is taken into his arms, for she knows that she need not care for anything else now:

> *… and before she knew what was happening, she was being held tightly by Chike. for a moment he seemed to breathe life into her, giving her exhausted body the energy it lacked, then as suddenly as he had embraced her, he moved away, and all she could hear was his low voice, urgent and insistent.*
> *"Come on, my own – run!"*
> *She did not ask where he was taking her, how long it would take.*[54]

Chike took Aku-nna to Ughelli, where he had decided to make her his bride. He had friends there who had already looked up jobs for them and also setup a house for the couple. Chike's love for Aku-nna is evident from the fact that even after her kidnapping he was sure that he would take her along to this new town and had sent a word to his friends to prepare accordingly :

> *… the thought that he could be forced to leave the town without Aku-nna never occurred to him- it was an unthinkable thought. As far as he was concerned, he was leaving, and he was taking Aku-nna with him even if she had been married to twenty Okoboshis.*[55]

The young couple is overjoyed to find themselves in the new town, in their new "zinced" house with cemented floor. 'Chike and Aku-nna were deliriously happy'. Chike couldn't stop kissing her and kept asking if she regretted coming with him at all. Aku-nna is filled with love and gratitude for him and tries to assure him of her love for him. Suppressing her own shyness, she takes him into a hug, and quotes the Old Testament wherein she pledges to take him for life as her own. The quote, though wrongly uttered, does not fail to show the sincerity of her emotions:

"Wherever thou goest, I will go. Your people shall be my people and your God my God".[56]

This pleased Chike to no end, as he had already begun to see her as his wife. He not only cared for her, but also her brother and mother. With the money that his father had given him for this new start in life, he planned to not only setup his own marriage, but also his in-laws. He reminded Aku-nna, that the most important people who should come to benefit from this marriage must be Nna-nndo and Ma Blackie. He intended to call her brother to live with them so that his education did not suffer and send some amount to Ma-Blackie regularly so that she would be independent of Okonkwo. Aku-nna is filled with gratitude for her husband to be and promises to serve him all his life which makes Chike laugh that her words might sound mercenary. Aku-nna tells him that she didn't care, for she knew that she was not marrying him for money:

> *He laughed into her hair. "To hear you say that people might think you are marrying me for my money."*
> *"Oh, no, not because of that, but for many other things-your kindness, your understanding and respect for people and the fact that you are suffering too, I mean your whole family. Oh, I don't know- I want to marry you for many, many reasons which I feel in my heart, although I can't name them all. Your money makes your life, and the life of our people, comfortable, but it be only an added comfort, not the main happiness."*[57]

Chike's father had given them money to buy a bed as his marriage gift for the new couple. As the lorry driver carrying them around prophesizes, their love was going to ensure that their marriage was a 'bed of roses' not of thorns. He even christened their bed 'Joy' and they discovered a totally new aspect of their love through their union on it. Chike was pleasantly surprised to discover that his love had still been saving herself for him. As the girl's virginity was highly valued in their society before marriage, he could not help but think about the rumor that Aku-nna and Okoboshi had started on their own wedding night. But for him it was the future that mattered. Chike had confessed to his father that all he wanted was Aku-nna's heart and happiness. As long he had those there was nothing else that he desired. Chike's stand is one of a true lover for whom nothing mattered apart from his love – neither social norms nor practicality. In a society where virginity could make or break the life of a girl and her family, his take on the subject not just showed his love for the girl but also the effect of modern western progressive education.

Aku-nna herself was full of dignified pride as she had successfully saved herself from Okoboshi even if she had had to take help of a lie that had disgraced her character in the eyes of the society. For her, the only thing the mattered was that 'she would never bring dishonor to the man she loved.' When Chike insists that their people must know of her purity, she disagrees and says that all this was no more important. They should just give them the bride price in peace because, as they say, if the bride price is not paid, the bride will die at child birth.

Aku-nna's revolt against her social customs was not completely successful. Though she had physically gotten away, chosen to love and marry a slave, her mind was still subjugated through the limiting social norms. Instead of bringing about ultimate self-fulfillment and self-actualization, her actions and her fear of the social customs attracted grave consequences. And Aku-nna's final destruction in the words of Lloyd Brown:

> *"…is itself a demonstration of the degree to which her will is dominated despite her conscious set of revolt."*[58]

While Aku-nna was trying to live her life of happy matrimony in the wake of her inner fears regarding the non-payment of bride price, Ibuza was thrown into a social outrage against the slaves Ofulues. The men of Ibuza tried their best to punish the Ofulues but the English laws came to their rescue. So, the people then began to turn their rage towards Okonkwo and his family, whose daughter started all trouble in the first place. All this had a really bad effect on Okonkwo as he took this degradation to his heart. He became ill and retaliated on Ma Blackie.

Though there was no formal system of divorce in the traditional African society, there were still ways of putting an end to unwanted marriage. Though there was no written documentation of a marriage or of a divorce, the community stood as witness to these events and their witnessing sanctioned these acts. In Ibuza, if a man no longer wanted to stay with his wife or if he wanted to divorce her, he would expose his backside to her in public. This meant that he had disowned his wife for all practical purposes and she no longer belonged to him.

Okonkow did just that. One evening, when the fever was too high, he walked straight into Ma Blackies hut, calling all his ancestors to be his witness, he removed his loin cloth and pointed his bare posterior towards Ma Blackie. Everyone was shocked, and ashamed as Ibuza men did not commonly take this step. Ma Blackie was also disturbed but her concern was primarily for the well being of her daughter. Having sent her son to Ughelli to live with Aku-nna and Chike, she just prayed for a safe delivery of her baby and that people of Ibuza got over what had happened quickly. She was receiving money regularly from Chike and thus lived comfortably.

In Ughelli, Aku-nna and her husband were enjoying what seemed to be an endless honeymoon after the local registry of their marriage. They had also taken a new home and moved their bed 'Joy' with them. All was good except for the worry in Aku-nna's mind about her bride price, for Okonkwo still refused to accept their marriage. Meanwhile Aku-nna gets pregnant and like all parents-to-be, totally in love, the two plan what they would call their child – if it would be a boy or a girl.

This joy is quickly overshadowed by the doctor's warning regarding Aku-nna's health. She is so young and small, been undernourished for so long, that her carrying her baby might be too taxing for her. Chike's fear of losing his love is apparent in his frustration. He believes that it is Aku-nna's constant worry over her bride price that is making her sicker and he assures her that his father would pay up at any cost:

> "You think about them so much that sometimes I think I don't even exist for you. Do you ever wonder what it would be like for me if you became ill...? I shall see that the bride price is paid...
>
> And you are not going to die and leave me. Do you understand?
>
> ... I don't want anything to happen to you-can't you see that you are my heart?"[59]

But even all his love is not enough to save the young girl from her imminent death. Try as much as they did, to change their destiny, the struggle ended with the self-willed death of Aku-nna in her premature caesarean child birth. Weak, she had always been, and the emotional and physical strain was too much for her, and she succumbed. Even in her last moments, she could not stop praising her love for being so kind to her and entrusts her brother to him. She is also overjoyed to hear that she had given birth to a girl as the belief was that when a couple loved each other a lot, they bore a girl child:

> "I told you so. I told you that I would not keep our love a secret.
>
> Now with our little girl, everybody will know. They will all know how passionately we love each other. Our love will never die...Let us call her Joy too, the same name we gave to the bed on which she was conceived."[60]

The loss of Aku-nna is too deep for Chike to bear, yet he is at peace to some extent, knowing that she died happy; at least she was now in peace. There would be no more haunting fears to trouble her. There would be no unpaid bride price to worry over.

The theme of love and marriage has been beautifully dealt with in *The Bride Price* by the novelist, the novel goes much beyond the parameters of a general love story throughout its portrayal of the folk lore and social customs of the Igbo people. Emecheta portrays the significance of racial and tribal identity and also condemns its negative aspects-its stronghold on the psyche of young girls like Aku-nna. Her insight, more realistic that any outright rejection sees the African woman perpetually involved in a struggle for self within the context of tribal solidarity.

We know, on the basis of sociological evidence spread all over the novel that Aku-nna does not die just because of some supernatural intervention. It wasn't just the bride price myth or her uncle's voodoo that killed her, but her own personal fear and diminution in the face of an alienated though successful and happy married life. Her fate and destiny is not just founded in the mysterious predispositions of inscrutable forces, but also, for the major part, on the function of social institutions and cultural traditions.

On one level, *The Bride Price* could be interpreted as the portrayal of love and marriage in the African context, intertwined with tribal religious belief, nearly in the tradition of the folk tale with its moral for a conclusion; as the language of the novel's concluding lines suggest :

> *So, it was that Chike and Aku-nna substantiated the traditional superstition they had unknowingly set out to eradicate. Every girl born in Ibuza after Aku-nna's death was told her story, to reinforce the old taboos of the land. If a girl wished to live long and see her children's children, she must accept the husband chosen for her by her people, and the bride price must be paid. It the bride price was not paid, she would never survive the birth of her first child. It was a psychological hold over every young girl that would continue to exist, even in the face of every modernization, until the present day.*
> *Why this is so, is, as the saying goes, anybody's guess.*[61]

Emecheta, through the love story of Chike and Aku-nna shows us the possibility of a successful rebellion and defiance of the age-old customs and the hope that someday, love, strong and solid enough, would be able to fight and survive in spite of all the social opposition and antagonism.

References

1. Emecheta, Buchi. (1976). *The Bride Price.* New York: George Brazilier Inc. p90.
2. Soyinka, Wole. (2002). *Death and the King's Horsemen.* (Norton Preface) New York: W.W. Norton & Company.
3. Gordon, April A. (1996). *Transforming Capitalism and Patriarchy: Gender and Development in Africa (Women and change in the Developing World).*
4. Emecheta, Buchi. (1976). *The Bride Price.* New York: George Brazilier Inc. p75.
5. *ibid*, p. 168.
6. *ibid*, p. 10.
7. *ibid*, p. 28.
8. *ibid*, p. 28.
9. *ibid*, p. 38.
10. *ibid*, p. 38.
11. *ibid*, p. 38.
12. *ibid*, p. 63.
13. Krige, Eileen. (1981). *Essays on African Marriage in Southern Africa.* Cape Town: Juta Publishers. p. 71.
14. *ibid*, p. 64.
15. Adichie, Chimamanda Ngozi. (2014). *We Should All Be Feminists.* London: Harper Collins Publishers. pp. 30-31.
16. *ibid*, p. 82.
17. *ibid*, p. 82.
18. *ibid*, p. 92.
19. *ibid*, p. 80.
20. *ibid*, p. 80.
21. *ibid*, p. 87.
22. *ibid*, p. 91.
23. *ibid*, p. 91.
24. *ibid*, p. 91.
25. *ibid*, p. 92.
26. *ibid*, p.92.
27. *ibid*, p. 93.
28. *ibid*, p.97.
29. *ibid*, pp. 97-98.
30. *ibid*, p. 98.
31. *ibid*, p. 98.
32. *ibid*, p.98.
33. *ibid*, p. 105.
34. *ibid*, p.105.
35. *ibid*, p.106.

36. *ibid*, p.107.
37. *ibid*, p. 104.
38. *ibid*, p. 114.
39. *ibid*, p. 115.
40. *ibid*, p. 115.
41. *ibid*, p. 116.
42. *ibid*, p. 116.
43. *ibid*, p. 116.
44. *ibid*, p. 103.
45. *ibid*, p. 118.
46. *ibid*, p. 118.
47. *ibid*, p. 126.
48. *ibid*, p. 132.
49. *ibid*, p. 134.
50. *ibid*, p. 138.
51. *ibid*, p. 139
52. *ibid*, p. 141
53. *ibid*, p. 141.
54. *ibid*, p. 145.
55. *ibid*, p. 147.
56. *ibid*, p. 148.
57. *ibid*, p. 149.
58. Brown, Lloyd. (1975). "The African Women as a Writer" in *Canadian Journal of African Studies*. Vol. 9, No. 3. Oxfordshire: Taylor and Francis Ltd. p40.
59. *ibid*, p. 161.
60. *ibid*, p. 167.
61. *ibid*, p. 168.

Chapter - IV

Things Fall Apart

Chinua Achebe's novels are mostly dedicated to understanding the effect and legacy "especially for Africa, for black people, for all deprived peoples" of the terrible disaster that proceeded from "Africa's meeting with Europe" in the period of high imperialism in the late nineteenth century. His novels stand as a hallmark of post colonialism, retelling us everything that the western world had ungraciously documented earlier. Achebe's Africa is not a 'long night of savagery', but a land of rich culture and tradition. His Africa stands tall as a land of social institutions and individual greatness. Along with redefining the African identity, his novels also represent the human relationships within the traditional society of the Igbo people. Achebe's first novel '*Things Fall Apart*', recreates the first impact of European invasion upon the old Igbo society and its effect on the tribal setup – the relationship between the people; how the social change brought about by the western interference affected the lives of individual men.

> *I had to the tell Europe that the arrogance on which she sought to excuse her pillage of Africa, i.e. that Africa was a Primordial Void, was sheer humbug; that Africa*

> *had a history, a religion, a civilization. We reconstructed this history and civilization and displayed it to challenge the stereotype and the cliché. Actually it was not to Europe alone that I spoke. I spoke also to that part of ourselves that had come to accept Europe's opinion of us.*[1]

Chinua Achebe's careful and confident craftsmanship creates a society wherein human bonding–love, friendship, marriage, and kinship is depicted in the most organic way. He highlights the native customs pertaining to marriage, be it winning a girl over a wrestling match, taking in multiple wives, as a symbol of power and wealth in society, or the secondary treatment of women in marriage, their limited role in decision making etc. Achebe depicts all these with unmatched finesse. The portrayal of love – for wife, family, children, community – is painted through great subtlety and restraint like Okonkwo, the hero of the novel, is never presented as an overly expressive man, especially when his kind and loving side is concerned, but his love for his wife Ekwefi and daughter Ezinma is shown in the novel in a very beautiful way. When Okonkwo's young daughter, Ezinma, becomes ill, he is so anxious and upset that he goes to the *obi*, or hut of Ekwefi, the child's mother and prepares medicine himself for the girl. He is not lacking in warmth, yet, afraid of being considered weak and effeminate like his father, he holds his love and concern firmly suppressed. So much so, that just the fear of being considered a coward drives him to kill a boy he had raised and loved as his own son. This fear becomes his undoing, and the murder of Ikemefuna, in a sense, initiates the fall of this tragic hero.

In '*Things Fall Apart*', Achebe deals with the theme of love and marriage through the depiction of the traditional society of the Igbo people, tracing the human emotions and bonding, along with the rituals and customs of the tribal society. The Igbo tribal set up was unique in its own individualistic structure; they never had any central organization or any kings. They rejected any inherited or hierarchical system of authority. It was this system that allowed a son of nobody to become village chief. A man was known by his own achievements, and not that of his father's. When Unoka, Okonkwo's father had died, he had taken no titles. On the contrary, he was heavily laden in debt. He had no land, no titles to show, nor had he more than one wife, all the things that proved a man of worth in the Igbo society had eluded him all his life. Though Unoka himself did not regret his unsuccessful life, his son did. Okonkwo was ashamed of him. His biggest fear was to be known like his father was – a failure in everything. And thus, all his life he had worked to prove his self-worth, distinct from the father he had unfortunately been born to. Fortunately for him, he lived in a society where a man was accepted for his own achievements, and not just by the inheritance from his father:

> *When Unoka died he had taken no title at all and he was heavily in debt. Any wonder then that his son Okonkwo was ashamed of him? Fortunately, among these people a man was judged according to his worth and not according to the worth of his father. Okonkwo was clearly cut out for great things. He was still young but he had won fame as the greatest wrestler in the nine villages. He was a wealthy farmer and had two barns full of yams, and had just married his third wife. To crown it all had taken two titles and had shown incredible prowess in two inter-tribal wars. And so although Okonkwo was still young, he was one of the greatest men of his time.*[2]

In Okonkwo's time, the largest social unit was the village group, which comprised of a few villages. Like Umuofia comprised of nine villages. Disputes were settled by public meetings, and where a common agreement could not be reached, an oracle would be consulted. These people's highly individualistic society may have developed partly for geographical reasons, for the Igbo lived in forests which were all but impenetrable, and each village was invisible to the next. Living thus enclosed, it is not surprising that the Igbo tended to be a tense, excitable and nervous people. In the old days only the trading between various markets and the practice of exogamy lessened the isolation of each village, for it was a custom that a man must seek his wife outside his own village and each family therefore maintained ties with a few other villages.

Achebe's *Things Fall Apart* tells primarily the story of Okonkwo, and theme of love and marriage can be traced through his character and people around him. Achebe gives a clear picture of the Igbo society and the institution of marriage in it through Okonkwo's three wives. His women are traditionally meek and submissive. Even if there triggers a stray spark in them, it is subdued by the beating of the man. Thus, the womenfolk feel tranquillity in obeying and following the patriarchal order of the clan. The wives were not permitted to question their husbands. When Okonkwo was entrusted with taking care of Ikemefuna, he calls his first wife and puts him in her care without any explanation. Even her natural curiosity is snubbed.

> *So when the daughter of Umuofia was killed in Mbaino, Ikemefuna came into Okonkwo household. When Okonkwo household. When Okonkwo brought him home that day he called his most senior wife and handed him over to her. 'He belong to the clan', he told her. 'So look after him'. 'Is he staying long with us?' she asked. 'Do what you are told, woman', Okonkwo thundered, and stammered. 'When did you become one of the Ndichie (elders) of Umuofia?' And so Nwoye's mother took Ikemefuna to her hut and asked no more questions.*[3]

Okonkwo, the hero of the novel, is an important and respected man in Umuofia, in the days immediately preceding the European colonization, around the late 1800s. He has been driven on to achievement, primarily, by his shame at his father's failure. His father, Unoka, who in his eyes, was a complete failure, was his biggest fear, in that he might become like him. In order to ensure that he did not end up like his father, Okonkwo ran away from everything that was a reminder of him- be it laziness, incurring debts, love for music or expressing kindness and love for anyone. According to Okonkwo, all these were signs of weakness, not suitable for real man. Okonkwo's father, Unoka, was a gentle but irresponsible man who loved playing the flute but who could not succeed in life because he did not work hard enough, and nor did he care enough about the values of his intensely competitive society, a society in which a livelihood was hard to get from soil and the man of status was the man who had a flourishing yam crop, many barns and multiple wives, Unoka never even took a title – another sign of man's achievements, For this, he was called 'Agbala', Okonkwo always tried twice as hard as most men to build his reputation different from his father's.

> *Okonkwo's fear was… the fear of himself, lest he should be found to resemble his father. Even as a little boy he had resented his father's failure and weakness, and even now he still remembered how he had suffered when a playmate had told him that his father was agbala…agbala was not only another name for a woman, it could also mean a man who had taken no title. And so Okonkwo was ruled by one passion – to hate everything that his father Unoka had loved. One of these things was gentleness and another was idleness.*[4]

Okonkwo built his farm with great effort and toil into a wealthy one. He had three wives and two tittles. Thus, he was successful man. But he is a severe man who cannot express his affection lest anyone think he is weak. For him, all soft emotions were signs of weakness. His *Chi* or personal god is said to be good.

> *If ever a man deserved his success, that men was Okonkwo…At the most one could say that his chi or personal god was good. But the Igbo people have a proverb that when a man says yes his chi says yes also.*[5]

Because of Okonkwo's determination he moulds his own fate – or for a time it a appears so. It was the high position he enjoyed in his society that resulted in his being chosen as an emissary of war to a neighbouring village Mbaino, where an Umuofia woman had been killed. That woman was the wife of Ogbuefi Udo. An ultimatum was dispcatached to Mbaino asking them to choose between war on the one hand, and on the other the offer of a young man and a virgin as compensation. Okonkwo returns with two hostage – a lad of fifteen and a young virgin. The girl was given to Ogbuefi Udo to replace his murdered wife and as the boy belonged to the whole clan, he was entrusted to Okonkwo, to be kept in his care till the decision was made as to what needed to be done with him.

Okonkwo hands over Ikemefuna, the lad from Mbaino, to his first wife, who takes care of him along with her children, as her own. We see the way he snubs her when she had just asked him as to how long Ikemefuna would be staying with them. This was the general state of affairs. The husband was the revered figure in the compound who could not be questioned about anything. The wives were expected to be simply silent slaves, doing their bidding. For example, the way Okonkwo forced his family to work during the planting season was too much for them, yet they never dared to complain.

> *During the planting season Okonkwo worked daily on his farms from cock crow until the chickens went to roost. He was very strong man, and rarely felt fatigue. But his wives and young children were not as strong – and he so they suffered. But they dared not complain openly.*[6]

Ikemefuna, entrusted with Okonkwo, begins to live in his compound, and gradually the love and care shown him by the wives and children of Okonkwo, especially the first wife and her son Nwoye, makes him feel at home. Nwoye becomes friends with the young stranger and begins a friendship, deep and strong, that even the permanent separation between the two cannot put an end to.

> *Nwoye's mother was very kind to him and treated him as one of her own children...He was by nature a very lively boy and he gradually became popular in Okonkwo's*

> *household, especially with the children. Okonkwo's son, Nwoye, who was two years younger, became quite inseparable from him.*[7]

In Nwoye's young eyes, Ikemefuna was no less than a hero, who knew everything. A child's pure love for an elder brother like figure is evident in their relationship. Ikemefuna seemed to know everything. He could make flutes from bamboo stems and even from the elephant grass. He knew the names of birds – all of them – and could set clever traps for the little bush rodents. For little Nwoye, it was no less than a superpower that Ikemefuna knew which trees make the strongest bows. Even Okonkwo loved the boy in his own suppressed way. He admired that lad and wished that his own son would turn out like him. He was very pleased to see the positive effect of Ikemefuna in the way he was influencing Nwoye, who new preferred staying outdoors with him or in his father's hut rather than tagging along with his mother as he used to earlier. But of course, Okonkwo would rather die than express his love for someone, and so he kept his emotions to himself.

> *Even Okonkwo himself became very fond of the boy – inwardly of course. Okonkwo never showed any emotion openly, unless it be the emotion of anger. To show affection was a sign of weakness; the only thing worth demonstrating was strength. He therefore treated Ikemefuna as he treated everybody else – with a heavy hand. But there was no doubt that he liked the boy, sometimes when he went to big village meetings or communal ancestral feasts he allowed Ikemefuna to accompany him, like a son, carrying his stool and his goatskin bag. And indeed, Ikemefuna called him father.*[8]

Just as the saying goes, that love cannot be really hidden, no matter how tough an exterior one might adopt, Okonkwo's love for Ikemefuna was also not a secret, and even more so, Ikemefuna's admiration for his father-figure. It was for this reason that the elders had advised Okonkwo to take no part in the boy's killing. After Ikemefuna had been living in Okonkwo's compound for three years, the Oracle of the Hills and the Caves ordained that boy should be sacrificed to the gods. The love that had developed among the children of the house for this new entrant is evident in the sorrow they all felt at his leaving even though it was told them that he was just being taken back to his home. Yet, they all feared that they might not see him again:

> *Nwoye went to his mother's hut and told her that Ikemefuna was going home. She immediately dropped the pestle with which she was grinding pepper, folded her arms across her breasts and sighed, 'Poor child' The next day the men returned with a pot of wine... Okonkwo got ready quickly and the party set out with Ikemefuna carrying the pot of wine. A deathly silence descended on Okonkwo's compound. Even the very little children seemed to know. Throughout that day Nwoye, sat in his mother's hut and tears stood in his eyes.*[9]

The elders had advised Okonkwo against taking a direct part in Ikemefuna's killing as he used to call him 'father'. But when the village men lead the boy along the forest path, Okonkwo is among them, and when the moment comes, Okonkwo is trapped by his own obsession, the need to appear absolutely strong. The death of Ikemefuna is one of the most moving passages in the novel. The boy had been told that he is being taken back home to his village. He has not been told that he is to be sacrificed, and though initially ill-at-ease, he slowly begins to look forward to meeting his family again. He wonders if his mother was dead or living. He walks singing to himself, feel of thoughts of about his new family and old. How he'd tell his mother about Okonkwo who had taken care of him, his children who had been like his own siblings – those along with a foreboding about the well-being of his mother, were the thoughts racing in his young lively mind. His love for his surrogate family is apparent and ironical to the reader who knows that his 'father' Okonkwo is going to end his life.

> *Although he had felt uneasy at first, he was not afraid now. Okonkwo walked behind him...how his mother would weep for joy and thank Okonkwo for having looked after him so well and for bringing him back...Ikemefuna felt like a child once more. It must be the thought of going home to his mother.*[10]

Little did the ill-fated lad knew that he was never going to see her again, the same man he called his father; whose mere presence behind him reassured him even in the dense forest, would turn out be his murderer:

> *One of the men behind him cleared his throat. Ikemefuna looked back, and the man growled at him to go on and not stand looking back. The way he said it sent cold fear down Ikemefuna's back. His hands trembled vaguely on the black pot he carried. Why had Okonkwo withdrawn to the rear? Ikemefuna felt his legs melting under him. And he was afraid to look back. As the man who had cleared his throat drew up and raised his matchet, Okonkwo looked away. He heard the blow. He heard Ikemefuna cry, 'My father, they have killed me!' as he ran towards him. Dazed with fear, Okonkwo drew his matchet and cut him down. He was afraid of being thought weak.*[11]

Dazed with fear, Okonkwo commits this appalling act. Such fear might be in the nature of other murderers as well, but for Okonkwo, this fear – the fear of appearing weak like his father, was his drive. Okonkwo's tragedy is that he never really confronts his fear and thus, can never explain himself. There is never a single person who can understand his anguish over the death of Ikemefuna, and if he could have a lessened his pain by sharing it with someone, maybe someone like his close friend Obierika, or one of his wives, just his own main flaw – that need to appear publicly strong and absolutely certain of his actions, prevents him for doing so. He is unable to even bring out his sorrow. Okonkwo is quite vocal in his love for his land, its culture and traditions, but can never bring himself to express his love for the people he actually cares about. That, in his eyes would be appearing weak.

So tangled is Okonkwo is his own idea of a strong man, that he is unable to express his love even for his own children. He is unable to comprehend the sensitive nature of his son and ends up distancing him further and further from himself through his words and actions. The boy, who already lived in fear of his father, for try as much as he did, he, just could not become the ideal strong man his father expected him to be at this young age, still found relief in his mother's stories and daydreams. It was his friendship with Ikemefuna, that gave him a kind of standing in front of this father. With this new brother, he felt he could win the world, including his father's affection, for Ikemefuna seemed to know everything. In Ikemefuna's company, he is able to live without his mother's stories and feigns annoyance over women whenever he is called by his mother or any of his father's wives to do the tasks expected to be carried out by men. This act helps him avoid Okonkwo's constant torture and beating.

> *Nwoye would feign annoyance and grumble aloud about women and their troubles. Okonkwo was inwardly pleased at his son's development, and he knew it was due to Ikemefuna. He wanted Nwoye to grow into a tough young man capable of ruling his father's household when he was dead and gone to join the ancestors...And so he was always happy when he heard him grumbling about women. That showed that in time he would be able to control his women folk.*[12]

In the eyes of Okonkwo, no matter how prosperous a man was, but if he could not control his women and children, he was not really a man. So, Okonkwo encouraged his boys to sit with him in his obi, his hut, and told them stories of violence and bloodshed. These stories were masculine stories of valour that he wanted to inculcate in his boy. Nwoye also pretends to take interest in the stories of tribal wars told by Okonkwo as that pleases his father to the core, though deep within, Nwoye loves the kind of stories his mother tells. But this pretence of liking manly stories saves him the torture of being beaten up and rebuked by his father whom he fears.

But the day Ikemefuna is killed, Nwoye feels something snap inside him. He knew that his own father is in some way responsible for his murder. Nwoye does not understand Okonkwo's motivations any more that Okonkwo understood those of Unoka, his father. Nwoye, in a tragic but inevitable pattern, becomes increasingly severed from Okonkwo and from his entire family.

> *As soon as his father walked in, that night, Nwoye knew that Ikemefuna had been killed, and something seemed to give way inside him, like the snapping of a tightened bow. He did not cry. He just hung limp.*[13]

His little mind had felt the same kind of sorrow when he had first heard the voice of an infant crying when walking through the forest. The women around him had all hushed up and quickened their steps. He had heard that twins were supposed to be an abomination in their society and so, upon birth, they were put in earthenware pots and thrown away in the dense forest, but this was the first time he had come across them. He felt chilled to the core, realizing the intense inhumanity practised around him. That day also, he had felt the same kind of heaviness and chill. He felt it again.

> *Then something had given way inside him. It descended on him again, this feeling, when his father walked in, that night after killing Ikemefuna.*[14]

Nwoye's heart, soft and full of love, is never really able to reconcile with the loss of his brother-like Ikemefuna, and especially the fact that his own father had a hand in it, and thus, he grows further and further apart from Okonkwo.

Okonkwo himself was not the least unaffected. He did not taste any food for two days after Ikemefuna's death. He drank palm-wine from morning till night, and could not sleep.:

> *Okonkwo did not taste any food for two days after the death of Ikemefuna. He drank palm-wine from morning till night, and his eyes were red and fierce like the eyes of a rat when it was caught by the toil and dashed against the floor...He did not sleep at night. He tried not to think about Ikemefuna, but the more he tried the more he thought about him...Now and then a cold shiver descended on his head and spread down his body.*[15]

Obierika, Okonkwo's friend, reproaches him for the death of Ikemefuna, and his part in it, but Okonkwo – needing to believe himself right, even against his own feeling, which he sternly casts aside – rejects the reproach and will not listen. Okonkwo is unable to accept the values of love and gentleness – he fears them too much. He fears that his acceptance of such emotions might weaken him in his own eyes and the eyes of his community. Okonkwo is presented in the novel as a man not lacking in warmth, but a person who would never surrender to these feelings that would show his warm side to the world. For him his coldness and stern exterior were signs of manly strength. Love was a woman's domain. And he was most certainly not one.

> *When did you become a shivering old woman', Okonkwo asked himself, 'you are known in all the nine villages for your valour in war, how can a man who has killed five men in battle fall to pieces because he has added a boy to their number? Okonkwo, you have become a woman indeed.*'[16]

Thus, reproaching himself for feeling sentimental about Ikemefuna's death, Okonkwo tries to get over his hidden guilt.

While portraying this kind of repressed love through Okonkwo's character, Achebe also talks about expression of love in the society, that in no way deteriorated the manliness of a man. He shows Obierika as an almost perfect character, a man who is not afraid of blood, a valiant warrior, a man with earned titles, a good father and a responsible man of community, yet one who does not shy away from showing love, be it for his friend or his children. While chiding Okonkwo for getting involved in Ikemefuna's killing, he tells him that no man could ever call him coward for he is not. Yet, if the oracle ever pronounced his son's sacrifice, he would not stop it, but also won't take part in it:

> *'You know very well, Okonkwo that I am not afraid of blood; and if anyone tells you that I am, he is telling a lie, and let me tell you one thing, my friend. If I were you I would have stayed at home… if the Oracle said that my son should be killed I would neither dispute it nor be the one to do it.'*[17]

While Okonkwo and Obierika are thus engaged in talks, another visitor comes along. Ofoedu comes along with the news of two deaths. He tells them that Ogbuefi Ndulue of Ire village had died. Now this comes as no surprise to the men as he was very old and had been ill for a while. His first wife Ozoemena, who was also very old, in fact too old to attend Ndulue in his illness, had left him in the care of his younger wives.

When the man died in the morning, one of the wives went to inform the senior wife, who 'rose from her mat, took her stick and walked over' to her dead husband's obi. There 'she knelt on her knees and hands at the threshold and called her husband, who was laid on the mat "Ogbuefi Ndulue", three times and went back to her hut.' Later in the day, when the youngest wife went to call her again to be present at the washing of Ndulue's dead body, she found Ozoemena also dead.

As per the Igbo custom, if a man and wife were dead at the same time, the woman's last rites would be performed before the man. Also, while drums were beaten to inform the whole village about the death of a man, the woman's death went silent; there were no drums beaten, no announcement made.

Achebe, once again takes opportunity, through his small digression in the novel to drive home the theme of love and Okonkwo's understanding of it. For when Obierika comments upon how strange it was for both the man and his senior wife to die just a few minutes apart, he talks about the love that the old couple shared, like they were 'one mind'. But Okonkwo is unable to fathom how a title-holding strong man could be expressive of his love for his wife. He is taken aback on hearing that Ndulue never did anything without telling his wife Ozoemena:

> 'It was always said that Ndulue and Ozoemena had one mind,' said Obierika. 'I remember when I was a young boy there was a song about them. He could not do anything without telling her.' 'I did not know that', said Okonkwo. 'I thought he was a strong man in his youth.' 'He was indeed,' said Ofoedu. Okonkwo shook his head doubtfully. 'He led Umuofia to war in those days', said Obierika.[18]

This simple conversation between the men highlights the concept of love that Okonkwo holds. For him, love and strength – to co-exist – is unimaginable. Okonkwo cannot conceive of a strong man who respects a woman's judgement. For him, women are to do what they are told and strong man is one who knows how to control his women and children by instilling in them the fear of his wrath. We see Okonkwo meting out unjust and harsh treatment to his wives and children several times. Though he protects his family from poverty and destitution, he is not able to foster the bond of understanding with his family, especially his eldest son Nwoye. Okonkwo never showed any emotion openly except the emotion of anger that pushed his son further and further away from him.

Yet Okonkwo is never presented as a man in whom warmth is lacking. The love and concern are there but are held firmly suppressed. When Okonkwo's young daughter, Ezinma, becomes ill, he is so anxious and upset that he goes to the obi, or hut of Ekwefi, his second wife and Ezinma's mother, and prepares medicine himself for the girl. When the child recovers from illness, however, Okonkwo cannot show his emotion. He would do all he can in his capacity for his family except acknowledge how much they meant to him. Okonkwo's concern for his child's safety is visible time and again in his care for Ezinma. Not only did he like her so much that he wished she were a boy, or prepare medicine for her when she was sick, but he also defied the words of Chielo, the village priestess and ran the risk of annoying Agbala, a goddess by following Ezinma when she was taken away by Chielo to pay a visit to the goddess in the cave.

Ezinma is feared to be an *ogbanje*, 'one of those wicked children who, when they died, entered their mother's wombs to be born again.' In a country where infant mortality rate is so high, it is not surprising that such a belief grew up – the children who died were always the same children, born again and again, fated to die again and again, the eternal bringers of anguish to their parents. Ekwefi had given birth to ten children, nine of them had died in infancy, and by the time Ezinma had been born, she had already resigned herself to the fate of giving birth to *ogbanjes,* for none of her children had lived beyond the age of three. But Ezinma had survived to the age of ten years, and Okonkwo and Ekwefi now hoped that this child had come to stay. The unconditional love of a mother and daughter is portrayed through Ekwefi and Ezinma:

> *Ezinma was an only child and the center of her mother's world. Very often it was Ezinma who had decided what food her mother should prepare. …Ezinma did not call her mother Nna like all children. She called her by her name, Ekwefi, as her father and other grown-up people did. The relationship between them was not only that of mother and child. There was something in it like the companionship of equals, which was strengthened by such little conspiracies as eating eggs in the bedroom.*[19]

The pregnancy which is supposed to be crowning glory for women had become only physical agony for Ekwefi without any promise of motherhood. Losing nine children wasn't easy. When her tenth child, Ezinma was born, Ekwefi 'accepted her, as she had accepted others – with listless resignation' at first, but when she lived past her third, fourth, fifth year, Ekwefi began to hope that maybe the gods had finally had pity on her, and her child had come to live:

> At first Ekwefi accepted her, as she had accepted others – with listless resignation. But when she lived on to her fourth, fifth and sixth years, love returned once more to her mother, and, with love, anxiety. She determined to nurse her child to health, and she put all her being into it… Everybody knew she was an Ogbanje… But she had decided to stay… Ekwefi believed deep inside her that Ezinma had come to stay.[20]

The love for Ezinma, and fear of losing her, force Okonkwo and Ekwefi to do all in their power to ensure that the *ogbanje* curse is broken. Okonkwo had asked a well-known medicine-man to dig up Ezinma's *iyi-uwa*, so that her bond with the world of *ogbanje* could be broken. Though all these things were done, yet time and again, the parents lived in fear of losing her. Whenever Ezinma fell ill, Ekwefi was filled with anxiety and would not rest till her daughter regained full health. Okonkwo himself took care to prepare medicine for the child and asked about her constantly till he was sure that she was well.

One night, when Chielo comes calling, bringing the message of Agbala, who wanted to see Ezinma, both Okonkwo and Ekwefi try to discourage her from taking the little girl along. But when the priestess heard none of them and took the little girl away, both the mother and the father cannot stop themselves. Even though they know that the goddess will be angry with them for following her messenger, they follow Chielo secretly, separately. Once outside the cave, they discover each other, and Ekwefi is filled with renewed love and gratitude for this man who never showed his emotions verbally yet cared so much as to follow her and their daughter in such a dark, scary night.

> *Ekwefi did not answer. Tears of gratitude filled her eyes. She knew her daughter was safe. 'Go home and sleep', said Okonkwo. 'I shall wait here.' 'I shall wait too. It is almost dawn. The first cock has crowed.'*[21]

Ekwefi and Okonkwo, both the parents, had stayed up all night at the mouth of the cave to see Ezinma emerge with Chielo, safe and sound. While everyone knew that Ekwefi had followed the priestess and her daughter, nobody except Ekwefi and the priestess knew that Okonkwo had been there too:

> *Okonkwo was also feeling tired and sleepy, for although nobody else knew it, he had not slept at all last night. He had felt very anxious but did not show it. When Ekwefi had followed the priestess, he has allowed what he regarded as a reasonable and manly interval to pass and then gone with his matchet to the shrine… he had become gravely worried.*[22]

Okonkwo, so worried for his child, is however, unable to show his concern through direct action, or words, as that would not be 'manly' of him.

Achebe paints love in *Things Fall Apart* with various colours. While the likes of Obierika and Ekwefi are vocal and unashamed to show their love for the ones they hold dear to them, Okonkwo lives in suppression and denial. He was always a man of few words, but when the matter of the softer emotions come up, it left him completely tongue-tied. Ekwefi recalls how she was in love with Okonkwo, and he cared for her too. The day he had defeated the Cat in a wrestling match, she had fallen for him, but he did not have enough money to pay her bride price and so she could not marry him initially. But later she could not contain her love for Okonkwo and left her husband for him. She remembers how he had, even then not said anything, but just made love to her to show his acceptance:

> *Ekwefi's mind went back to the days when they were young. She had married Anene because Okonkwo was too poor then to marry. Two years after her marriage to Anene she could bear it no longer and she ran away to Okonkwo. It had been early in the morning. The moon was shining. She was going to the stream to fetch water. Okonkwo's house was on the way to the stream. She went in and knocked at his door and he came out. Even in those days he was not a man of many words. He just carried her into his bed in the darkness and began to feel around her waist for the loose end of her cloth.*[23]

This incident shows the way Igbo society functioned. While the payment of the bride price was essential, the society's acceptance of a woman's choice to walk out of a marriage she is not happy in, is also commendable. Achebe's novels mirror the Igbo society in all aspects. Talking about the institution of marriage, his novels reflect the social customs and traditions pertaining to it, and more specifically the play of gender roles is highlighted. Achebe, when interviewed by Raoul Granqvist, a post-colonial expert, author and Associate Professor of English at Umea University, Sweden, insisted that "The Igbo sensibility has never been comfortable with anything so absolute and clear-cut as "Man is Boss". This statement has important implications for Achebe's writing because he upholds the system of "diffuse authority" in Igboland explicitly and insistently. He contends that traditional Igbo societies laid emphasis on the decentralization of authority, and the distribution of power across a broad front in such a way that the possibility of a consensus to use authority oppressively against women was limited. Though the Igbo were a patriarchal society, the role of woman was also important. And even if women had lesser say in important matters, their existence could never be totally denied. Ekwefi, Okonkwo's second wife, stands as a flagbearer of gender equality, who is vocal in her outbursts, and bold enough to speak her mind when she feels like. Though the husband was supposed to be the 'owner' she never lets her spirits be ruled by Okonkwo. And Okonkwo also knows her well and perhaps loves her most for her strength and boldness. It is an example of Ekwefi' bold individuality that she dared to leave her husband for another man when she could not suppress her love for the latter.

Chinua Achebe never attempts to underplay the evils within the Igbo society but presents it as he knew it. Through Obierika's daughter's wedding rituals, Achebe highlights many a custom associated with the African marriage. The settlement of the bride price, one of the most important components of an African marriage, is dealt with in great detail, and he also highlights the distinctive features of marriage and bride price in different societies within Africa:

> *In this way Akueke's bride-price was finally settled at twenty bags of cowries. It was already dusk when the two parties came to this agreement… As the men ate and drank palm-wine they talked about the customs of their neighbours. 'It was only this morning,' said Obierika.'that Okonkwo and I were talking about Abame and Aninta, where titled men climb trees and pound foo-foo for their wives.' 'All their customs are upside down. They do not decide bride-price as we do, with sticks. They haggle and bargain as if they were buying a goat or a cow in the market.' 'That is very bad,' said Obierika's eldest brother. 'But what is good in one place is bad in another place. In Umonso they do not bargain at all, not even with broomsticks. The suitor just goes on bringing bags of cowries until his in-laws tell him to stop. It is a bad custom because it always leads to a quarrel.' 'The world is large,' said Okonkwo. 'I have even heard that in some tribes a man's children belong to his wife and her family.'*[24]

The men, laughing at the idea of the mother's claim over her children, depict the underprivileged status of women in a marriage. The women have neither the courage nor the freedom to go against the decisions of the males or to voice their opinions different from their's.

They can bear their children, tend to them, but cannot assert their rights over them. The following Igbo proverb proves it:

'Onwune nwata na enwe ewu bun a aji'.

Translated as, 'a child's ownership of a goat is only skin-deep.' It means that no matter how well a child looks after the goat given to him by his father, yet he cannot exercise control over it. Similar is the fate of women in Igbo society whose perplexing condition is portrayed by Achebe in his novels. These women take care of the needs of their husbands and look after their children yet have no say in the decisions pertaining to their own or their children's lives.

Achebe's depiction of marriage in the African society paints the gender defined roles of the man and woman. Although women have an integral part to play in their chores of the clan, they hardly get their due share of importance because all the tasks expected to be done by them are considered as menial or inferior. In the novel, we are told about the inferiority of women through different situations and circumstances. For example, women are not allowed to plant yam, the king of crops as that is the "man's crop". They could only grow "women's crops" like coco-yams, beans and cassava".

> *His (Okonkwo's) mother and sisters also worked hard enough, but they grew women's crops, like coco-yams, beans and cassava. Yam, the king of crops, was a man's crop.*[25]

Although women put in equal amount of labour, or, as a matter of fact, more labour than men, their hard work was hardly ever recognized and rewarded. On the other hand, men's task in the Igbo society is to look after their household by providing yam that would last from one Yam Festival to the next; on the other hand, women plant crops, cook for and serve their husbands, and also carry their crops to the market to sell, bear children and take care of them.

Another unique feature of the African marriage that Achebe displays is the practice of polygamy. It is as natural in African society to have multiple wives as to have multiple barns and children. The more they are in number, the higher the man's status in the society. The admiration and yearning of a wife for her husband to get other wives is a trait that makes the African women quite unique. The first wife enjoys the position of the chief wife, whose approval of other wives makes possible for the house to be run smoothly, without hassles. The wives find it easier to carry out the chores for the husband when they have other wives of their husband in the house. For example, we saw the chief wife of Ndulue, Ozoemena, too old to take care of her husband herself, handing over the responsibility to the younger wives.

When Okonkwo, in the very beginning of the novel, is shown asking Nwakibie for yam seeds to plant, the whole custom of wine-bringing and drinking among the co-wives of Nwakibie highlights the superior position of the chief wife. Okonkwo had not inherited a barn or a title, or any young wives from his father, and thus, had to fend for himself as well as his mother and sisters.

Possessed by a fear of a contemptible life and shameful death like his father's, he was determined to make his life a worthy one. And thus, he decided to take a loan of yam seeds to plant. For this loan he went to Nwakibie, taking along a 'pot of palm-wine and a cock':

> *There was a wealthy man in Okonkwo's village who had three huge barns, nine wives and thirty children. His name was Nwakibie and he had taken the highest but one title which a man could take in the clan. It was for this man that Okonkwo worked to earn his first seed yams.*[26]

The subordinate position of women, as compared to the men is evident when Achebe tells us that when all the men present had 'drunk two or three horns, Nwakibie sent for his wives.'[27] At first only four wives came to attend this ceremony as the other wives were not home perhaps. But even those that came could not begin drinking as they had to wait for the chief wife to have the first drink among them, and she was still on her way:

> *When everyone had drunk two or three horns, Nwakibie sent for his wives. Some of them were not at home and only four came in. 'Is Anasi not in?' he asked them. They said she was coming. Anasi was the first wife and the others could not drink before her, and so they stood waiting. Anasi was a middle-aged woman, tall and strongly built. There was authority in her bearing and she looked every inch the ruler of the women folk in a large and prosperous family. She wore the anklet of her husband's titles, which the first wife alone could wear. She walked up to her husband and accepted the horn from him. She then went down on one knee, drank a little and handed back the horn.*
>
> *She rose, called him by his name and went back to her hut. The other wives drank in the same way. In their proper order and went away.*[28]

The chief wife by virtue of being the first, the senior-most among the women of the household, enjoys a higher social standing and often, holds the confidence of the master of the house, deriving a certain prestige from her position. But her social supremacy need not translate into actual ruling within the household, as she has almost no control whatsoever over her co-wives. In fact, it is better to be the favorite wife rather than the chief, as the favorite one would be the special one, chosen by the husband himself. Okonkwo's household is a good example of camaraderie between the co-wives, where they enjoy the obvious advantage of helping each other in looking after the babies, preparing the food, etc.

Okonkwo's wives, all three of them, lived together without the drama of competition and rivalry, taking care of the household together. They lived like sisters and loved each other's children as their own. This is in stark contrast to the world of jealousy and rivalry in Emecheta's, *The Bride Price*, wherein Okonkwo's wives spare no chance to put down each other. But here, they help each other and even lie to their husband, if the need be, to save each other. For example, when Okonkwo's first wife requires some fire, Ekwefi sends Ezinma with live coals in a piece of broken pot, and Nwoye's mother thanks her, calling her Ezigbo, which means 'the good one'. In another instance, Okonkwo had gotten angry with his youngest wife Ojiugo for not cooking the afternoon meal. When he discovered that she was not home, he asked where she was. Ekwefi informed him that she had gone to 'plait her hair'. When he asked if she had taken along her children, his first wife said that they were in her hut, eating. Then he asked is Ojiugo had asked her to feed them, and Nwoye's mother lies by answering in the affirmative so that Ojiugo could be saved from her husband's wrath:

> *Okonkwo bit his lips as anger welled up inside him. 'Where are her children? Did she take them?' he asked with unusual coolness and restraint. 'They are here,' answered his first wife, Nwoye's mother. Okonkwo bent down and looked into her hut. Ojiugo's children were eating with the children of his first wife. 'Did she ask you to feed them before she went?' 'Yes', lied Nwoye's mother, trying to minimize Ojuigo's thoughtlessness.*[29]

In yet another incident, when Okonkwo is angry with Ekwefi for cutting a few banana leaves and beats her, the other two wives try to stop him 'from a reasonable distance'.

Another aspect of marriage shown by Achebe is the practice of wife-beating. Wife-beating, a part of domestic violence cannot be said to be specific to African marriage as its instances are witnessed across the world, in almost all countries, but the way the Igbo men had the privilege to beat their wives, and its being considered their right, is quite alarming. Okonkwo's youngest wife, Ojiugo, is beaten by him for the reason that she went to their neighbor's place to plait her hair without preparing Okonkwo's afternoon meal. This enrages Okonkwo to the extent that he did not think twice on beating Ojiugo during the Week of Peace. The period before planting the crops in observed as a sacred week during which the people of Umuofia live in peace and avoid hurting their clansmen either by using harsh words or through violence. They avoid fighting even if a heinous crime like adultery is committed as any kind of violence in this period invites the wrath of the earth goddess, Ani, without whose blessings, nothing would grow:

> *Okonkwo was provoked to justifiable anger by his youngest wife, who went to plait her hair at her friend's house and did not return early enough to cook the afternoon meal… when she returned he beat her very heavily. In his anger he had forgotten that it was the Week of Peace. Ezeani, the priest of the earth goddess… seemed to pay no attention (to Okonkwo's explanation) … He brought down his staff heavily on the floor. 'Your wife was at fault, but even if you came into your obi and found her lover on top of her, you would still have committed a great evil to beat her.' His staff came down again. 'The evil you have done can ruin the whole clan. The earth goddess whom you have insulted may refuse to give us her increase, and we shall all perish.'*[30]

Ojuigo is beaten heavily by her husband for such a trivial error, and the others, including Ezeani, the priest of the earth goddess, are annoyed and concerned over this act of Okonkwo only because it is the Week of Peace.

A similar case occurs during the New Yam Festival. Okonkwo is uncomfortable and restless because he hates sitting idle for days waiting for a feast. His anger crosses all limits when he confronts his second wife, Ekwefi, and comes to know that she has cut some leaves off the banana tree to wrap food. Without hearing anything further, he beats Ekwefi and nobody dares to stop him. His other wives, who realize that his anger was in vain as the banana tree had just lost a couple of leaves, try in vain to plead from a distance to let her go. Yet none have the courage to intervene and stop him:

> *Okonkwo's second wife had merely cut a few leaves off it to wrap some food, and she said so. Without further*

argument Okonkwo gave her a sound beating and left her and her only daughter weeping. Neither of the other wives dared to interfere beyond an occasional and tentative, 'It is enough, Okonkwo', pleaded from a reasonable distance.[31]

These two incidents reflect "hegemonic masculinity" in the society, a term coined by Raewyn W. Connell in 1980. The term analyses the power inequalities prevalent in the society by mentioning that the masculine gender enjoys the dominant position through their specific and peculiar attributes that consist of strength, courage, vigour, fearlessness, aggressiveness and decisiveness. Hegemonic masculinity is next to patriarchy as its basic concept is:

> *"understood as the pattern of practice (i.e., things done, not just a set of role expectations or an identity) that allowed men's dominance over women to continue."*[32]

Achebe, however, cannot be held guilty of propagating violence against women as in the same novel, he also shows an instance where a trial by the clansmen is held against a wife beater. Chinua Achebe has himself said:

> *The writer cannot expect to be excused from the task of re-education and regeneration that must be done. In fact, he should march right in front.*[33]

In a communal ceremony of the society, the chosen village men dressed up as ancestral spirits and mythical characters and came together to settle village disputes. In one such meeting, Uzowulu complained that his brothers-in-law had beaten him up and taken his wife and their sister, Mgbafa back with them and now refused to pay back the bride price he had paid for her. The brothers of the wife tell the egwugwu that they did so to save their sister, who had already suffered a miscarriage due to her husband's beatings. The last time she was beaten so badly that the neighbours had to interfere and save her. So, they say that they'd send her back to her husband only if he promised to never beat her again. The egwugwu decided that Uzowulu was at fault for being so brutal with his wife, and so, he should request his wife to come back with the promise that he would not beat her again:

> *'Go to your in-laws with a pot of wine and beg your wife to return to you. It is not bravery when a man fights with a woman.'*[34]

Achebe portrays the Igbo culture in all its complexities, highlighting the social customs and the society. The Igbo, known for their capacity to accept, absorb and change, are shown through the novel in different lights. The man-woman relationship, the expression and repression of emotions, position of women and the status of marriage – all form the core of Achebe's novels. Tradition, as exemplified in folk tale and custom, as well as historical material, reveals women possessing strength and determination, as well as organization. There is sufficient evidence that the earth goddess, Ani, was the primary deity. Ani's bosom was the ultimate resting place for all men and women. But, still, the women are shown as not possessing enough power to speak against male domination. A woman, among women, could rule, but not in society as large. For example, a priestess like Chielo, or chief wife like Anasi. Their power was limited – area-specific. The shocking depiction of violence against women in *Things Fall Apart* reimposes the perception that African society is dominantly patriarchal where the position of women in the society is vulnerable and weak. Okonkwo's misogyny is encoded in the acts of violence and aggression, which he perpetrates on the women of his family.

For example, Okonkwo was not a good shooter, and he knew it, but could not take it when Ekwefi takes a jibe at his weakness and runs to beat and shoot her:

> *But although Okonkwo was a great man whose prowess was universally acknowledged, he was not a hunter. In fact, he had not killed a rat with a gun. And so, when he*

called Ikemefuna to fetch his gun, the wife (Ekwefi) who had; just been beaten murmured something about guns that never shot. Unfortunately for her, Okonkwo heard it and ran madly into his room for the loaded gun, ran out again and aimed at her as she clambered over the dwarf wall of the barn. He pressed the trigger and there was a loud report accompanied by the wail of his wives and children. He threw down the gun and jumped into the barn, and there lay the woman, very much shaken and frightened but quite unhurt. He heaved a heavy sigh and went away with the gun.[35]

While on the one hand the above extract shows Okonkwo's aggression and vanity – how he would not allow a woman to make any disparaging remark against him – on the other hand, the last line of the same extract proves that though blinded by anger, he did not lose his care and concern for long, just like his anger came as a flash, it also went away in a flash and he cared enough to check that his wife was not really hurt. But this luck deserts him during the last rites of Ezeudu, one of the village elders. He was the same elderly men who had warned Okonkwo not to have anything to do with Ikemefuna's death. At Ezeudu's funeral, Okonkwo's dane-gun goes off accidently and kills the dead man's son. Because the killing of a clansmen is a crime against the earth, Okonkwo is banished from Umuofia for seven years. The neighbors, including his friend Obierika, help him to pack during the night. But when dawn comes, they can no longer raise a hand to help him. They come back like avenging furies compelled into his ritual destruction. They set fire to his houses and kill his animals, for they are 'cleansing the land which Okonkwo had polluted with the blood of a clansman.' They are acting correctly in their own eyes, with every social sanction that their community could provide. Their feelings of friendship and sympathy for Okonkwo becomes subservient to their 'group mystique.' They are doing what is expected of them and what they expect of themselves.

Thus, through a chance incident, Okonkwo loses everything that he has worked all his life to obtain. Okonkwo, unable to 'rise beyond the destiny of Chi', is exiled from his own land, the land that he loved more than his own self and forced to seek refuge in his mother's ancestral land, Mbanta. Though he was well received there, he could never stop regretting his loss of Umuofia – his fatherland. He had to spend seven years in exile, and in these seven years he prospered in Mbanta, yet he did not stop regretting his loss of Umuofia even once:

> *The seven wasted and weary years were at last dragging to a close. Although he had prospered in his motherland Okonkwo knew that he would have prospered even more in Umuofia, in the land of his fathers where men were bold and warlike. In these seven years he would have climbed to the utmost heights. And so, he regretted every day of his exile. His mother's kinsmen had been very kind to him, and he was grateful. But that did not alter the facts. He had called the first child born to him in exile Nneka – 'Mother is Supreme' – out of politeness to his mother's kinsmen. But two years later when a son was born, he called him Nwofia – 'Begotten in the Wilderness.'*[36]

Out of all the feelings of warmth that Okonkwo successfully managed to suppress, perhaps, there was only one that was stronger than any fear of appearing weak or effeminate, and that was his love for his land. It was this love that he seldom tried to contain. When Obierika visits him in Mbanta and tells him about the white man's advent into Umuofia, Okonkwo is filled with a sense of duty to preserve his native land from these foreign transgressors and can barely finish up the due time of exile. He wants to go back to his land as soon as he can, to stop its disintegration. Okonkwo knew that his village had changed in his absence, but the magnitude of this change brought by the white man, was beyond his imagination. He has to see to believe.

When at last Okonkwo is able to return to Umuofia, he realizes the extent to which it has changed. He has lost his place among the nine masked spirits, the Egwugwu, who wear the ancestral masks and act as a judicial council in cases which cannot be settled amicably by the councils of men. He has lost his chance to lead his people and lost the years when he might have taken high titles. Nevertheless, he plans to rebuild his compound and reputation by marrying his daughters to men of high repute in Umuofia and by initiating his sons, the four who remained after Nwoye joined the missionaries, into the *Ozo* society, the members of which are supposed to be the highest title holders. But Okonkwo's return to his land is nothing like he planned:

> *Okonkwo's return to his native land was not as memorable as he had wished. It was true his two beautiful daughters aroused great interest among suitors and marriage negotiations were soon in progress, but, beyond that, Umuofia did not appear to have taken any special notice of the warrior's return. The clan had undergone such profound change during his exile that it was barely recognizable.*[37]

All his life Okonkwo had believed in suppression of all emotions except anger. For him, any other emotion was being effeminate. But the one love he was not keen on concealing was his love for his land, his clan and culture. He was proud of it and believed in upholding it at all costs. And thus, when he saw his clan breaking apart, he was very sad.

> *Okonkwo was deeply grieved. And it was not just a personal grief. He mourned for the clan, which he saw breaking up and falling apart, and he mourned for the warlike men of Umuofia, who had so unaccountably become soft like women.*[38]

Umuofia had changed beyond recognition. The new Christian mission had claimed many, including Okonkwo's son Nwoye. The government of the English was now established, and the court was set up too 'where the District Commissioners judged cases in ignorance.' Ignorance, because this judge had no inkling of the ways of the Igbo people. The customs that they had followed for centuries were pronounced as illegal overnight without sparing a thought for their cultural sentiments. Court messengers had been appointed to interpret and act as go-betweens. Although they were Africans and some even Igbo, they were foreigners to Umuofia, belonging to another society, having learnt in a different medium. The courts and the English district officers did not understand the status of the village elders and the men of title. Okonkwo was understandably appalled:

> 'What is it that has happened to our people? ... Does the white man understand our custom about land?';

Obierika's reply sums up the cruel inevitability of the situation:

> 'How can he when he does not even speak our tongue? But he says that our customs are bad; and our own brothers who have taken up his religion also say that our customs are bad. How do you think we can fight when our own brothers have turned against
> us? The white man is very clever. He came quietly and peaceably with his religion. We were amused at his foolishness and allowed him to stay. Now he has won our brothers, and our clan can no longer act like one. He has put a knife on the things that held us together and we have fallen apart.[39]

Tension and misunderstanding mount in Umuofia. The natives and the missionaries engage in constant conflict, with one calling the other's god false. The zeal of the converted Christians is especially bordering on fanaticism. One such over-zealous convert, Enoch, tears off the mask of an egwugwu, an ancestral spirit, exposing the human face and the man whose sacred duty it is to wear the mask and bear the possession by the spirit:

> It happened during the annual ceremony which was held in honour of the earth deity. At such times the ancestors

of the clan who had been committed to Mother Earth at their death emerged again as egwugwu through tiny ant-holes. One of the greatest crimes a man could commit was to unmask an egwugwu in public, or to say or do anything which might reduce its immortal prestige in the eyes of the uninitiated. And this was what Enoch did.[40]

This act of Enoch amounted to the killing and defiling of an ancestral spirit, so it infuriates the whole clan, especially the elders. They demand the mission head to leave so that they could burn down the church. Acting out of his own very different concepts, not understanding their views any more that they understand his, the English missionary, Mr. Smith, bravely refuses to go. The villagers then, dressed up as egwugwu administering justice, burn the church. But Mr. Smith, not one to take such act lying low, goes to the District Commissioner and the white judge decrees that the villagers must be punished. He calls six village leaders, among them, Okonkwo, on the pretext of holding a meeting. But once they reach, they are arrested and humiliated. They are released after much humiliation and shaving off hair and beating, but that too, only when the village has paid a heavy fine for their release. Once free, all the men of the village, with the chiefs, hold a meeting. But the government court messengers arrive to break up the meeting. Okonkwo, his deep pride mingling with his hatred for the whites, draws his matchet and kills one of the messengers expecting other villagers to follow his lead. But he gets to know soon that the days of his power and the days of Umuofia's power, are both, over. Instead of killing the remaining messengers, the villagers let them go. He knows that Umuofia will not go to war against the strangers. He returns to his compound and hangs himself.

Suicide is an offence against the earth, and in a bitter scene Okonkwo's great friend Obierika has to ask the District Commissioner and his men to cut Okonkwo down from the tree where he had hung himself, and bury him, for he can only be buried by strangers, for no villager would touch the body of a man who's committed suicide; such was the custom of Umuofia. In a last passionate outcry, Obierika mourns the death of his friend, Okonkwo, and tries to express his tragedy:

> *"That man was one of the greatest men in Umuofia. You drove him to kill himself; and now he will be buried like a dog..." He could not say any more. His voice trembled and choked his words.*[41]

But the District Commissioner does not understand. He goes away thinking that Okonkwo's story, that of a man who had killed a messenger and hanged himself, may possibly make a good whole chapter, or at least a 'reasonable paragraph' in the book he is writing, titled 'The Pacification of the Primitive Tribes of the Lower Niger'.

Achebe, in the novel, focuses primarily on the tragedy of Okonkwo, a man who does not only fall because of the forces working from outside, but also due to his own pressures from within. Neither is all evil in the Igbo society blamed on the white men but is shown from the internal perspective as well. Okonkwo is a man who is very greatly damaged by the external circumstances of his life. His primary wish is to be revered by all as a man of great wealth, power and control – the antithesis of his father. It is this wish and his fear of unmanliness, once again, kindled by his hatred for his father, that pushes him to commit violence against the good within. In the same way, the old Igbo society is destroyed, as Achebe makes quite clear, both by inner flaws and outer assaults. In portraying the personal tragedy of Okonkwo, and the collective tragedy of Umuofia, Achebe has spun his tale beautifully around the culture and customs of the Igbo society, giving us a fair glimpse into the cultural practices of the people.

While the theme of love is explored through various prisms – parent-child love, fraternal bond, love for one's land and family, the Igbo matrimony is highlighted through various instances. Obierika's daughter's wedding is a detailed account of the marriage customs and the relationships between Okonkwo and his wives explores the conjugal dynamics in the African society. The practice of polygamy, and the status of chief wife, relationship between co-wives are all showcasing the nature of an African marriage. Gender inequality, a part and parcel of the traditional African marriage, is highlighted again and again through short stories that are narrated by different characters through the course of the novel, or episodes like wife-beating and abusing, or putting the women-folk down.

Although the central action of the novel is of man's experience, Achebe has created a separate world of women in his novel. In this world, the women live happily, helping each other, caring for each other, far removed from the aggression and crippling pressures of the man's world, created by the men themselves.

Some stories overtly depict the superiority of women, but their in-depth study reveals the true significance. The story of the Mosquito (man) and the Ear (woman) narrated by Okonkwo's mother is one such example. The Mosquito gives a marriage proposal to the Ear but the Ear, not finding him to be a suitable match for itself, mocks at the Mosquito and declines the offer. This rejection is humiliating for the Mosquito and since then whenever he passes the Ear, he reminds her by buzzing into the Ear that he is still alive and flourishing:

> *When he (Okonkwo) was a child his mother had told him a story about it. But it was as silly as all women's stories. Mosquito, she had said, had asked Ear to marry him, whereupon Ear fell on the floor in uncontrollable laughter. 'How much longer do you think you will live?' she asked. 'You are already a skeleton.' Mosquito went away humiliated, and anytime he passed her way he told Ear that he was still alive.*[42]

Analyzing the story from a woman's perspective, it is evident that such intense is the feeling of rejection for males that they find it difficult to cope with it, especially when it comes from a female. Even though the females are given the supreme authority in the clan, in the form of Agbala or the Earth Goddess, yet the final verdict always comes from the males because they are not ready to look inferior to their counterparts in any way as that would hurt their male ego. In the story, the female Ear exercises her right to taking decision for herself, but then she is condemned for the whole life to face the wrath of the Mosquito:

> "… the Mosquito was taunting the Ear in revenge for the insult with which his suit had been once rejected?"[43]

The act of giving the final decision by a man is also proven in the first egwugwu episode of *Things Fall Apart*, wherein, the egwugwu judge favorably for Uzowulu, reprimanding him for beating his wife yet asking her to get back to him when he comes to request her return, instead of punishing him strictly for his animal-like behavior. They, i.e., egwugwus, hold their ritual meeting, and then come out with their verdict, knowing well that while the woman would obey whatever they decided, the man would never hear letting her away, no matter how wrong he be. The wife was his property, and he would accept no other decision but obtain her again, whichever route they might suggest:

> "Don't you know what kind of man Uzowulu is? He will not listen to any other decision", replied the other.[44]

Things Fall Apart shows the meek and submissive wife in Okonkwo's first wife, Nwoye's mother, and the bold and rebellious wife in Ekwefi, thus showing the different kind of women characters in the African marriage. While the society was largely patriarchal, not every woman bowed down to it in absolute submission. Okonkwo's second wife is one such free, rebellious spirit. She walked out of her first marriage because she was not happy, and united with her first love, Okonkwo, in whose heart she holds a special privileged position even though he might not verbally express it. Okonkwo knows she is bold and strong, yet he does not always mind her strong-headedness and feels sympathetic towards her emotional outbursts. He understands her loss of nine children and her fear of losing her last surviving daughter Ezinma. His love for her and her daughter is evident when he follows them the night Chielo takes away Ezinma. The wife traditionally had to take permission of her husband before venturing out on her own. But Ekwefi's love and concern for her daughter makes her forget all the rules and regulations of the clan. Highlighting the power of a mother's love that gives the woman courage and strength to stand against all odds and fight for the things they consider right. The fact that Okonkwo, instead of being angry with her, followed them into the forest to ensure their well-being, is evidence enough to prove his soft-hearted temperament that he always tried to hide, even from himself.

Okonkwo's love for Ezinma is more than what he feels for any of his other children. This father-daughter relationship between the two has been drawn beautifully in the novel. Even while scolding her and ordering her to "sit like a woman!" Okonkwo cannot help but admire Ezinma's strong temperament. He wants her to fit the mould, yet regrets her not being a boy. All his life, he cannot come to terms with the fact that the one child he could count upon to take forth his legacy, is a girl, and thus, not fit to be his true successor. This, however, never weakens the bond they share:

> *Okonkwo was especially fond of Ezinma. She looked very much like her mother, who was once the village beauty. But his fondness only showed on rare occasions.*[45]

Ezinma understands her father to a great extent and also tries her best to help him out in every way she can, in spite of the limitation of being 'a girl'. Okonkwo, on his part, also realizes the qualities of his daughter, but all his love cannot help him overcome the fact that she was not his son, but a daughter. During his exile, he did not need to explain to the girl as to why he wanted his daughters to wait for marriage till they got back to Umuofia. She understood that their getting married when they got back would help Okonkwo regain his social status to a great extent. She understood his unspoken words. Theirs was a special bond:

> *Okonkwo was very lucky in his daughters. He never stopped regretting that Ezinma was a girl. Of all his*

children she alone understood his every mood. A bond of sympathy had grown between them as the years passed.[46]

Ekwefi and Ezinma's relationship is also a special one. In fact, the novel deals with the parent-child love and relationship in a very beautiful way. The friendship between Nwoye and Ikemefuna shapes Nwoye's life entirely. Obierika and Okonkwo are also depicted as best of friends. In fact, it was Obierika who ensured that Okonkwo got proper value for his yams in his years of exile. And Okonkwo's love for his land is the running motif of his life and death.

The sister-like love and bond that the co-wives share is reflected not only in the happy co-living of Okonkwo's three wives, but also in the relationship shared by their children. Ezinma enjoys great influence over Obiageli. Ezinma is also ever-ready to help her father's other wives with any household chores that she is capable of doing.

The African marriage is depicted in all its intricacies. Right from the marriage settlement of Obierika's daughter to wife-beating – no major facet has been left out in the novel. In *'Arrow of God'*, Achebe has written a very interesting piece of dialogue between Akubue and Ezeulu in regard to the relationship between husband and wife. In the novel, Ezeulu narrated an incident in which his father advised his friend to treat his wives politely and get his work done. Advising the same to his friend Akubue, Ezeulu states:

> *In out custom a man is not expected to go down on his knees and knock his forehead on the ground to his wife to ask her forgiveness or beg her favour. But, a wise man knows that between him and wife there may arise a need for him to say to her in secret: "I beg you." When such a thing happens nobody else must know it, and that woman if she has any sense will never boast about it or even open her mouth and speak of it. If she does it the earth on which the man brought himself low will destroy her entirely.*[47]

This advice of his father is adopted by Ezeube who applies it whenever he has to deal with his wives. According to Ezeube, women should be treated as inferior beings but still men should try not to hurt their ego and in return, the image and prestige of men should be taken care of by the wives. Such thought, however, is never harbored by Okonkwo, for whom, his wives are his property, and nothing else. Even though he might love them to some extent in his heart deep within, for all practical purposes he was their master, and they, the servants. In the novel, his second wife, Ekwefi is bold and rebellious and enjoys more freedom than the average wife as Okonkwo loves her above all his other wives. But this magnanimous love for his second wife, too, does not prevent him from beating her. He beats her whenever he wishes to, so that she may not begin considering herself above her husband. At other times, he beat his wife just to vent out his own frustration.

Traditionally, women in marriage, are condemned to oppression, suppression and non-existence. They become the voiceless beings, forced to bear the brunt of subjugation, given no other choice for themselves. Narrating the life of the typical woman in a traditional African marriage, Achebe has shown the difficulties and trauma they had to bear – not permitted to ask questions – children mutilated or thrown away in the name of abomination – getting beaten by their husbands. According to the norms of the society, it is the right of their husbands and nobody could object or interfere in between to stop such brutality being committed against them. Talking of wife beatings, Adewale Rotimi has said that wife beating was believed to be a part of African culture as it has been mentioned in African proverbs too. Some of the proverbs that deal with wife-beating are:

> *"Opa ti a fin a iyaaale ni a ofina iyawo"* (The whip which was used to beat the most senior wife is still being kept for her juniors) *"Pa mi nku nse ori kunkun si oko."* (It is only a woman who risks being beaten to death that disobeys her husband)[48]

The incidents of wife-beating have been portrayed in the texts of most African writers. Chinua Achebe in *Things Fall Apart* evinces how Okonkwo used to beat his wives. In one instance, he beats his third wife, Ojiuogo, because she goes to her friend's place to plait her hair and fails to return early enough to cook the afternoon meal. Okonkwo could not bear such carelessness on the part of his wives as according to him they are meant to keep him happy. When she returns after getting her hair done, she is beaten black and blue by Okonkwo who does not even bother to consider the Week of Peace in which any kind of violence is prohibited, including beating one's wife. The Week of Peace, also called The Sacred Week, is observed to please the Goddess Earth, but Okonkwo does not fear the Earth Goddess or any other such mighty being when it comes to meting out punishment to his wife. All that mattered to him was that his wife had failed to carry out her duties towards him. Also, it is worth noting that the villagers and the priest condemn him and fine him not because he beat his wife, but because he beat her in the Week of Peace.

A similar case occurs once again in the novel when Okonkwo pours out his anger and frustration on his second wife, Ekwefi. During the celebrations of the New Yam Festival, people make merry and, as a ritual, no task is done. But because Okonkwo is a hardworking man, and hates sitting idle, so on the day of the festival he gets so irritated that his irritation gives way to anger. To satisfy his anger, he starts looking for a person and a reason to vent his anger upon. Finally, he gets an opportunity when he sees his second wife, Ekwefi, has cut off some banana leaves from the banana tree to wrap food in it. On seeing this, Okonkwo starts beating her to which Ekwefi responds by murmuring ill of him behind his back. She makes a snide remark about his shooting, and because Okonkwo was actually a bad shot, such a comment coming from his wife, makes him blind with rage. Unfortunately, for Ekwefi, Okonkwo hears her and runs behind her to shoot her. Thankfully, the bullet does not hit her.

Women in Achebe's novels fear their husbands and cannot muster up enough courage to question them. And once in a while if they do dare to ask, even the most valid of questions, they are humiliated or brutally shut up, but never respectfully answered. A case in point is Nwoye's mother who wanted to know the length of Ikemefuna's stay with them. Instead of giving a satisfactory answer, Okonkwo scolds her for asking a question at all. She is supposed to mutely follow his instructions, without ever questioning what she is asked to do.

The wives are shown as weak in the wife-husband relationship, yet these weak women never hesitate in discharging their duties. They bear responsibilities of the clan and inculcate in their children the culture of their region through story-telling. The instances in the text reveal that although females are expert at inculcating in their children the traditions and customs of Africa, males do not lag far behind in learning the art of story-telling. The man and the women, both try to imprint their culture and customs in the minds of their children through oral art. The difference lies in the kinds of stories narrated by both the genders. Females narrate the stories of sun, moon, sky, animals, good and evil and males narrate stories of war and valour, courage and bloodshed. As African culture attaches immense value to story-telling, the stories describing the culture of Africa could not have been complete without the mentioning of this art in the novel. The African women's ability of telling stories to their children has been mentioned repeatedly through various short stories in the novel, all teaching some values or life skills.

In *Things Fall Apart*, Okonkwo does not like the kind of stories that his wives tell. He wants his sons to grow up listening to masculine stories that are about war and men. Whenever he finds his son Nwoye taking interest in the kind of stories his wives told, Okonkwo could not help but scold and beat him as he does not want his son to grow up effeminate, into a meek and feeble man. This thought process of Okonkwo is evident through the following passage:

> *Okonkwo encouraged the boys to sit with him in his Obi, and he told them stories of the land – masculine stories of violence and bloodshed. Nwoye knew that it was right to be masculine and to be violent, but somehow, he still preferred the stories that his mother used to tell, and which she no doubt still told to her younger children – stories of*

> *the tortoise and his wily ways, and of the bird eneke-ntioba who challenged the whole world to a wrestling contest and was finally thrown by the cat. He remembered the story she often told of the quarrel between Earth and Sky long ago, and how Sky withheld rain for seven years until crops withered and the dead could not be buried because the hoes broke on the stony earth. At last Vulture was sent to plead with Sky… At last Sky was moved to pity… That was the kind of story that Nwoye loved. But he now knew that they were for foolish women and children, and he knew that his father wanted him to be a man. And so he feigned that he no longer cared for women's stories. And when he did this he saw that his father was pleased, and no longer rebuked him or beat him. So Nwoye and Ikemefuna would listen to Okonkwo's stories about tribal wars, or how years ago, he had stalked his victim, overpowered him and obtained his first human head.*[49]

The above extract gives clear distinction between the husband and the wife – and their masculine and feminine stories, and how both the genders stick to their kinds of stories. Children are however, always excited about listening to stories, though they feel more attached to the mother's stories perhaps. Storytelling, traditionally, is a forte of women within the household, but maybe because of the immense importance attached to this art, men, too, try their hands at it, not wanting to stay behind their female counterparts in any way.

Achebe shows the condition of the African wife, in all her glory within the household yet subservient to her husband. While the husband is the privileged ruler in his own right, the wives are meek and feeble in general. Even if there is an exception in the like of Ekwefi, even her bold and assertive self cannot totally escape the dominance of her man.

The wives are portrayed traditionally subservient and weak, playing a distinctly secondary role to their husbands. They are seen as a prize for the affluent men and are believed to have no identity of their own. Achebe's men, like Okonkwo, are strong and voraciously violent.

They are bestowed with the titles of the clan and their male prowess is voluptuously proliferated by marrying many women. In the clan, men have the freedom to keep as many wives as they could feed. The novel displays the society's bias towards the masculine gender by depicting that the privilege of marrying many women is a man's entitlement, but the woman has no such privilege. She must either stick to the man she had been married to, under whatever circumstance he keeps her, or leave him for another, like Ekwefi did.

The wives worked day and night to provide for the husband and their children, yet their work was considered menial in comparison to their husband, even equal or lesser hard work. In Igbo society, gender specific tasks are allotted to the men and the women. Though deep within, Okonkwo is proud of Ezinma's boldness and sharpness that are considered male attributes, he not only teaches her to carry out tasks meant to be done by females but also scolds her for not behaving like women. The patriarchal ideology of the clan does not allow women to supersede men in any respect.

The portrayal of love and marriage in Achebe's novel, *Things Fall Apart*, is evident throughout, in spite of the focus being laid on the traumatic effect of the colonial invasion on the Igbo clan. Okonkwo's love for his family and his fatherland – one suppressed, the other overtly expressed, finds depiction in the novel, along with the love between the brother-like friends – Nwoye and Ikemefuna, and Okonkwo and Obierika. The happy co-existence of Okonkwo's three wives is also something unique because co-wives usually end up being rivals for their husband's attention. But such an angle has not been explored here. Ekwefi and Ezinma's bond is also as strong as a mother-daughter relationship can get.

The position of chief wife is explored through various instances and characters like Anasi and Ozoemena and Okonkwo's first wife – all of them treated with preference in any social occasion, where the younger wives pay due respect. It is important to note that the senior wife's permission is essential to be obtained before getting a new wife. The wives, all different in temperament and nature, have one thing in common – that they are all perceived as inferior beings, who are better off serving the males. Each and every woman, no matter how dominant and influential in her home or her village, could not be considered as enjoying equal status with men. Most African societies had a strong bias favouring the male superiority. The basic framework of the African society is one of patriarchy, where, as elsewhere, men rule and dominate.

Although these female characters are submissive and subjugated, yet they do not stay confined to the chores of their respective compounds. They grow crops and sell their produce in the market and also help their husband in planting and harvesting his crops, thereby lending a helping hand to their husbands and fathers for the smooth functioning of their household. Further still, they cannot step out of their compound without having fulfilled all their assigned duties there. In many cases the economic responsibility became a burden. Though contributing in every possible way, these women became mute spectators with respect to the matters of their state or homestead. They are either never allowed to give their opinion, or if they do, are not heeded. For instance, when Okonkwo wants to hold a feast to thank his kinsmen in Mbanta for hosting him for seven years, he asks his wives to work for it, but does not entertain their suggestion:

> *Okonkwo called his three wives and told them to get things together for a great feast. 'I must thank my mother's kinsmen before I go', he said. Okonkwo never did things by halves. When his wife Ekwefi protested that two goats were sufficient for the feast he told her that it was not her affair.*[50]

Thus, the wife has no power against her husband in the eyes of society, or even herself. Her meekness defines her in the Igbo society. Achebe primarily portrays his women as the weak second sex in a marriage. Be it a love marriage or an arranged marriage, Ekwefi or Ojiugo, all women are reduced to an equal footing in marriage, subjugated, subservient. Even when Achebe talks of a couple, very much in love, like the old Ndulue and Ozoemena, the social set up was such that Ndulue, a man of valour and titles, had had to take other wives to establish his worth in the eyes of the people, for in their eyes, a man's status was measured by the number of wives he kept, and Ozoemena had had to accept junior wives of her husband, perhaps gladly, keeping with the norms of the day.

The setting up of the marriage, and various rituals pertaining to it has also been described in great detail through Obierika's daughter's marriage, thus giving a fine view of the African marriage. The determining of the bride price, followed by the girl Akueke's, appearance before her suitors, and the ensuing celebration, has all been noted down with beautiful portrayal of the native culture. The whole village took part in the wedding ceremony, showing that marriage in Africa is anything but a private affair.

Achebe highlights the African marriage customs through his novels. Polygamy, bride price, household division of labour, wife beating etc. are all dealt with, in the novel, with a deep understanding of the native culture. The wives of Okonkwo lead a subservient life, that can be witnessed through the evidences in the novel where they have no allowance to do anything according to their will. Even a hair braiding requires the husband's permission. The customs and taboos that forced the woman to take a subjugated position are aplenty. For example, the wife had to kneel in front of the husband while serving him food. It was her prime duty to ensure that he got his meal hot and ready on time, failing which she would get a beating that she could not even cry against.

The multi-dimensional aspects of love have been analysed in this chapter, based on the relationships shared by Okonkwo and his wives, the love between him and Ekwefi defines the basic love, desire and concern between man and wife, while his relationship with the the other two wives is more of a socially sanctioned union than a mating of hearts. Ezinma's relationship with both her parents shows the love between parents and child, while Nwoye and Ikemefuna exhibit brotherly love. The love between friends is beautifully shown through Obierika and Okonkwo's friendship and then again through the comfortable understanding between Ekwefi and Chielo. Okonkwo's love for his land forms the basis of patriotic love explored in the chapter that moves the entire life and also brings about an end to Okonkwo. The theme of marriage has been analysed mainly under the lens of feminism, showing the heavy burden laid on women by the household chores, the submissive attitude of the wife that she must adopt towards her husband; the generally acknowledged right of a man to beat his wife; and finally, the fact that marriage does not necessarily give rise to intimacy between spouses. These are the general conclusions that can be drawn about an African marriage through Achebe's *Things Fall Apart*.

References

1. Achebe, Chinua. (1990). "African Literature as Restoration of Celebration", an essay in *Kunapipi* 12, no.2.
2. Achebe, Chinua. (1958). *Things Fall Apart*. New Delhi: Modern Classics, Penguin India. p.6.
3. ibid, p.12.
4. ibid, p.11.
5. ibid, p.20.
6. ibid, p.11.
7. ibid, p.21.
8. ibid, pp. 21-22.
9. ibid, p.42.
10. ibid, pp. 43-44.
11. ibid, p.44.
12. ibid, p.38.
13. ibid, p.44.
14. ibid, p.45.
15. ibid, p.46.
16. ibid, p.47.
17. ibid, pp. 48-49.
18. ibid, p.50.
19. ibid, p.56.
20. ibid, p.58.
21. ibid, p.80.
22. ibid, p.32.
23. ibid, p.80.
24. ibid, p.53.
25. ibid, p.18.
26. ibid, p.15.
27. ibid, p.15.
28. ibid, pp.15-16.
29. ibid, p.22.
30. ibid, p.22.
31. ibid, p.28.
32. Connell, Raewyn W. and Messerschmidt. (2005). "Hegemonic Masculinity: Rethinking the Concept" in SAGE Journals, *Gender and Society*. 19.6. p.832.
33. Achebe, Chinua. (1975). "The Novelist as a Teacher", in Morning *Yet on Creation Day:* Essays. *London:* Heinemann African Writers Series. p.72.
34. ibid, p.68.
35. ibid, p.29.

36. ibid, p.119.
37. ibid, p.133.
38. ibid, p.133.
39. ibid, p.129.
40. ibid, p.135.
41. ibid, p.151.
42. ibid, p.55.
43. ibid, p.191.
44. ibid, p.69.
45. ibid, p.33.
46. ibid, p.126.
47. Achebe, Chinua. (1964). *Arrow of God*. New York: Anchor Books. p.172.
48. Rotini, Adewale. (2007). "Violence in the Family: A Preliminary Investigation and Overview of Wife Battering in Africa". *Journal of International Women's Studies*. 9.1. p.236.
49. ibid, p.39.
50. ibid, pp.120-121.

Chapter - V

Conclusion

This study has been carried out with the objective of analyzing and critically establishing the position of love and marriage as constant themes in the novels of Elechi Amadi, Buchi Emecheta and Chinua Achebe. An analysis of the development of African literature in English, alongwith the study of these writers' specific novels taken for this research work, namely, *The Concubine*, *The Bride Price* and *Things Fall Apart*, as well as the inferences drawn from their critical reading has formed the body chapters. The conclusion forms together the findings and arguments into a coherent whole consisting of generalizations flowing from analysis. In the introductory chapter of this research work, a critical analysis of the development of the African novel in English from the historical perspective has been carried out in the first part. The second part of this first chapter holds a detailed study of the different aspects of love and marriage portrayed in the African novels. The various types of matrimonial alliances permitted in the African society have been analysed in this part. The next three chapters are a fleshed-out analysis of the selected texts. The three novels have been analysed in the second, third and fourth chapters respectively, to prove the treatment of love and marriage as constant themes in these novels and to establish their importance in the African society.

The first part of the first chapter analyses the newfound scholarly interest in the study of African literature, that has flourished in the recent past. The 'land of the savage', which was viewed under the colonists' prejudiced lens has been discovered as a place of abundant literary richness and cultural ingenuity. The same African continent which had earlier been described in literary works as 'The Dark Continent' or 'A Long Night of Savagery' is now rightly considered as a land of long rich cultural legacy endowed with a varied corpus of literary traditions, passed on from one generation to the next through the oral medium. The orature of Africa, that was preserved in the form of folklores, poems and songs etc. helped in ensuring that the Africans could easily adapt these into their writing when the time came for it. The oral narratives were deftly transformed into the written form to save them from getting lost under the colonial rule.

The novels, in the written form completed the task that the narrators did in oral narratives. These stories encapsulated in culturalism and traditionalism, instilled in the young minds, the ritual practices and traditions of the various clans. The similarity of the novel with oral narrative carved for it a special place in the African cultural tradition. Such novels not only worked towards preserving their unique culture but also served as a medium for the Africans to tell the world what they really were, as opposed to what they had been presented as. These novels became a tool in the hands of the Africans who wanted to put forth their own perception of their society, which must definitely be closer to reality. In their works they tried to capture the minds of culturally grounded Africans. As these writers knew the tradition of their place and were well aware of the many customs and beliefs of their people, it was easier for them to portray the reality of Africa as compared to the foreign colonizer. With the help of their missionary education and by using their colonizer's tongue, Africans found it easier to reach out to the wider audience to present the true picture of their nation's culture and traditions. Writers like Soyinka and Achebe actively addressed the issue of the African past, and its distortion by the western writers. Chinua Achebe, fondly called the "father of African literature" and Africa's greatest storyteller, shows the deep influence of Africa's cultural traditions in all his works, mostly deliberately, to stress upon the richness of African culture. For example, he makes use of the Igbo folk stories and proverbs abundantly to exhibit philosophical thought of the people. He wrote:

> *I would be quite satisfied if my novels (especially the ones I set in the past) did no more than teach my readers that their past – with all its imperfections – was not one long night of savagery from which the first Europeans acting on God's behalf delivered them.*[1]

With the increased interest of Africans in novels, as well as of the readers worldwide, now willing to know more about this long-neglected part of the world, the African novelists felt the urge to pen down their own experiences. They began writing more about their own life and society. Some wrote of the pre-colonial Africa, in its original state, while some chose to write about the transforming lives under the colonial effect. The civil wars tearing apart the lives of their people post-independence still continues to be a favourite motif in the novels of Africa. Achebe, Amadi, Emecheta, Nwapa, Ngozi, Thiong'o etc. are just a few big names among a multitude of good writers that have portrayed the African reality breaking the myth of a dimwit populace and barbaric society propagated by the likes of Conrad and Cary.

But while the world has expanded its focus of study from political and social to inter-personal and domestic relationships as far as the study of American and European literature is concerned, the primary interest in Africa is still largely limited to the post-colonial studies.

The search for a personal anchorage and the restlessness in modern man is beautifully depicted in most modern works, and is subject of widespread scholarly interest to the critics across the world. The themes of love and marriage, inter and intra-personal relationships and the domestic space have begun to inspire research work in a marked shift from the political and social angle that dominated most studies earlier.

Historians have addressed the rise of romantic love and marriage and their breaking up in the western world, while anthropologists have explored the ways in which globalization has reshaped local ideas about those same topics. Yet, as far as studies focusing on African literature are concerned, littérateurs are still more comfortable dealing with the themes of post colonialism and cultural conflict as opposed to the human relationships in Africa. Love and marriage in Africa has been peculiarly ignored, resulting in a serious lack of understanding about such vital elements of social life – a glaring omission given the intense focus on love, matrimony and sexuality in the African society.

The second part of the introductory chapter deals with the importance of love and marriage as constant themes in literature and the focus has been mainly put on literature of Africa, dealing with the representation of love and marriage in them. The importance of love as a theme in African literature has been presented, citing the examples of some novels written by the Africans, showcasing the culture and society of Africa. Works like *The Marriage of Anansewa*, *The Bride Price* and *The Concubine* have dealt with the theme of love expansively through their pages, and hence have been analysed for the purpose of this research. The representation of various aspects of love, like, man-woman relationship, parent-child relationship, friendhip and an individual's love for his native land etc, have been pointed out to portray the recurrent thematic importance of love in the literature of Africa. Also, the various types of matrimonial alliances shown by the African novelists in their works, presenting the real picture of the land has also been anlysed in this chapter, along with the different aspects of an African marriage like the settling of marriage, settlement and payment of the bride price, gender equations, polygamy, widow remarriage etc.

This research work has sought to understand the importance of love and marriage in the African social scenario through the novels of Elechi Amadi, Buchi Emecheta and Chinua Achebe. In a substantive introduction and three chapters dealing with a novel each of these three writers, this thesis argues for the importance of paying attention to the many different cultural and historical strands that constitute love and marriage in Africa. The Eurocentric gaze on the exploration of finer emotions and relationship in Africans have tended to look at African love through the lens of provider love, that is, love based on the man's ability to provide financially for the woman, implying that African do not have the capacity to feel or express romantic love. However to do this is to impose an inappropriate and prejudicial eye upon African modes of loving, desire and matrimonial alliances. The African way of love and marriage may appear different from the way in which the people of the West express love and exercise marriage, but that does not mean that Africans are incapable of communicating and experiencing love for each other or enjoying the institution of marriage. They have done so from time immemorial and this study has sought to analyse and emphasise the importance of the ways in which Africans show love, court one another, marry and have families, on the basis of the texts selected for this research work.

Dealing with the young people's ideas about love and courtship, various rituals associated with marriage, the different types of matrimonial alliances permissible in the African society, the kind of relationship shared by man and wife, the gender roles allocated to the partners in a marriage, polygamy, bride price, widow remarriage etc. all these aspects throw a vivid and compelling look at the treatment and role of love and marriage in African society as seen through these novels. They not only portray the present social scenario but also express hope for the future. *The Bride Price*, for example, brings to light a lot of things that is wrong in the Igbo society of Ibuza, through the portrayal of Aku-nna's parents' marriage and later her uncle-cum-stepfather's household and mentality, yet Emecheta presents the transformation of the timid girl into a woman holding her own, one who dares to love and stand by it, breaking the age-old system of caste and oppressive tradition, heralding a progressive society for future.

In the African society, especially the ones presented by these novelists, that is, Amadi, Emecheta and Achebe, love and marriage form the basis of domestic relationships and the society at large. Love plays an instrumental role in the development of characters in all three novels taken under this research work. Various aspects of love and its forms have been beautifully painted in these novels. Love, across literature, stands out as a force to reckon with, and these novels present the all encompassing power of love, that can win over anything and everything any given day based on its purity and honesty.

Amadi presents love as a force of desire as well as an emotion that enables supreme sacrifice and compassion. Ekwueme's love for Ihuoma is not only fuelled by his desire for her, but also through mutual respect, kindness and compassion. He feels sorry for the young widow initially but gradually gets attracted towards her. His love is not superficial, inspired only by her beauty. In fact, he loves her poise and grace, her self-respecting demeanour as well as her caring attitude towards everyone. In her, he is able to find the motherly love that is missing in Ahurole by far. For Ahurole is a petulant child, not yet mature enough to understand the demands of a relationship. In Ekwueme's madness for Ihuoma, Amadi explores the adamance of a lover and the force of love exhibited through Ihuoma's kindness that can win over any ailment. The way Ihuoma nurtures him back to health is symbolic of the healing power of love. Later, when the hero gets to know of Ihuoma's reality (about her past life), he is least bothered and not at all afraid. He is happy to be able to get even a moment in this life with Ihuoma if that is all he were to get before becoming victim to the wrath of the Sea-King. And true enough, Ekwueme dies a hero in the eyes of the reader.

The other form of love that Amadi deals with in the novel is that of jealousy or rivalry. Ahurole's jealousy of her husband's desire for Ihuoma makes her do the unthinkable. Ignoring the warnings of Anyika, the village *dibia*, or the medicine man, she goes ahead and administers a love potion to her husband that has an extremely negative reaction. Far from falling in love with her, the potion works in such a manner that Ekwueme loses his sanity, and even in his madness he yearns for Ihuoma, way more than before. Under the influence of the medicine, he stops caring for what the society would say and openly shows his love for the woman he had always set his heart upon. Ahurole's jealousy only drives him farther away.

On the other hand, the Sea-King's rivalry with any human who dared to love Ihuoma and thought of marrying her has a more sinister aspect. The Sea-King put an end to the life of every man that dared to love his concubine. Starting from the death of Emenike, then Madume, and finally Ekwueme, this supernatural force continues to exhibit his love and possessiveness towards his concubine from her past life. He spares no one, no matter how true the love might be. The Sea-King, in his jealousy, does not even think of the effect his wrath might have on Ihuoma. Twice she is left shattered in the novel, failing to understand where her fault lay. Having no memory of the past life in this present human incarnation, the poor woman comes across as a victim of one-sided love by the parahuman force on which she had no control.

Emecheta's portrayal of love is more intertwined with the mores of society and its dictates. Though playing with the psychological hold myth has on customs and people, Buchi Emecheta has chosen to underline scientific explanation to the victory of the myth rather than blaming the supernatural forces, highlighting the strength of love that could mould a timid girl into a rebel of the society. After her father's death in Lagos the thirteen-year-old girl Aku-nna, along with her mother and brother, returns to live in the family village Ibuza, and is inherited by her father's brother, an ambitious would-be chief, who later inherits her mother too and gives her the long-desired pregnancy that she had been anxious for. Aku-nna is allowed to continue her schooling under the belief that it would increase her bride price for the benefit of her avaricious uncle.

She falls in love with her teacher, Chike Ofulue, who is an '*Osu*', but their marriage is forbidden by the ancient tribal taboo since his family is descended from slaves. After Aku-nna is kidnapped by the son of a leading Ibuza family, her own family is obliged to agree to her marriage with her abductor, as per the ancient custom of the village. Chike, her lover, dramatically saves her from her abductors before the marriage formalities are complete and they elope to another village where they both find jobs and a comfortable home. Their union not only defies the taboo against inter-marriages of 'free' and 'slave' families, but it also challenges an ancient belief that any woman who marries against the will and wishes of her family and whose bride price remains unpaid would die in childbirth.

Though the doctors had already pronounced Aku-nna's pregnancy difficult citing her weak and malnourished body that was not fit enough to carry a child, yet her belief in the myth of the bride price plays constantly in her mind. Chike's family does its best to to put Aku-nna's mind at rest by offering the customary bride price. But bent on vengeance and full of spite, Aku-nna's uncle refuses to accept the match or the bride price. Superstitious dread takes hold of Aku-nna and the ancient curse seems to hold sway when she dies in childbirth. Though Emecheta has presented the hold of the curse, her logical explanation of Aku-nna's death, and the description of the happy matrimony Aku-nna had enjoyed with Chike proves that though defeated by her circumstances, her love had given her unprecedented strength. Her joy, a reflection of the love she got from Chike could not have been possible without the intensity of love she enjoyed with him. For Aku-nna and Chike, their love was the power that enabled them to build a life together going against the norms of society. It was their love that gave them the strength to follow their heart and live a life of marital bliss however shortlived it might have been, rather than suffering under the yoke of customs and tradition all their life, harbouring just regrets on what could have been. They lived happily as long as they could and this was the power that they got from their love for each other – to build a life away from family, away from their village, finding completion in each other.

Achebe's concern in *Things Fall Apart* is primarily the clash of cultures, but on a closer reading, the theme of love runs glaring through the novel. Love here, is not just the love between man and woman, but is represented through multiple characters in a wide range of relationships, in defferent aspects. While the quintessential man-woman love finds its representation in the man-wife relationship of Okonkwo and Ekwefi, his second wife, there are various other forms of love that find portrayal through the inter-personal relations between other characters.

Okonkwo and Ekwefi's love is the kind of primeval love that has existed since always, even before the formation of civilization. Sexual desire and the will to stay together, layered with concern for each other form the highlight of their love. Various instances in the novel suggest that Okonkwo loved and respected Ekwefi for her free spirit and quick tongue even if his inflated ego took offence at the slightest of banters with her.

Platonic love, defined by friendship, kindness and compassion also runs across the novel through the relationship shared by Okonkwo and Obierika, Nwoye and Ikemefuna, Ekwefi and Chielo. These three pairs exhibit the finest example of love in friendship in the behavior they exhibit for each other. Kindness, concern, compassion form the highlight of the kind of love they shared with each other.

Parent-child relationship and the mutual love they hold for each other is best explored by Achebe through the depiction of Ezinma, and her relationship with both her parents. The comfort, ease and understanding that she shares with Ekwefi and Okonkwo forms the basis of their love for one another. Ezinma's love for Okonkwo is highlighted through her waiting for return to Umuofia before accepting any marriage proposal. Not only does she wait herself, but also convinces her sister to wait so that they can get back to their village and court boys from influential families there, which would help Okonkwo in regaining his social stature. Okonkwo too, full of love for his daughter, many a time, wishes Ezinma were his son and successor.

Another major kind of love portrayed by Achebe in his novel is patriotic love. Okonkwo's love for his land, its culture, traditions and customs is the central moving force in his life. His desire to prove himself worthy of his land, the desire to save it from the foreign invasion and interference moves the major plot of the novel. His love for the land he was born into, his father's land holds his heart inspite of the fact that he had no love lost for his father. In fact, if anything, he abhorred him and dreaded becoming like him. Yet, his preference for Umuofia weighs stronger than any other emotion he ever had – love for his wives, children, friends or even the mother's land. Achebe explores Okonkwo's patriotism throughout the novel, and when Okonkwo sees his land and its people failing him, he prefers to kill himself than witness its decline.

Love has always had a place in every society and culture since the beginning of time. Love binds people, love blinds people. Love builds lives of togetherness, or love may put someone in an overwhelming state of euphoria or break a heart in two. Its power is remarkable. It can change someone forever, or drive him and her to do insane things, that are completely out of their character. Love can never die; it lives on eternally in the heart of every man and woman who have been blessed to find someone to love. Literature has also existed for ages. Its power is no less than the power of love. Literature has for centuries, not just reflected the various aspects of love, but also changed the views and beliefs of individuals and moulded society as well. Love is inself one of the most powerful elements in life. It provides the underlying impetus and thematic content in many works of literature, and the three novelists taken under study in this research work have beautifully presented the power of love in their works. Their novels have explored love in its various forms and expressions. Their novels studied in this research work prove that love is the driving force of life, the force that unites man to woman and a friend to another friend, the magnetism uniting mother to child and child to mother, lover to lover, friend to friend, and man to land.

However, love is not always portrayed as a liberating, life-giving force in literature, as is evident in all three novels taken under this study. Love can be an eternally life giving power as well as an oppressive, even fatal force. Ihuoma's supernatural lover, the Sea-King brings grief and regret to her by snatching the life of her husband and lover due to his envy. Ahurole's love for Ekwueme proves fatal for her own marriage to him. Aku-nna's love for Chike makes her an outcaste in her own village, with her friends and family turning away from her. Okonkwo's love for his masculinre image makes him go against his heart and take part in the killing of Ikemefuna, distancing him from his own son. And later, his love for his land and his inability to accept the change in the people due to the foreigner's advent makes him take his own life, once again proving how fatal love can be. The power of love and its impact on the characters in the novels highlight the thematic importance of love.

Apart from the theme of love, one of the most elaborate cultural traditions practiced in the novels taken for analysis in this research work is the custom of marriage. John Mbiti in the book *African Religions and Philosophy* relates that marriage is a complex affair with economic and religious aspects which often overlap so firmly that they cannot be separated from one another. For Africans, marriage is the focus of existence. It is the point where all the members of a given community meet: the departed, the living and those yet to be born. Marriage is a duty, a requirement. A person who does not participate in it is considered a failure by the society.

The family plays an instrumental role in the individual's life and matrimony. The family, most often functionally (not just emotionally), encompasses a wide range of relatives, including grandparents, parents, children, brothers and sisters, cousins, aunts and uncles, etc. Even when all these people do not live in the same house or compound, the sense of communal responsibility, obligation and authority is wide ranging and strongly felt and encouraged.

The individual is of less importance as compared to the collective tribe. The domestic relationships, even between husband and wife and their own children is not independent of the society's interference. Each personal decision-making is influenced by a large variety of individuals and social situations. Issues of love affairs, matrimonial alliances, birth control, child planning, sexual conduct, education, allocation of economic resources, etc. are all often a part of group discussions before any decision is finally made in their regard. The traditional village community dictates the individual's life in a large way. A case in point is the village meeting to chastise Okonkwo for beating his youngest wife during the Week of Peace in *Things Fall Apart*.

Emmanuel Obiechina points out in '*Culture, Tradition and Society in West African Novel*':

> *The identification of the individual with the group of which he forms part, and with its social and cultural outlook, is the very essence of traditionalism. It finds expression in the individual's acquiescence in the beliefs and customs of the group and his sharing with the rest of the group a feeling of social unity. His individual self-interest is always subordinated to the overall interest of the group. This is an important traditional value which the novelists*

emphasize contrasting it with the opposite value based on individual self-interest in the modern urban situation.[2]

In almost all the novels we can witness the societal impression about marriage being a source of security and legitimate support for the woman. The role of a wife is confined to the domestic space, catering exclusively to the male wants. The general refusal to accept any flexibility in this role reflects the attitude of the Africans – men and also women, to a great extent. The gender division is deeply etched in the minds of the people, playing a major role in not just shaping their perspective but also the society as a whole. For example, in all the three novels taken up for study in this work, it is prominently mentioned how it is a man's job to grow yams and no matter how many more crops the wife might grow and sell in the market, the man is still the master, and the one allowed to grow the king of crops, yam! Masculinity is revered while femininity is looked down upon.

No novel highlights this distinction more appropriately than Achebe in *Things Fall Apart*. In *Things Fall Apart*, Okonkwo is driven by his fear of femininity. His furious manhood overpowers everything "feminine" in his life, including his own conscience. For example, when he feels bad after being forced to kill his adopted son, he asks himself: "When did you become a shivering old woman?"[3] It is also argued that one's chi, or personal god, is the 'mother within'. This understanding further demonstrates how Okonkwo's hyper masculinity corrupts his conscience, as his contempt for his own mother and other women prevents him from being in harmony with his chi. He views all things feminine as distasteful, in part because they remind him of his father's laziness and cowardice. His father was considered an *agbala*—a word that refers to a man without title, but is also synonymous with 'woman'. Thus, Okonkwo not only regrets his father's lack of success, but attributes it to a lack of masculinity. Okonkwo's feminization of all things lacking success or power is a common theme throughout the novel. His obsession with maleness is fuelled by an intense fear of femaleness, which he expresses through physical and verbal abuse of his wives, his violence towards his community, his constant worry that his son Nwoye is not manly enough, and his wish that his daughter Ezinma had been born a boy. The women in the novel, meanwhile, are obedient, quiet, and absent from positions of authority – despite the fact that Igbo women were traditionally involved in village leadership. Nevertheless, the need for feminine balance is highlighted by Ani, the earth goddess, and the extended discussion of "Nneka" ("Mother is supreme") in chapter fourteen, when Okonkwo is living in exile from Umuofia. Ekwefi's perseverance and love for Ezinma, despite her many miscarriages, is seen as a tribute to Igbo womanhood, which is typically defined by motherhood. Okonkwo's defeat is also viewed by some as a vindication of the need for a balancing feminine ethos. It can also be argued that Okonkwo's failures are tied to his contempt and fear of women and his inability to form quality personal relationships with the women in his life—his wives, his children, and his own mother. Indeed, it is argued that Okonkwo's violent and vehement anti-women position is the exception, not the norm, within his community of Umuofia and the wider Igbo society. Still, the secondhand treatment of the woman in marriage is more than obvious in the multiple depictions of the suppressed subjugated wife in almost all the novels.

Molara Ogundipe-Leslie discusses in *'The Female Writer and her Commitment'* that:

> *The myth of the unchanging, naïve rural woman seems to coincide with the actual social practice and tendency of men to discourage change and innovation in women's lives.*[4]

Women were supposed to stay confined in their roles of daughter, wife, mother, and any transgression from it dislodged the angel from her pedestal, landing her down, not even fit for the ground on which men walked. She was deemed no longer fit to reenter the domestic space. When Aku-nna lies to Okoboshi in *The Bride Price* about her loss of virginity to Chike, he feels cheated. Not even once does he repent abducting the girl without her consent to marry, instead he abuses her physically and verbally, saying that 'she was nothing but a common slut'[5].

Elechi Amadi has also beautifully portrayed this predicament of women in his novel *Estrangement*. Alekiri had built up an extra-marital relationship in the absence of her husband Ibekwe, during the war. Ibekwe is unable to accept this transgression inspite of ample proof of his own promiscuity in the meanwhile. He thinks that his wife has stepped beyond the limits of her role as a wife and thus there is no forgiveness for her. Despite all her efforts she is unable to convince him to restart their marital life together. Once the woman has been dislodged from her traditional role as a wife and mother, she is no longer fit to re-enter domestic space. She is for all purposes considered an outsider and a transgressor of the patriarchal social norms. Woman's condition, inspite of diverse changes in the society, essentially remains the same. She is constantly marginalized and her problems are never quite appreciated by her husband and immediate family. It is, as Mariam Ba has pointed out in an interview:

> *In the family, in the institutions, in society, in the street, in political organizations, discrimination runs supreme. Social pressure shamelessly suffocates individual attempts at change. The woman is heavily burdened by mores and customs, in combination with mistaken and egoistic interpretations of different religions...*[6]

Buchi Emecheta has sketched the role of a woman, trying to fit into the role deigned by the society in *The Bride Price* through the character of Ma Blackie. Inspite of more than a decade of marriage to Ezekiel Odia and two children, she is still made to feel insufficient because she had not given birth to more sons. Just one was not enough in society where marriage was mainly orchestrated to procure maximum number of children, especially sons. She is constantly taunted by her husband as well as the neighbours and is sent off to the village to consult the dibia, or the medicine man, regarding her 'infertility'. Later, when Ezekiel Odia dies, she gets married to his brother as per the Igbo custom. This comes as no surprise that inspite of having lived in the city of Lagos, she adheres to the rules of Ibuza because marriage would not only provide security and legitimate support to her and children, but also a renewed chance at motherhood, for which she had been craving so long. Her life is representative of the married women in the African society, whose primary purpose in life is to bear children – the more the better.

Emecheta's another work, *The Joys of Motherhood* deals with the aspiration of a married woman, Nnu Ego, whose sole ambition in life is to have children who would take care of her in her old age. Unfortunately, even after bearing multiple children, most of whom die, leaving her childless for the major part of her life, and finally having a few who live, none are there to take care of her in the end; thus, leaving her longing for the joys of motherhood all her life. The title of the novel is derived from Flora Nwapa's novel *Efuru*, which reads:

> *Efuru slept soundly that night. She dreamt of the woman of the lake, her beauty, her long hair and her riches. She had lived for ages at the bottom of the lake. She was as old as the lake itself. She was happy, she was wealthy. She was beautiful. She gave women beauty and wealth but she had no child. She had never experienced the joy of motherhood. Why then did the women worship her?*[7]

Such was the society's construct that for a woman, to be married and bear children, was essential not only to elevate her in the eyes of the society, but also to prove self-worth in her own eyes. Efuru's only daughter from her first marriage had died and her husband had eloped with another girl. She was unable to get pregnant again in her second marriage and thus was mistreated and humiliated by her second husband who openly favoured his other wives, who were his children's mother, to her. Though she is later chosen by the goddess of the lake, Uhamiri, to be one of her worshippers, and hence is respected by all, yet because of being childless, she is unable to get the love of her husband and lives a life of frustration. Nwapa's Efuru, like the lady of the lake that she dreams about, is beautiful and wealthy, but because she is childless, she is bewildered and frustrated. She is a clever and successful trader, yet when she fails to deliver a child to her husband, her existence is reduced to a shadow in the mystical world of gods and goddesses. Just like Ma Blackie, her life is also an enactment of the life of a tribal African woman, expected to fulfill the conventional role of wife and mother for a worthy place in society. Not all the reverence (of the people for her mystical status) or the money she got with this service could help her establish her worth in the eyes of the people, husband or her own self. She was always thought of as incomplete because she had no children.

Another aspect of marriage highlighted in the novels under this study is the limited freedom to choose one's partner. The young boys and girls were encouraged to court each other with the approval of the guardian, yet, the choice of marriage was largely dependent on the parental acceptance. In case of the parent's (read father's) disapproval, the couple was left only with two choices – either to forget their affair or to elope.

In Amadi's *The Concubine*, Ihuoma says no to Ekwueme's proposal for marriage citing how angry and disappointed his parents would be if he were to break off his long-standing marriage to Ahurole and marry her instead – a widow with three children:

> *"And think of your parents, and the girl's parents too. They would be very angry with you and even more so with me. Indeed I would be the laughing stock of all the women in the village. Ekwe, please give up the idea."* [8]

The sanction of the parents was a must for marriage, not just for social acceptance, but also for the peace of mind of the couple involved. Without the approval of the parents, the question of the bride price remained unanswered leading to more complexities, as seen in Emecheta's *The Bride Price*. The belief that the bride price if unpaid would continue to torement the newly weds, leading to the death of the bride in childbirth haunts the lead character Aku-nna who had eloped with her lover, Chike. Her step father Okonkwo in this anger refuses the multiple offers made by Chike's father for the bride price. Aku-nna dies haunted by the myth of the bride price while delivering her first child.

Another notable feature of the African marriage presented in the novels is the general camaraderie between the co-wives. There is a sense of togetherness and a community feeling among the women that sustains them even in their days of intense psychological crisis and loneliness. Though there is, but naturally, a kind of rivalry between them sensed from time to time, yet they enjoyed each other's company and support each other like sisters most of the times. The wives of Okonkwo in *The Bride Price,* especially the first wife, are in a constant struggle to show their superiority over the other co-wives. Yet when the moment of crisis arrives in the form of Aku-nna's abduction, they all moaned her loss together, cursing the abductor for carrying away the girl of the house. The relationship between the co-wives of Okonkwo in *Things Fall Apart* is not only healthier but also more genuine. These women not only enjoy each other's company but seem to form a united sisterhood which acts as a bulwark against the demands of a patriarchal social set up. The shared experiences and common cultural responses to female oppression leads to a solidarity among them which is evident in the way they stand for each other and try to protect each other. They try their best to alleviate Okonkwo's anger whenever they feel one of them is in danger of getting a sound thrashing from him and also care for the other's children as their own. Katherine Frank comments in *Women Without Men: The Feminist Novel In Africa:*

> *Given the historically established and culturally sanctioned sexism of African society there is no possibility of a compromise, or even truce with the enemy. Instead, women must spurn patriarchy in all its guises and create a safe, sane, supportive world of women: a world of mothers and daughters, sisters and friends.*[9]

The different attitudes of women, portrayed in different novels by these novelists show the heterogeneous nature of women in the African marriage. Some accept the husband as the god incarnate and ask no questions, forever bowed down in submission, they do every bidding of his, obliged that he asked. There are some others, however, who rise in defiance of this mute slavery and assert their own individuality. Both these variants can be seen in Okonkwo's household in *Things Fall Apart* in the character of his first and second wife. The domesticity of the first wife works in stark contrast to Ekwefi's independent spirit – bold, confident and holding her own even in front of a fierce and short-tempered man like Okonkwo. The insignificance of the first wife is glaring in the writer's neglect in allowing her to own even a name of her own. Keeping in line with her lack of individuality; shadowed by her complete submission to her husband, Achebe does not even care to refer to her as anything but the 'first wife' throughout the novel. That is her whole identity – someone's wife. That's it. On the other hand, the other two wives, who do dare to assert their identity or follow their will even if it means going against the husband's wishes, have at least some individuality left in them, and thus have themselves called by their own names – Ekwefi and Ojiugo.

But even if women like Ekwefi dared to assert their individuality at times, the general state of women was such that inspite of all the freedom that a woman could enjoy in her own right, she is always shown as holding a disadvantageous position as compared to her husband. The wife had to take care of the house, the husband, the crops and farms, of selling the produce in the market, yet she always stood on the lower end of the gender equation. The wives, all different in temperament and nature, have one thing in common – that they are all perceived as inferior beings, who are better off serving the males. Each and every woman, no matter how dominant and influential in her home or her village, could not be considered as enjoying equal status with men. Most African societies had a strong bias favouring the male superiority. The basic framework of the African society is one of patriarchy, where, as elsewhere, men rule and dominate. To quote Hafkin and Bay:

> *Though women had a substantial measure of economic independence and a voice in political affairs in many parts*

of the continent, they were not dominant, as some have said they were not equal.[10]

These novelists have highlighted the complex nature of the gender relations where on account of the strict nature of patriarchal social norms, the wife is always the second sex, the smaller partner in marriage. In such a rigid social structure, where sex roles are clearly demarcated, there is very little scope for a woman to protest. Francis Imbuga, in his play *The Married Bachelor* clearly brings forth this disparity when Mary tells her boyfriend Denis that she has a child by another man. He refuses to accept her, even though he himself has a son by another woman. Elechi Amadi in his novel *Estrangement* highlights a similar plight in the case of Alekiri. She had started an affair with Dansuku when her husband Ibekwe was away in the war, with no news of his return. Alekiri contemplates on her relationship with Ibekwe and remembers that her husband had a girlfriend too before marriage but she had never bothered about it, nor questioned her husband ever in this regard. She comes to the conclusion that marriage in itself is a faulty institution:

> *Marriage is a sham, a make-belief. It is not worth it…Men only love themselves. To them women are mere property. Touch their property and they are mad. And in their madness, the destroy the property. Marriage is not worth it. Better to have a lover. Men value lovers more than wives. If I were his lover he would not treat me so badly.*[11]

In the novel, Alekiri, disillusioned by Ibekwe's treatment, understands 'marriage' to be a kind of emotional death-trap and never wants to get into it again. Yet her fear of staying single and lonely in a world where marriage is considered an essential security for women brings her to accept Dansuku's proposal for marriage. Women are conditioned in such a way that they can rarely establish an identity independent of a man. The daughter, the wife, the sister etc… these are the roles that the world has put on a pedestal and more often than not, the woman dies trying to perfect these roles, rather than try to have an individual identity. To belong is the highest honour. And the woman in marriage, or even during the courtship, does everything in her capacity to keep proving that she belongs to the man, the master in this relation of unequals.

This wish of the woman to 'belong' is also visible in Aku-nna's submissive attitude towards Chike. Inspite of the fact that Chike was madly in love with her and respected her, and he would never have forced her against her will to do anything, yet time and again she keeps trying her best to please him and nurture his ego lest he should feel hurt or bad in any way, keeping her own likes and dislikes aside. She cares nothing of her own discomfort while ensuring that he was having his will fulfilled, as that was what she had seen her mother and aunts do…this was the cultural conditioning she had received as a girl since childhood. Though Chike was nothing like the typical men she had seen all her life, yet she behaved like the typical mute, ready-to-please girl she had always been raised up as:

> *"I love you, Chike. Please teach me how to give you joy."…Soon she learned how he wanted her to give him pleasure.*[12]

In an earlier instance, when Aku-nna and Chike had just professed their love to each other, Chike is overcome with emotions for her and starts kissing her. Now, although this could be seen as a very natural act for lovers, the fact that Aku-nna did not really like it, yet gave in without the slightest of dissent just to please Chike, once again highlights the gender dynamics in the African society. The joy on his calling her 'Akum' which means, 'my wealth', shows how she loves the idea of being 'owned' by a man like Chike. Her submissive attitude and the willingness to please him a kind of slave mentality handed down to women over generations is obvious over and over again:

> *He did not know what else to do but to start kissing her the way Europeans did in films. Aku-nna knew one was*

supposed to enjoy being kissed but she did not know how to enjoy it. She had read in old copies of True Romances that kissing was meant to do something to a girl. Well, it had done nothing for her, but she let him have his play. All she wanted was to make him happy…[13]

In *Things Fall Apart* we witness a similar response in the behavior of Okonkwo's first wife, who is habituated to perform all her duties towards her husband and her household and even when the husband demands something out of the ordinary, she does not have the freedom to question or seek explanation from him. She is simply to do as told without asserting her own thoughts on any matter. When Okonkwo entrusts her with Ikemefuna, she is told that she needs to take care of him like her own child. Her basic enquiry about how long the boy would stay with them is snubbed rudely by Okonkwo:

'Do what you are told, woman', Okonkwo thundered and stammered.[14]

Granted, that Okonkwo himself did not have the answer to this question as the elders of the village were to decide the fate of Ikemefuna some other time later, yet instead of rebuking his wife for such a genuine question, he could have answered properly. But this basic respect of a man for his wife is something that seems to be largely missing in the African society. On the other hand, the wives are constantly in service of their husbands, barely raising their voices while speaking to them, let alone talking back.

The subdued, submissive, slave-like behavior of these women is representative of the cultural conditioning of women which force them to depend upon men. Simone de Beauvoir has pointed out this predicament of women in the context of European women, which seems equally valid for African women too:

The privileged place held by men in economic life, their social usefulness, the prestige of marriage, the value of

> *masculine backing, all this makes women wish ardently to please men. Women are still, for the most part, in a state of subjugation. It follows that woman sees herself and makes her choices not in accordance with her true nature in itself, but as man defines her... Representation of the world, like the world itself, is the work of men; they describe it from their own point of view, which they confuse for the absolute truth.*[15]

All the novels studied in this research work reflect the social realities in terms of love and marriage in Africa. The purpose of this study has been to highlight the thematic importance of these two themes in the works taken under the study. The treatment of love as a liberating experience empowering an individual to break away from the shackles of cultural monotony has been beautifully expressed in these three novels. Also, the power of love that can take lives and break the psyche is also treated with sensitivity in the novels under study. The treatment of marriage can be said to be full of duality, portraying both the negative and positive aspects of the institution in terms of society and individual relationships. While on the one hand, we see marriage offering the sanctioned joy of togetherness to a couple, we also witness its crippling effect on the individuality of the person, especially if the person belongs to the female gender.

This study focuses on an analysis of the selected texts for the study, with particular focus on the themes of love and marriage. The study analyses love and marriage and their role in the development of the characters. These two relationships work to empower the characters, as well as weaken them from the core as per their situation in life. While the effect of love seems to be equal on both parties in the relationships under analysis in the selected novels, the effect of marriage undoubtedly sways in favour of man; such is the state of gender equation in the African society.

The true test of woman continues to be the marriage institution. In this closed-in arena, every married woman is to fight out her survival as an individual. The marriage paradox lies in the fact that it is both sublimating and subsuming. Through it, a woman attains a status acclaimed by society and fulfills her biological need of procreation and companionship. Through it too, the woman's place of a second-class citizen is emphasized and too easily, she is lost in anonymity to the benefit and enhancement of the household. The woman in marriage is conditioned to believe that she is married and thus traditionally bound to be subjugated completely to her husband and his family – her earnings, her attention and her entire self now belongs to him who has wed her, or to his family. She has no hold on her own life. The payment of the bride price made by the husband's family has enslaved her to them for life.

Though the women in marriage are sometimes able to move from a state of powerlessness to a state of self-awareness and maturity where they are able to take decisions for themselves, to break away from all forms of oppression and to assert their individuality, like Ma Blackie, who finally stands in support of her daughter and removes the pins from the doll that her husband had kept for voodoo, or black magic on Aku-nna, yet such examples are far and few. Most of the women live and die in silence, suffering under the yoke of patriarchy, considering it their destiny to be oppressed and suppressed. The girls, from an early age, are made to internalize and believe that marriage is the only institution through which they can assert their womanhood or individuality. Thus we see a girl, not even having reached the age of puberty, Aku-nna, dreaming of making her father proud of her by marrying a man who would pay a heavy bride price for her. This was her idea of gaining love and respect from her father. Such ideas, internalized by the female characters, help in upholding the patriarchal nature of the society and in flourishing of their oppression. Traditionally accepted practices like the bride price, wife-beating, widowhood rites, polygamy etc. continue to keep the women in a secondary position. However, the characters in the novels taken for this study show that all of them did not simply accept their fate. In fact, they reacted in the best way they could, and whenever given an option, they rebelled against this system. Hence, we witness Ihuoma finally listening to her heart and thinking about her own happy future with Ekwueme, Aku-nna eloping with Chike to start a new life away from the constraints of Ibuza and Ekwefi asserting her will and using her words to express her thoughts whenever she could.

The treatment of love, like marriage, forms the basis of this research work, and the selected texts have been analysed from the point of view of this theme to outline its importance in the selected works under this study.

Amadi in *The Concubine* depicts the hold of love on Ekwueme which is so powerful that he cannot turn from it inspite of the strict social code. Ekwueme had been engaged to Ahurole since childhood and everyone expected them to get married any day now that they were both of marriageable age. But he had fallen in love with Ihuoma, and nothing, that anyone, including Ihuoma herself could say, could discourage his feeling for her. His father suspicious of his feeling for the young widow takes it upon himself to discourage his son from harbouring feelings for Ihuoma and talks of getting him married to Ahurole at the earliest:

> "... *Tomorrow I am going to start negotiations on Ahurole. I have informed her parents and relations. Everything is ready. We can't go back. I tell you it is almost an abomination to break off an enagement like this. It is unheard of. No one will ever side with you. 'Ekwueme's heart jumped into his stomach. A sickening sensation assailed him. His father was right, of course. Worse, tradition was decidedly against him and thought of kicking against it unnerved him. It would be sensational news in the village. Then he thought of Ihuoma. Suddenly his father was no longer there. In his phase Ihuoma stood smiling wistfully, a deep affection glowing in her eyes. Energy surged through him and his eyes shone.*[16]

The very thought of Ihuoma fills him with renewed energy to fight the society for his love. Although Ihuoma declines his proposal due to the social constraints and propriety, his love for her does not falter. He gets married to Ahurole because Ihuoma wants him to. But even marriage cannot take his mind off his first love. Ahurole filled with envy, uses a love potion on him, which has a reaction and turns him mentally deranged.

Even in this madness, he seeks just one person – and that is Ihuoma. Ahurole runs away fearing discovery of her act and punishment for it, but Ekwueme has no care in the world except to see Ihuoma day and night. Ihuoma also finally gives in to her emotion, in the face of Ekwueme undying passion and nurses him back to health. When the two finally agree on marriage, another hurdle comes in the form of the spirit world. The exquisitely beautiful Ihuoma turns out to be the concubine of the Sea-King, cursed to a human life by him for her action in her last life. Even as his concubine she had fallen in love with a mortal and had yearned to live on earth with him. Sea-King miffed with this act of hers yet too much in love with her to punish her severely decides to humour her and gives her a life on earth as a human.

Though he has condemned her to human life, yet his love and possessiveness for her is such that he cannot bear any man as her husband even in this life and ends up bringing death to anyone who dares to own her. Ekwueme's love however, empowers him so much that he does not back down even in the phase of supernatural beings working against him:

> 'Dede, I do not know whether you believe this or not. It does not matter. One thing is clear, I shall marry Ihuoma. She is a human being and if marrying a woman like her is fatal mistake. I am prepared to make it. If I am her husband for a day before my death my soul will go singing happily to the spirit world. There also I shall be prepared to dare the wrath of four hundred Sea-Kings for her sake.[17]

The doomed love of the ordinary mortal, Ekwueme, finds sublimity when faced by the immortal vengeful wrath of the Sea-King in *The Concubine*, laying importance on the power of love that brings an ordinary man in level with the gods. Though Ekwueme is not spared the wrath of the Sea-King and meets untimely death just like other men who dare to love or desire Ihuoma, yet his valiant love wins the hearts of the readers; and he comes out as the fearless hero who dares to love against the norms of his society and stick by it even against supernatural powers, in the face of imminent death.

The issue of marriage in African society is also dealt in great detail in the novel. Be it the settling of marriage between children by their parents, or the bride price settlement, each small aspect of an African marriage is very realistically portrayed, giving a clear glimpse of the society in context. The issue of widowhood finds a sensitive depiction in the novels of Amadi and Emecheta through their portrayal of the difficulties faced by Ihuoma and Ma Blackie after their husbands' demise.

Both the novelists have dealt with the customs and cultural practices involved with widowhood, like the shaving of the hair of the widow, her staying in mourning for a year, wearing old clothes in that period etc. In some societies, traditions prescribe harsh injunctions for widows. They are denied the use of ornaments, perfumes, flowers, fine clothing, no braiding of hair, etc. In most cases, widows are shaved as a mark of respect for their departed husbands and they are denied all other beautiful things that women cherish. Drawing a parallel between the conditions of widows in Africa and India, Remi Akujobi writes in his paper *"Yesterday You Were Divorced. Today I Am A Widow": An Appraisal of Widowhood Practices and the Effects on the Psyche of Widows in Africa* that in other societies too widows are denied three basic meals a day, they are to sleep on the bare floor and are to observe celibacy and other untold hardships.

In *Shadow Lives: Writings on Widowhood* edited by Uma Chakravarti and Preeti Gill, a broad historical canvas of meanings surrounding the social category "widow", especially in India was clearly painted. The book states that widows are practically exploited in India. They are oppressed and are seen as "shadows of womanhood". The same can be said for the widows in Africa because the diversity and complexity are interwoven in the common experience of loss, deprivation, helplessness and hopelessness.

The death of a loved one brings trauma, grief and a total reconstruction of one's life. Widows experience economic hardship, emotional and social problems and pass through a period of loneliness that affects them to the core. They go through phases of bereavement which include phase of numbing which is the immediate reaction to the loss of the spouse, phase of yearning and searching, and phase of reorganization of their lives, joining the pieces of their disorganized life. In all these phases, a woman's companion is only uncertainty. We see these phases poignantly depicted through Ihuoma's loss.

Looking at widowhood in African societies through the novels taken under study, it is not so hard to have an on-the-spot verdict on the plight of widows. It may not be wrong for one to conclude that economic rather than any other interest is responsible for the treatment widows receive in society. Human greed which exists in African societies very much like others makes it possible for the easy exploitation of the widows, the urge to acquire material wealth, particularly what is considered "free" wealth controls the treatment of widows in society. All other activities, be it the taking away her right to inheritance, right to cultivate yams or the system of levirate marriage, all serve the same purpose. We witness this attitude in Okonkwo's treatment of Ma Blackie in *The Bride Price*, looking to acquire everything that had once belonged to his now deceased brother.

In the same light, the dehumanizing and humiliation the widow passes through in society is all a ploy to make her economically weak and voiceless. Once again, the insistence of the villagers of Ibuza on Ma Blackie discarding her good clothes after the death of Ezekiel Odia and Okonkwo telling them to let her be comes to mind. His interest in her was purely economical. He wanted her to agree to marry him under the levirate marriage system so that he could have a stronger claim on Ezekiel's property and his daughter Aku-nna's bride price in future.

Ihuoma too has to face such humiliating conditions but she had no backing like Okonkwo. Instead, her dead husband's brother only wants her to stay devoted to his dead brother even if she marries elsewhere again as he did not want to see his brother's compound to be overgrown with weed. He has no desire for her but only respect. Nor is he desirous to usurp his late brother's property. However, the general view of a widow as a disadvantaged woman is seen in Madume's attitude toward

Ihuoma after Emenike's death. At first he feels he would be doing her a favour by marrying her now that she was a widow with three children. Also, he has his eyes set on a particular piece of land that had belonged to Emenike and was now in charge of Ihuoma. When Ihuoma spurns his advances, he tries to abuse her and physically overpower her that makes the poor woman shout out for help, and rue the moment that took her husband away and gave villains like Madume the idea that she was easy to get.

Life is a continuous battle for many widows in Africa: marriage, children, religion, tradition, customs, illness and death are everyday hassles for most individuals. But widow in African societies often find these traits of life to be particularly difficult due to the continuing oppression from their different communities. The oppression of widows as stated before occurs through a variety of channels, including religion and tradition. Tradition in this case acts as a victimizer to the widow because in her grief, she is still considered a failed woman but she cannot escape tradition nor can she escape her expectations. These two things so condition the woman that she believes that she is somewhere responsible for her plight; and the condition she is in is not unwarranted.

The issue of widow remarriage is also sensitively dealt with in the novels. Ekwueme and Ahurole's marriage had been fixed by their parents when they were little children, thus there was no question of seeking their thought on the match:

> 'You know,' he said, 'my parents selected Ahurole as soon as she was born. I could hardly pull a bow by then. I really had no choice.' 'That is the usual thing. You dare not go against it...'[18]

Growing up, the two knew well what lay in store for them in terms of marriage, and that they had no individual choice in this regard. Yet, the lad falls in love with another woman and this comes as a source of great consternation to their families and they hurry up their marriage rituals to ensure that the word of the parents does not fall empty. The social set-up, where a widower could easily be the first husband of a girl, but that a widow could be the first wife of the man was absolutely unthinkable, shows the gender inequality persistent in the African society. Ihuoma, the young widow whom Ekwueme falls in love with, is quite clear in rejecting his proposal:

> 'Ekwe, listen,' the woman began. 'You know very well I like you. How can I deny it? You like me too, otherwise you would not want to marry me. But you need a young maiden who would obey you and give you the first fruits of her womb. Do not cheat yourself. I am too old for you. You would soon grow tired of me. My children would be a constant burden on you. No Ekwe, I do not want to spoil your life. Since your childhood you have been engaged to Ahurole. She is young, well-behaved and beautiful. Go and marry her instead.'[19]

But of course, there are numerous examples of older man taking on young virgin for his wife. The wife has to be the mother to children older than her many a time in such marriages and it is considered absolutely normal by all.

Ma Blackie too is married for a second time to her deceased husband's brother. This showcases another significant rule that we get to witness in an African marriage, that is, how the wife is a family property. Okonkwo takes on Ma Blackie as his fourth wife, inheriting everything that his brother had acquired in his lifetime, including his wife. Even after the death of the husband, his family continues to be the guardian and the widow's keeper. Whether the brother of the deceased marries the widow as in *The Bride Price*, or not as in *The Concubine*, yet he continues to be the custodian of his brother's widow. Marriage proceedings in respect of a widow were not long-drawn or protracted. The main thing was the payment of the bride price to the family of the deceased husband after seeking permission from the deceased husband's family as the woman would continue to belong to her husband's family even after being widowed if her bride price was not paid back to that family. For example, we witness Ekwueme seeking Nnadi's consent to marry Ihuoma. Nnadi 'had no objections to the marriage provided Emenike's compound was not allowed to fall to pieces.'[20] The novel presents the social scenario through Ihuoma's life and her lovers.

Buchi Emecheta's *The Bride Price* is preoccupied with the love story of Aku-nna and Chike that goes against social conventions and defies the age-old concepts of class and caste to establish the supremacy of love above all. Aku-nna is an introvert who finds a confidante and her confidence in Chike and their friendship soon turns into love. But the fact that Chike was an *osu*, the son of a prosperous farmer slave, presents a problem for their relationship due to social divide between them. The theme of forbidden love triumphing over a tradition that allowed minimum freedom to to young hearts brings to force the reality of new Africa – the modern land that has seen a vast change from the old ways due to modern education and missionary interference in day-to-day life. The title of the novel is derived from a practice which is still very much in vogue in most African societies i.e., the payment of bride price.

The bride price refers to a previously agreed upon amount paid by a groom to the family of the woman he is marrying. This practice, based on the idea of give-and-take relationship between man and woman, is inherently transactional; the girls are considered property that can be bought and sold. This practice shows the deep-rooted gender-bias in the society, which is also the cause of domestic and gender-based violence to a great extent. Such practice encourages commodization of women and strips them of autonomy and personhood. In Ibuza, as in many African communities, girls are brought up with the idea that they are to be a source of wealth to their families through the bride price they'd procure, and Aku-nna was brought up no different.

The South African philosopher and social critic, Mokokoma Mokhonoana, has commented that *Lobola (bride price) is a retired broke father's last hope to paying off his debts.* We see this thought substantiated in Emecheta's *The Bride Price,* wherein Aku-nna's step -father has his hopes pinned on her future bride price to further his own social ambitions of buying titles for himself using that money. Aku-nna, herself, had nothing more to desire than a lavish marriage with a heavy bride price while her own father lived as she wanted to do him proud.

This shows the general conditioning of the society where the girls were commodities to be bought and sold for higher bride price or to get a greater number of wives. Both helped in the increase in social standing in Africa.

As such, girls received lifelong training to prepare them to be 'good women' who would attract large bride prices. After her father's death Aku-nna is allowed to continue schooling only because it was believed that educated girls fetch a higher bride price. She has little value in the eyes of her uncle, now – stepfather Okonkwo, than an item for auction. Her mother, too busy in her new husband's household politics, has little time for her. The uncertainty of her future and her utter powerlessness against a tradition that threatens to swallow her sends Aku-nna into deep despair. In such hopeless conditions, Chike comes as knight in shining armour who promises to save her from the confines of a society where she can hardly breathe.

Their love story is a story of discovery. Aku-nna and Chike, both fettered by tradition, discover the power of their love that helps them to move beyond the confines of their society. Aku-nna was born into a tradition that allowed her no autonomy, no way to control the decisions that shape her life. Hers was a community that considered it normal and legitimate for a girl to be kidnapped into marriage, or have a lock of hair cut off by a man unable to afford a bride price. Theirs was a community where 'every young man is entitled to his fun' but the blame 'usually went to the girls'. Here girls existed forever in survival mode, taking whatever precautions they could, but always prepared for the worst.

On the other hand, Chike Ofulue is rich, handsome and the headmaster of a local school. Unfortunately, he is of slave ancestry and so, he cannot marry Aku-nna – the one woman he wants. As Ogugua warns Aku-nna:

> *"You must be very careful. That man, that teacher – he's not one of us, you know. No decent girl from a good Ibuza family is allowed to associate with him. My father would rather see his daughter dead than allow such a friendship.*[21]

The *osu* caste system in the Igbo culture was not much different from the servile position of women in society. The descendants of the slaves, girls and women – were all viewed in a subordinate light. *Osu*, by definition are 'a people sacrificed to the gods in Igbo community.' In some circumstances, prisoners captured during inter-tribal wars were taken as slaves by their captors, which automatically marked them as part of the *osu* caste. Members of the slave caste in the Igbo society were ostracized, and prevented from intermarrying with the freeborn. Though the practice was eventually outlawed by colonial rule, the sentiments that held the slaves apart from the community still persist in the lifetimes of their descendants.

Yet, both Aku-nna and Chike, longing to move beyond the confines of their society, fall in love with each other. Inspite of the odds against them, they elope to Ughelli and live a life of their dream if only for a short while. Be it the passivity of Ma Blackie, Okoboshi's kidnapping of Aku-nna or Okonkwo's relentless demeanour towards her, she fights against all of these with the newfound power of love for Chike and moves with him to set up a new happy world. Though the hold of tradition does not entirely weaken, significant in her anxiety regarding her bride price, yet the fact that the little meek girl could survive so long against the negative forces says something about her grit and determination fuelled by love.

Aku-nna tries her best to save herself, but ultimately, the ropes of myth and tradition strangle her, taking her life. After she elopes with Chike, Okonkwo is so embittered that he refuses to accept the more than generous bride price offered by Chike's father. In Ibuza tradition, the myth prevailed that any girl who married without the payment of her bride price would surely die during her first childbirth. Aku-nna – young, malnourished and under a mountainous psychological stress – unwittingly fulfills this prophecy when she dies giving birth to her daughter Joy. Nonetheless, she lives a life of her choice, albeit it was short-lived, and dies in the arms of her love, Chike, finally at peace within.

Her last words to her husband prove how fulfilled she felt in her short span as an independent woman, not bound by baseless traditions.

This feeling of liberty in itself, was quite rare for women in her society, and she was grateful to have been lucky enough to experience it:

> "…how passionately we love each other, our love will never die. …Promise me that you will be happy, because you have made me so happy, so…"[22]

Emecheta has painstakingly highlighted the many cultural practices related to love and marriage that originate from, and in turn, legitimize the insidiously discriminatory view of certain members – usually women – of the society as inferior. Through Aku-nna's life, as well as those of other female characters, Emecheta explores the theme of love and marriage by showing the enslavement of women by traditional practices such as the bride price, widowhood rites, courting games, marriage by abduction and the *osu* caste system, and love of the young couple winning over all.

The role of love in *Things Fall Apart* goes much beyond the boy-girl relationship and is explored in a multi-faceted way by Chinua Achebe. While the most primitive man-woman love finds recurrence through the relationship of Okonkwo and Ekwefi, as well as the strong narrative about the love story of the elderly couple Ndulue and Ozoemena. Fraternal love between Okonkwo and Obierika is also noteworthy, and so is the bond between Nwoye and Ikemefuna. The love of parents for the child i.e., parental love, is beautifully depicted through Okonkwo and Ekwefi's relationship with their daughter Ezinma; and above all Okonkwo's love for his land, its culture and tradition becomes the driving motif of the novel.

The plot set in pre-colonial Africa and the first intrusion of the westerners into the Igbo life, and the disbalance thereby created that goes on to tear apart the traditional society is seen mostly in the context of post-colonial literature. Most literary studies have focused on the clash of cultures and its effect on the individual and society at large. The disintegration of the society that fails to stand united against the foreigner is the tragedy that has been much explored, but the theme of love and marriage has largely gone unnoticed in the novel due to the primary focus on the aforementioned angle.

This research work has sought to trace the angles of love and marriage in the novel through the relationships shared by the various characters in it. The love, portrayed through various characters and their relationships with each other, not only shows the importance of such fine emotion in the Igbo society, but also breaks the false image of barbaric Africa created by the likes of Joseph Conrad and Joyce Cary. These writers had presented the most superficial picture of not only the country, but also of African characters – portraying them as uncivilized and unruly savages.

Achebe, through his novel *Things Fall Apart*, creates the pre-colonized African village Umuofia and explores in-depth, the relationship between individuals, and individual and society, to show how a person's emotional and psychological development is shaped. He gives us in Okonkwo a protagonist we can identify with, yet view from an objective vantage point. His uppity behavior with his wives is something that every socially-aware reader can recognize as a sad reflection of the patriarchal times we have lived in for too long now; while his fear for his child's life and hopes from them is identifiable with every parent's concern for their child. Okonkwo's blind love for his father's land is worthy of respect, and his tragic end leaves us wondering if this man had an alternate choice, having lived all his life guided by his idea of the male principle.

Addressing the recurrent theme of marriage in the novels of Africa, along with the largely ignored topic of love, especially the angle of romantic love, this research work seeks to establish their importance in African literature and society. Just like the people all across the world, the Africans too are concerned about finding, losing and keeping love. Yet given the paucity of scholarly attention to the subject, those who are not very familiar with the continent or its literature, may be excused for holding the misconception that inter-personal relationships like love and marriage are of little importance in African life. According to Jennifer Cole and Lynn M. Thomas:

What explains this inattention to the topic of love in Africa outside the continent, even as discourse about love have flourished in the continent remains a mystery.[23]

That love and marriage are indispensable parts of not just individual life experiences but the concern of African society at large is reinforced through the novels of Elechi Amadi, Buchi Emecheta and Chinua Achebe, and hence a worthy subject for in-depth study when dealing with Africa. For the Africans, these inter-personal relationships not just bound two individuals but stressed on the kinship altogether, taking ahead the cultural ideologies and traditions of the society.

According to Cole and Thomas, the Africans love discussing love. African singers sing about it, advice columnists and novelists write about it and television programs and movies depict it in all its permutations. Yet scholarly disinterest in the topic is quite puzzling. Cole and Thomas in *Love in Africa* have argued that the failure of most research works across the world to engage with love and marriage is in part a product of the West's history with Africa. Since Europeans justified their slave-and colonial-era domination by depicting Africans as moronic, hypersexual and barbarous people without the emotional or intellectual depth required for nobler sentiments and relationships. Thus, the rest of the world which for long has walked behind the western world has also neglected the study of these aspects in African literature.

However, the study of these twin themes gives a finer understanding of the cultural practices of the country. A close study of these novels shows various aspects of the African life which otherwise would remain unknown to us. For example, the Africans traditionally had no formal system like a divorce yet the annulment of marriage, though rare, did take place. Emecheta mentions in *The Bride Price* as to how Okonkwo had called in the villagers to his compound and showed his naked posterior to Ma Blackie to disown her. This was all a man had to do to practically leave a wife. In another instance, in *Things Fall Apart*, Achebe has mentioned how Ekwefi walks out of her first husband's home one morning and comes to her love and becomes his second wife gladly. Even this was accepted by the society. This undoubtedly presents the Igbo society in a progressive light, showing the Africans no less human and vulnerable to aesthetic feelings than any other character in world literature.

Love and marriage are closely intertwined with the social and cultural norms of the Africans and hence a complete understanding of the African way of life calls for an earnest study of the novels in the light of these two themes as studied in this research work. The topic and conclusion of this research has succeeded in giving a new dimension to the study of love and marriage in African literature.

References

1. Achebe, Chinua. (1975). "The Novelist as a Teacher, in *Morning Yet on Creation Day: Essays*". London: Heinemann African Writers Series. Vol.9 p.8.
2. Obiechina, Emmanuel. (1975). *Culture, Tradition and Society in the West African Novel*. Cambridge: Cambridge University Press. p.202.
3. Achebe, Chinua. (1958). *Things Fall Apart*. New Delhi: Modern Classics, Penguin India. p.47.
4. Ogundipe-Leslie, Molara, (1987). "The Female Writer and her Commitment in Eldred Durosimi Jones" *et.al.* eds. *Women in African Literature Today*. London: James Currey Ltd. Trenton, N.J.: African World Press. p.8.
5. Emecheta, Buchi. (1976). "The Bride Price". New York: George Brazilier Inc. p.139.
6. Ba, Mariam, quoted in Schipper de Leeuw. (1987). "Mother Africa on a Pedestal: The Male Heritage in African Literature and Criticism". *Women in African Literature Today. A Review*. pp.46-47.
7. Nwapa, Flora. (1966). *Efuru*. London: Heinemann African Writers Series. p.81.
8. Amadi Elechi (1966). The Concubine. London: Heinemann African Writers Series. p.91.
9. Frank, Katherine (1987). *Women Without Men: The Feminist Novel in Africa in Women in African Literature Today*, eds. Eldred Durosimi Jones, *et.al.*, Trenton, *NJ: African World Press*. p.15.
10. Hafkin, Nancy J. & Bay Edna G.(1976). *Women in Africa – Studies in Social and Ecnomic Change*. Stanford: Stanford University Press.
11. Amadi, Elechi. (1986). *Estrangement*. London: Heinemann African Writers Series. p.118.
12. Emecheta, Buchi. (1976). *The Bride Price*. George Brazilier Inc., New York. pp.153-154.
13. Emecheta, Buchi. (1976). *The Bride Price*. New York: George Brazilier Inc. p.98.
14. Achebe, Chinua (1958). *Things Fall Apart*. New Delhi: Modern Classics, Penguin India, p.12.
15. Beauvoir, Simone de, quoted by Robert Fatton Jr. Gender. *Class and State In Africa in Women and the State in Africa* by Jane L. Parpart and Katheleen A. Staudt op. cit. Colorado: Lynne Rienner Publishers. p.53.
16. Amadi, Elechi. (1966). *The Concubine*. London: Heinemann African Writers Series, p.107.
17. Amadi, Elechi (1966). *The Concubine*. London: Heinemann African Writers Series, p.197.
18. Amadi, Elechi. (1966). *The Concubine*. London: Heinemann African Writers Series, p.91.
19. Amadi, Elechi (1966). *The Concubine*. London: Heinemann African Writers

Series, p.91.
20. Amadi, Elechi. (1966). *The Concubine*. London: Heinemann African Writers Series, p.193.
21. Emecheta, Buchi. (1976). *The Bride Price*. New York: George Brazilier Inc. p.70.
22. Emecheta, Buchi. (1976). *The Bride Price*. New York: George Brazilier Inc. p.167.
23. Cole, Jennifer and Lynn, Thomas M. (2009). *Love in Africa*. Chicago: The University of Chicago Press. p.280.

Bibliography

Primary Sources

Achebe, Chinua, (1987). *Anthills of Savannah.* London: Penguin Books.

Achebe, Chinua. (1958). *Things Fall Apart.* New Delhi: Modern Classics, Penguin India.

Achebe, Chinua. (1964). *Arrow of God.* New York: Anchor Books.

Achebe, Chinua. (1975). "The Novelist as a Teacher", in *Morning Yet on Creation Day: Essays.* London: Heinemann African Writers Series.

Achebe, Chinua. (2013). *No Longer At Ease.* USA: Important Books.

Amadi, Elechi. (1966). *The Concubine.* London: Heinemann African Writers Series.

Amadi, Elechi. (1969). *The Great Ponds.* London: Heinemann African Writers Series.

Amadi, Elechi. (1973). *Sunset in Biafra.* London: Heinemann African Writers Series.

Amadi, Elechi. (1982). *Ethics in Nigerian Culture*. London: Heinemann African Writers Series.

Amadi, Elechi. (1986). *Estrangement*. London: Heinemann African Writers Series.

Emecheta, Buchi. (1976). *The Bride Price*. New York: George Brazilier, Inc.

Emecheta, Buchi. (1977). *The Slave Girl*. New York: George Braziler, Inc.

Emecheta, Buchi. (1979). *The Joys of Motherhood*. New York: George Brazilier Inc.

Emecheta, Buchi. (2005). *The Moonlight Bride*. New York: George Braziller, Inc.

Secondary Sources

Achebe, Chinua (1989). *Hopes and Impediments: Selected Essays.* New York: Doubleday.

Achebe, Chinua. (1984). *The Trouble with Nigeria.* London: Heinemann African Writers Series.

Adebowale, Bayo. (2006). *Lonely Days.* Nigeria: Spectrum Books Limited.

Adichie, Chimamanda Ngozi. (2014). *We Should All Be Feminists.* London: Harper Collins Publishers.

Adichie, Chimamanda Ngozi. (2017). *A Feminist Manifesto in Fifteen Suggestions.* London: Harper Collins Publishers.

Aidoo, Ama Ata. (1977). *Our Sister Killjoy.* New York: Longman Publishers.

Akpan, Ntieyong U. (1972). *The Struggle for Secession 1966-1970: A Personal Account of the Nigerian Civil War.* London: Frank Cass and Company Ltd.

Albert, Edward. (2005). *History of English Literature.* London: Oxford University Press.

Amadi, A.C. (2002). *Widowhood in Igboland: Women's Tragedy.* (B.A. Long Essay) Nnamdi Azikiwe University, Awka.

Amuta, Chidi. (1989). *The Theory of African Literature: Implications for Practical Cliticism.* London: Zed Books.

Amuta, Chidi. (1989). *The Theory of African Literature: Implications of Practical Criticism.* London and New Jersey: Zed Books.

Ba, Mariam (1979). *So Long A Letter*. London: Heinemann African Writers Series.

Barry, Peter. (2010). *Beginning Theory: An Introduction to Literary and Cultural Theory*. New Delhi: Viva Books Private Limited.

BBC, (1993). BBC English Dictionary. London: Harper Collins.

Beauvoir, Simone de (1949). *The Second Sex*. London: Vintage Classics.

Beauvoir, Simone de, quoted by Robert Fatton Jr. Gender. *Class and State In Africa* in *Women and the State in Africa* by Jane L. Parpart and Katheleen A. Staudt op. cit. Colorado: Lynne Rienner Publishers.

Biswas, Chandrani. (1998). *Women and War: A Study of the Novels of Emecheta, Ekwensi and Amadi*. New Delhi: Book Plus.

Boehmer, Elleke. (2009*). Stories of Women: Gender and Narrative in the Post Colonial Nation*. Manchester: Manchester UP.

Brown, Lloys W. (1975). Review of *The Black Mind: A History of African Literature*, by O.R. Dathorne. Indiana UP: Research in African Literatures 6.1.

Brown, Llyod W. (1981). *Women Writers in Black Africa*. Westport, Connecticut: Greenwood Press.

Burns, Sir Alan. (1972). *History of Nigeria*. London: George Allen and Unwin Ltd.

Butler, Judith. (1999*). Gender Trouble: Feminism and the Subversion of Identity*. New York: Routledge.

Cartey, Wilfred. (1969). *Whispers from a Continen t: The Literature of Contemporary Black Africa.* London: Heinemann African Writers Series.

Chand, Neerja. (2005). *Beyond Feminism: Gender Perspectives on Buchi Emrcheta.* New Delhi: Book Plus.

Condell, Diana and Liddiard. Jean. (1987). *Working for Victory: Images of Women in the First World War 1914-1918.* London: Routeledge and Kegan Paul Ltd.

Cook, David. (1977). *African Literature: A Critical View.* London: Longman Publishers.

Cott, Nancy F. (1987). *The Grounding of Modern Feminism.* New Haven and London: Yale University Press.

Cox, Brian C. (1997). *African Writers Vol.1-2.* New York: Scribners.

Curry, James. (2008). *Africa Writes Back: The African Writers Series and the Launch of African Literature.* Athens: Ohio University Press.

De. St. Jorre, John. (1972). *The Nigerian Civil War.* London: Hodder and Stoughton Ltd.

Desai, Anita. (1963). *Cry, The Peacock.* New Delhi: Orient Paperbacks.

Desai, Anita. (1982). *Where Shall We Go This Summer?* New Delhi: Orient Paperbacks.

Douglas Killam & Ruth Rowe, (2000). eds., *The Companion to African Literatures.* London, Bloomington: James Currey & Indiana University Press.

Driver, Dorothy. (1991*). Correspondent. JCL. Vol.XXVI, No.1.* London: Hans, Zell Publication.

Emenyonu, Ernest N.(1987). ed. *The Essential Ekwensi: A Literary Celebration of Cyprian Ekwensi's Sixty-Fifth Birthday*. Ibadan: Heinemann Educational Books (Nigeria) Ltd.

Ezeibgo, T.A. (1996). *Gender Issues in Nigeria: A Feminine Perspective*. Lagos: Vista Books Ltd.

Fanon, Frantz (2001) *The Wretched of the Earth*. UK: Penguin Publishers.

Figes, Eva. (1970). *Patriarchial Attitudes: Women in Society*. London: Faber and Faber Ltd.

Frank, Katherine (1987). *Women Without Men: The Feminist Novel in Africa* in *Women in African Literature Today*, eds. Eldred Durosimi Jones, et, al. Trenton, NJ: African World Press.

Gailey, Harry A. (1971). *The Road to Aba: a Study of British Administrative Policy in Eastern Nigeria*. London: University of London Press Ltd.

Gordon, April A. (1996). *Transforming Capitalism and Patriarchy: Gender and Development in Africa (Women and change in the Developing World*. Boulder, Colorado: Lynne Rienner Publishers.

Gugelberger, George M.(1985). ed. *Marxism and African Literature*. London: James Curry Ltd.

Hafkin, Nancy J. & Bay Edna G. (1976). *Women in Africa – Studies in Social and Ecnomic Change*. Stanford: Stanford University Press.

Hafkin, Nancy J. and Edna G. Bay(1976). eds. *Women in Africa: Studies in Social and Economic Change*. Stanford, California: Stanford University Press.

Hallett, Robin. (1975). *Africa Since 1875*, Vol.2. London: Heineman.

Hardy, Thomas. ((1895). *Jude the Obscure.* New Delhi: UBSPD.

Hartmann, Susan M. (1982*).* *The Home Front and Beyond: American Women in the 1940s.* Boston, Massachhusetts: Twayne Publishers.

Hatch, John. (1971*).* *Nigeria: A History.* London: Secker and Warburg Ltd.

Ivezbaye, Dan. (1979). *Issues in the Reassessment of the African Novel* in African Literature Today.

Jones, Eldred Durosimi (1987). et.al., eds. *Women in African Literature Today: A Review.* London: James Curry Ltd., Trenton, New Jersey: Africa World Press.

Korieh, C.J. (1996). "*Widowhood among the Igbo of Eastern Nigeria*", M.Phil. Thesis, University of Bergen, Norway.

Koso Thomas, Olayinka. (1987). *The Circumcision of Women: A Strategy for Eradication.* London and New Jersey: Zed Books Ltd.

Krige, Eileen (1978). *Social Sytem and Tradition in South Africa: Essays in honour of Eileen Krige.* (Written in collaboration with William John Argyle and Eleanor Preston Whyte). London: Oxford Universiy Press.

Krige, Eileen and Krige, Jack. (1943). *The Realm of a Rain-Queen: A Study of the Patterns of Lovedu Society.* London: Oxford University Press.

Krige, Eileen. (1981). *Essays on African Marriage in Southern Africa.* Cape Town: Juta Publishers.

Lasebikan, E. (2001). "*African Culture and the Quest for Women's Rights: Ageneral Overview*", in Docas O. Akintunde (ed.). Ibadan: Sefer Books Ltd.

Macebuh, Stanley. (1980). *Poetics and the Mythic Imagination*. United States of America: Three Continents Press.

Masterplots II (1987). *Women's Literature Series [2]*. New York: Salem Press.

Masterplots II (1995). *Women's Literature Series [3]*. New York: Salem Press.

Mcmillan, Carol. (1982). *Women, Reason and Nature: Some Philosophical Problems with Feminism*. Oxford: Basil Blackwell Publisher Ltd.

Millet, Kate. (1972). *Sexual Politics*. Great Britain: Abacus Edition, Sphere Books.

Mills, Sara, (1989). et.al., eds. *Feminist Readings/Feminists Reading*. Hertfordshire: Harvester Wheatsheaf.

Moi, Toril (1985). *Sexual/Textual Politics: Feminist Literary Theory*. London and New York: Methuen and Co. Ltd.

Munro, Alice. (2001). *Hateship, friendship, courtship, loveship, marriage*. London: Chatto & Windus.

Ngozi, Chimamanda Adichie. (2006). *Half of a Yellow Sun*. London: Harper Collins Publishers.

Ngozi, Chimamanda Adichie. (2013). *Americanah*. London: Harper Collins Publishers.

Niven, Alistair. (1981). *The Concubine: A Critical View. Edited by Yolande Cantu*. London: Collings in association with the British Council.

Obeichina, Emmanuel. (1975), *Culture, Tradition and Society in the West African Novel*. Cambridge: Cambridge University Press.

Obiechina, Emmanuel. (1975). *Culture, Tradition and Society in the West African Novel.* Cambridge: Cambridge University Press.

Ogundipe-Leslie, Molara,. (1987). *The Female Writer and her Commitment in Eldred Durosimi Jones et.al. eds. Women in African Literature Today.* London: James Currey Ltd. Trenton, N.J.: African World Press.

Okely, Judith. (1977). *Gypsy Women: Models in Conflict.* New York: Halsted Press.

Okoye, P.U. (1995). *Widowhood: A National or Cultural Tragedy.* Enugu: Nok Publishers.

Okpewho, Isodore (1976). *The Last Duty.* New Jersey: Prentice Hall Press.

Postcolonial African Writers. (1998). *A Bio-Bibliographical Critical Sourcebook.* London: Fitzroy Dearborn Publishers.

Shamim, Amna. (2017). *Gynocentric Contours of The Male Imagination: A Study of The Novels of Chinus Achebe and Ngugi Wa Thiong'o.* New Delhi: Idea Publishing.

Showalter, Elaine. (1989), ed. *Speaking of Gender.* New York: Routledge.

Soyinka, Wole. (1988). *"Who's Afraid of Elesin Oba?" Art, Dialoge and Outrage: Essays on Literature and Culture.* Ibadan: New Horn Press.

Soyinka, Wole. (2002). *Death and the King's Horsemen.* New York: W.W. Norton & Company.

Stephanie Newell. (2002). *Literary Culture in Colonial Ghana: 'How to Play the Game of Life',* Bloomington, Indiana: Indiana

University Press, 2002, p. 135, ch. 7, "Ethical Fiction: J.E. Casely Hayford's *Ethiopia Unbound*".

Suri, Twinkle. (2006). *A Room of Their Own: Women's Voices in Africa*. New Delhi: Books Plus.

Suri, Twinkle. (2006). *A Room of Their Own: Women's Voices in Africa*. New Delhi: Book Plus.

Sutherland, Efua T. (1975). *The Marriage of Anansewa*. Essex, UK: Longman group Ltd.

Thiong'o, Ngugi wa (1977) *Petals of Blood*. Harare: Zimbabwe Publishing House.

Town, Ann. (2009). "The Status of Women as a Standard of Civilization." *European Journal of International Relations 15.4*. 681-706. Print.

Umeh, Marie Linton. (1996). *Emerging Perspectives on Buchi Emecheta*. Trenton, New Jersey: Africa World Press Inc.

Walker, Alice. (1983). *The Color Purple*. London: Orion Books Ltd.

Walker, Alice. (1994). "In Search of Our Mothers' Gardens" in *Anthology of African American Literary Criticism from the Harlem Renaissance to the Present*. Ed. Angelynn Mitchell. Durham & London: Duke UP.

Walters, Margaret. (2005). *Feminism: A Very Short Introduction*. Oxford: Oxford UP.

Wright, Edgar. (1973). *Critical Evaluation of African Literature*. Washington D.C.: Inscape Publishers.

Webliography

"African Literature - MSN Encarta"

"African literature" at infoplease.

Achebe, Chinua (1965). *"English and the African Writer"*. Transition copyright 1997, published by Indiana University Press on behalf of the Hutchins Center for African and African American Reasearch at Harvard University. https://www.jstor.org/stable/2935429

Achebe, Chinua. (1990). *African Literature as Restoration of Celebration*, an

Ba, Mariam, quoted in Schipper de Leeuw. (1987). *Mother Africa on a Pedestal: The Male Heritage in African Literature and Criticism.* Women in African Literature Today. A Review. http://hdl.handle.net/1887//7788

Brown, Lloyd. (1975).*The African Women as a Writer* in Canadian Journal of African Studies. Vol. 9, No. 3. www.tandfonline.com

Cole, Jennifer and Lynn, Thomas M. (2009), *Love in Africa*. The University of Chicago Press. https://www.press. uchicago.edu

Connell, Raewyn W. and Messerschmidt. (2005). *Hegemonic Masculinity: Rethinking the Concept* in SAGE Journals, Gender and Society. https://doi.org/10.1177/ 0891243205278639

essay in Kunapipi 12, no.2. https://ro.uow.edu.au

essay in Kunapipi 12, no.2.https://ro.uow.edu.au/kunapipi/vol12/iss2/3

George, Joseph. (1996). "*African Literature*", in *Understanding Contemporary Africa*. Edited by April A. Gordon and Donald L. Gordon. https://trove.nla.gov.au/version/ 26687189

Things We Inherited: Voices from Africa Curated by Liyou Libsekal (2015) https://cordite.org.au

http://www.marxists.org/history/international/socialdemocracy/ clarion/ index.htm

http://ezinearticles.com/Culture-and-Tradition-in-the-Pre-Colonial-Africa-in-Elechi-Amadis-The-Concubine&id=5697945

http://africanweddingtraditions.com/quotes-on-marriage.html

https://www.thebookbanque.com/literary/review/emecheta-bride-price

http://africanweddingtraditions.com/quotes-on-marriage.html

https://www.thebookbanque.com/literary/review/emecheta-bride-price

https://en.wikipedia.org/wiki/African_literature

https://www.researchgate.net/publication/274078768_ELECHI_ AIIADI'S_GREAT_PONDS_AND_PETROLEUII_ EXPLOITATION_IN_NIGERIA_THE_CHALLENGE_ OF_RESOURCE_CONTROL

https://archive.org/details/greatponds00amad

https://www.researchgate.net/publication/275796353_Estrangement

http://www.imrfjournals.in/pdf/MATHS/ENIRJ-Volume-5-Issue-1-2016/11.pdf

eprints.covenantuniversity.edu.ng

Lindfors, Bernth. (1975). *Critical Perspectives on Amos Tutuola*. Three Continents Press. https://books.google.co.in

Mikell, Gwendolyn. (1995) *African Feminism: Toward a New Politics of Representation, Feminist Studies*. https://philpapers.org

Ogunyemi, Chikwenye Okonjo. (1985) *Womanism: The Dynamics of the Contemporary Black Female Novel in English.* https://doi.org/10.1086494200

Palmer, Eustace (1978) *Twenty Five Years of Amos Tutuola*. The International Fiction Review.5(1). Retrieved 20 January 2015. https://journals.lib.unb.ca

Rodman, Selden (20 September 1953) *Book Review of The Palm-Wine Drinkard*. New York Times Book Review. https://books.google.co.in

Rotini, Adewale. (2007). *Violence in the Family: A Preliminary Investigation and Overview of Wife Battering in Africa*. Journal of International Women's Studies. 9.1. https://core.ac.uk>download>pdf

Strong-Leek, Linda. (2011). "Reading aWoman: Chinua Achebe's *Things Fall Apart* and Feminist Critique." *African Studies Quarterly* 5.2 (2001):n.pag. Web. 17 Feb. 2011. http://web.africa.ufl.edu/asq/v5/v5i2a2.htm

Thiong'o, Ngugi wa (1981).*Decolonising the Mind: The Politics of Language in African Literature* (Studies in African Literature Series). https://ngugiwathiongo.com

West, Anthony (5 December 1953) *Book Review of The Palm-Wine Drinkard*. New Yorker. https://jstor.org

West, Rebecca. (2013). "Mr Chesterton in Hysterics: A Study in Prejudice". The Clarion Nov. 1913 in British Social Democracy, Transcriber Ted Crawford. n. pag. Web. 2. Dec. 2013. http://www.marxists.org/history/international/social-democracy/clarion/index.htm

Made in the USA
Monee, IL
27 March 2023